Library of
Davidson College

IRELAND

From the Act of Union • 1800
to the Death of Parnell • 1891

*Seventy-seven novels and collections
of shorter stories by twenty-two*
Irish and Anglo-Irish novelists

selected by
PROFESSOR ROBERT LEE WOLFF
Harvard University

A GARLAND SERIES

The Life of John Banim

Patrick Joseph Murray

with an introduction by
Robert Lee Wolff

Garland Publishing, Inc., New York & London
1978

For a complete list of the titles in this series,
see the final pages of this volume.

Introduction copyright © 1978 by Robert Lee Wolff

All rights reserved

This facsimile has been made from a copy in
the Yale University Library (In.B225.W857).

The volumes in this series are printed on acid-free,
250-year-life paper.

Library of Congress Cataloging in Publication Data

Murray, Patrick Joseph.
　　The life of John Banim.

(Ireland, from the Act of Union, 1800,
to the death of Parnell, 1891)
Reprint of the 1857 ed. published by W. Lay, London.
Includes bibliographical references.
　　1. Banim, John, 1798–1842.　2. Novelists,
Irish—19th century—Biography. I. Title. II. Series.
PR4057.B2Z79　　1978　　　823'.7　[B]　　78-12228
　　　　　ISBN 0-8240-3474-0

Printed in the United States of America

The Fiction of
"The O'Hara Family"
John Banim (1798–1842)
Michael Banim (1796–1874)
Harriet Martin (1801–1891; see No. 23)

I

John and Michael Banim, writing together as "The O'Hara Family,"[1] with John calling himself Barnes O'Hara and Michael calling himself Abel O'Hara, were the first novelists of Ireland who were wholly of Irish Catholic origin (Lady Morgan's MacOwen grandparents hardly count). The Banims' father, Michael Banim, senior, owned a farm but was also proprietor of a small shop in Kilkenny (Leinster) where he sold powder and shot and fishing tackle. He was the first member of his family to leave the soil. He was eager that his sons should have a good education, but in the end could not afford it for both of them; so Michael, the elder, who had begun to read for the bar, went into the shop.

John attended the famous college at Kilkenny, in the Middle Ages an appendage to the Cathedral of St. Canice, refounded after Cromwell's spoliation, chartered in 1684 by the first Duke of Ormonde, whose family seat was Kilkenny Castle, chartered again by James II in 1689, and moved to its most recent site in 1780. Here Swift, Congreve, Berkeley, and others had been educated; it was sometimes known as "the Eton of Ireland." After two years there, John left to study art at the Royal Dublin Society, boarding in the house of a poor and parsimonious Protestant friend of his father whose domestic

v

economy he found revolting. At eighteen, back at home in Kilkenny, teaching drawing and so launched on his artistic career, he and the illegitimate daughter of a Protestant landowner fell in love. He was rejected by the girl's father, and her death soon afterwards plunged him into deep grief and into a period of dissipation. Traces of these episodes are to be found in his fiction.

In 1820 John Banim left Kilkenny for Dublin, where he became a journalist and assisted his fellow artists to obtain a royal Charter of Incorporation, but soon decided to devote himself fully to writing and completed (1820) a poem he called "Ossian's Paradise." In manuscript it elicited agreeable comments from Sir Walter Scott and was then published as "The Celts' Paradise" (1821). Richard Lalor Sheil (1791–1851), an Irish barrister only a few years older than Banim and already a successful playwright, with his long career as a politician still in the future, became Banim's friend and adviser. He may have collaborated with John on a tragedy, *Damon and Pythias*, which was successfully produced in London (May 1821) with the great Macready as its star and Charles Kemble also in the cast. After writing a pamphlet on George IV's forthcoming visit to Ireland, Banim in 1822 married and moved to London to seek his fortune. His gentle and admiring elder brother, Michael, gave him moral support at every turn. Before John left for London, the brothers planned to collaborate on a series of Irish tales. To the partnership Michael brought far less literary talent and no training as a writer but a more intimate personal acquaintance with Irish peasant customs than John in his life as student, artist, and journalist had ever acquired.

In London, John was engaged by a new journal called

the *Literary Register*, which, however, lasted less than a year, during which Banim first suffered symptoms of the disease that eventually crippled and killed him. At this early stage, before his own career was launched, Banim found himself called upon to advise and help another young Irishman, Gerald Griffin, who was to prove even more talented than he, at the very beginning of his search for fortune in England. He also published anonymously in 1824 a volume of essays entitled *Recollections of the Dead Alive*, satirizing the foibles of the day, including the craze for phrenology, log-rolling book reviewers, and ignorant art critics. There was nothing specifically Irish here. Ireland, however, was to be the subject of the "Tales," whose first series (3 vols., 1825; No. 16 in the Garland series) was now under way; Michael, in Kilkenny, was composing in the rare intervals of leisure from the shop the first story, *Crohoore of the Bill-Hook*, and sending it in brief installments to John, and John was working on the other two, *The Fetches* and *John Doe*.

II

The relatively few modern critics who have commented on "The O'Hara Family's" work have never been quite sure how much credit should be given to Michael Banim for his contributions; and the latest and most authoritative, Professor Flanagan, has quietly denied him any:

> Michael was neither a well-educated nor an ambitious writer. The controlling genius was always John's; he wrote most of the important novels and made exten-

sive revisions of Michael's contributions. For this reason it seems sensible to depart from the usual practice of referring to "the Banim brothers."[2]

But this is cavalier procedure indeed. John's surviving letters to Michael indicate that it was Michael who wrote *Crohoore of the Bill-Hook*, though John undoubtedly revised it, as Michael did all of John's work. When John had received the first part, for example, he wrote Michael, "So far as it goes, I pronounce that you have been successful. Here and there, I have marked such particular criticisms as struck me . . ."; and, as the story advanced, "I think I recognise our tithe-proctor, Peery Clancey; the portrait is so accurate I could not mistake the gentleman. Your next door neighbour, Mickle Ryan, is your original, and you have not outstepped nature, or misrepresented facts, in the slightest degree. . . . You tell me you intend to cut off the proctor's ears: slice them close to his head by all means; do not leave a shred; no honest man will say that he does not deserve the cropping."[3] It is of considerable importance to accept Michael's authorship, since *Crohoore* is the first, longest, and best of the novels making up the first series of *Tales*. It astonished its readers in 1825 with its power as it still astonishes us. And if the power was somewhat crude and showed the traces of Michael Banim's inexperience, this is no reason for denying him the credit for its authorship that John Banim himself always gave him.

Crohoore is set in eighteenth-century rural Kilkenny, where the reader finds himself in the household of a prosperous Irish Catholic farmer, employing many farmhands and domestic servants, a household of a kind not to be found in any previous novel of Irish life. A horrible murder and kidnapping, the search for the missing girl, the ambiguous role of the local "whiteboys," the persecution of the peasant population by the tithe-proctors (those local Irish Catholic laymen charged by the established Church of Ireland [Protestant Episcopalian] with the collection of the tithes for the support of its clergy), the prevalence of deep superstition: these are the striking features of *Crohoore*. Still laboring under the penal laws, with fresh memories of the time when (it was said) Protestant troops had pursued Catholic priests like hunted animals, ground down by rackrenting, the peasant "found himself ... compelled to contribute to the support, in splendour and superiority, of that very rival church ... to pay to its ministers the hard-earned pittance he could not afford to his own." Or, as a peasant sings after a "prefatory yell,"

> They must lave off their tithin' an rackin' iv acres,
> Or we'll roast 'em as brown as a loaf at the baker's;
> An we'll nip off their ears, an' we'll lave their heads bare,
> As they do wid the calves in the county Kildare.[4]

Eventually the reader actually sees the whiteboys slice the ears from the head of Peery Clancy, the wretched tithe-proctor. Before the actual operation is performed, the victim is buried up to the neck, and somebody suggests that if an acre of tithe-proctors could be sown in this fashion, it would make a wretched crop indeed. The crop, says another, would be hemp, to make "caravats" (neckties) for any whiteboy who might be caught. Our sympathies for Clancy are hardly aroused, however, because we have also come to know the horrible sufferings of the Delany family, which Clancy has ousted from their shelter because they cannot pay the tithe. Delany finds mere ear-cropping insufficient punishment for Clancy; until forcibly prevented, he is ready with a stone to bash Clancy's brains out. In this world of lawlessness and terror, only the human decencies—friendship, love, loyalty—make life bearable. *Crohoore* abounds in examples of these: between parents and children, between betrothed lovers, between foster-brothers, between masters and servants. It remains a minor masterpiece despite its infelicities of style.

The two other tales in the first series were both largely by John Banim, who sent them to Michael for his criticism. *The Fetches* is set in Kilkenny and its environs in the eighteenth century; its theme is a romance between two young lovers, and the psychological impact upon their minds of the working out of an ancient Irish superstition: the meaning of the apparition or "Fetch" of a living person. The novel is highly romantic, and the scenes along the banks of the Nore amidst John Banim's own favorite youthful haunts are lovingly drawn. But it was in the third story, *John Doe*, later reissued as *Peep O'Day*, that John Banim's talents were most clearly revealed. The splendid opening chapter, however, was by Michael. It describes a "pattern," or rural feast day in honor of a patron saint, including, as it so often did, a general "scrimmage," or skirmish among the men present: fighting for the sake of fighting; John had never attended such a celebration, but Michael had.

Thereafter *John Doe*, set in County Tipperary (Munster) near Clonmel, belonged to John. Ireland in all its strange complexity is introduced to two agreeable young English officers on garrison duty. John Doe himself is the leader of the whiteboys, who call their captain after the imaginary legal personage to emphasize his anonymity, and are themselves locally called "Shanavest" (old waistcoat) or "Caravat" (cravat) depending on their costume. By terrorist methods John Doe hopes to lower rackrents and prevent the payment of tithes. But who is John Doe, and where is he? The English officers, one in particular, have the duty to search him out, a task complicated by the fact that this same officer—a Protestant, of course—has fallen in love with a Catholic girl, daughter of a local landowner who seems to be menaced by the banditti.

Lacking the raw power of *Crohoore*, *John Doe* is better told and faster moving. It includes two memorable priests, one of them a witty and sophisticated and forceful shepherd of his flock, the other a drunkard, making what money he can by performing marriage ceremonies and asking no questions. Both are on excellent terms with the local Church of Ireland clergyman, and all three join forces to try to prevent the population from giving aid and comfort to the whiteboys, who are menacing priests as well as laymen. For the first time in Irish fiction, moreover, the reader is taken to visit an illegal still, and can study the art of preparing potheen. As so often, whiskey plays a major part in the lives of the characters, one of them singing, in Irish,

> Oh, whiskey, the delight and joy of my soul!
> You lay me stretched on the floor,
> You deprive me of sense and knowledge,
> And you fill me with a love of fighting;

> My coat you have often torn from my back;
> By you I lost my silken cravat;
> But all shall be forgotten and forgiven,
> If you meet me after mass next Sunday!⁵

This first series of the *Tales* (1825) was well received. Gerald Griffin wrote to his brother that they were "most vigorous and original things; overflowing with the very spirit of poetry, passion and painting," and were "astonishing in nothing so much as in the power of creating an intense interest without stepping out of real life, and in the very easy and natural drama that is carried through them, as well as in the excellent tact . . . in seizing on all the points of national character which are capable of effect." He did not mean *The Fetches*, he added, which was merely "a romance . . . but . . . a splendid one." In the shop windows of London Griffin had seen pictures by first-rate artists showing scenes from the *Tales*, although a mere month before their appearance John Banim had been wholly unknown.⁶

On May 1, 1825, only three weeks after the *Tales* were published, John Banim was already writing to Michael that by Christmas he would have completed a three-volume novel to be called *The Boyne Water*, a historical tale of the decisive battle of 1690 and of the years leading up to it from the accession of James II in 1685. By way of preparation, John not only read the standard works but visited the scene and walked over the terrain himself: the coast of Antrim, Londonderry, Lough Neagh, and the battle site near Drogheda. He intended to visit as well Limerick and its environs so much nearer home, where the last phases of the war took place, and the peace—so generous to the Catholics but never allowed to become effective—was signed; but Michael Banim took over this part of the job for him.

III

Completed on schedule and published early in 1826, *The Boyne Water* (3 vols., 1826; No. 17), as Professor Flanagan remarks, "set a standard which no other Irish historical novel was to meet."[7] It could never have been written without the example of the enormously popular historical fiction by Sir Walter Scott, pouring forth from the presses ever since *Waverley* (1814). When John Banim wrote, *Redgauntlet* (1824) was Scott's most recent novel. Readers of *The Boyne Water* will be struck by the fidelity—almost comic at times—with which Banim follows his model. But, just as each of the best of Scott's novels has a point to make beyond the resolution of its characters' personal problems and of the historical crises within which they are caught up, so *The Boyne Water*, ostensibly a story of 1685–1691, is also a strong plea for religious toleration in Banim's own day, and—specifically—for Catholic Emancipation, in 1826 the major political question in the public's mind.

At the very end of the novel, after the Treaty of Limerick has failed of ratification in 1695 and the penal era is well under way, the novel's Protestant hero in Ireland writes hopefully to his brother-in-law, its Catholic hero in exile on the Continent, that

> The descendants of the men who have sanctioned, and by that means caused the deliberate breach of their own treaty, made in the field, will awake to

> vindicate, as far as in them lies, the name of their ancestors. A son, jealous of his father's honor, pays his father's debts ... and Englishmen will yet pay their fathers' debt of faith to Ireland. The Treaty of Limerick will yet be kept.[8]

In 1826, this "prediction" could have but one meaning: the English, one hundred and thirty-four years after the signing of the treaty, were now obliged to honor it by emancipating the Catholics.

The entire novel, indeed, has been leading directly to this conclusion. Robert Evelyn and his sister Esther, of a Protestant landowning family with a house on the Antrim shore of Lough Neagh, encounter Edmund M'Connell and his sister Eva, of a Catholic noble family related to the Earl of Antrim, who live on the Atlantic shore of the Irish Sea near Glenariff. Immediately after the accession of James II in 1685, the two young couples fall in love. Despite their own innate religious toleration, they are caught up in the strife that precipitates and follows the Glorious Revolution of 1688, and are forced to take opposite sides. The fear and hatred between Catholic and Protestant in Ulster have ancient roots, most recently watered by the ghastly Catholic massacres of Protestants in 1641, still vivid in the minds of many of the characters in the novel. The extreme Protestants fear that the new Catholic King will encourage a second round. They are typified by the historical George Walker, militant anti-Papist and soldier-divine, who becomes one of the governors of Londonderry during its protracted siege, and then its bishop. A friend of Evelyn's family, he commands troops at the Battle of the Boyne, and is killed in single combat against a Dominican Friar, O'Haggarty, who is precisely his mirror-image, as bigoted a hater of Protestant heretics as Walker is of Catholics. O'Haggarty also dies in their encounter.

Serving on the side of William III, but without much enthusiasm, Evelyn is enabled by his duties to become personally acquainted with both William and James II; at times he is a privileged prisoner of James's forces, and so comes to know Sarsfield, while at others he serves as aide-de-camp to Schomberg in William's armies. M'Connell, whose family suffers atrocities at the hands of the Protestants, becomes far more committed to James's side than Evelyn to William's, and eventually takes command of a Rapparee band of freebooters helping the Catholic cause. Protestant or Catholic, these figures from the upper classes or from the pages of history books usually have only intermittent life. Banim excels in the drawing of Irish Catholics of lower degree: Moya Laverty, a peasant girl who cherishes a hopeless passion for Robert Evelyn, and several times appears in the nick of time to save his life; Galloping Hogan, the Rapparee leader (a historical person), commander of the force that seizes and occupies and eventually burns down Evelyn's family house on Lough Neagh; Rory na-Chopple, a horse thief who knows the language of horses and can talk them into doing his bidding and who, for all his smiling face, is a ruthless killer who enjoys the sport; and Carolan, the blind harpist with a strong feudal attachment to the M'Connells (based on the celebrated Torlogh Carolan [Ó Cearbhállain], 1670–1738). These persons are as fully realized as Scott's best characters of a similar sort, such as Meg Merrilies, the gypsy woman in *Guy Mannering*. And there are a good many symbolic noble hounds and even an eagle, as so often in the pages of Irish novelists.

In dealing with the leading historic figures, Banim is at pains to show that William is a cold-hearted but fair-minded general, determined not to be stampeded by Protestant extremists and not to be entrapped into persecuting Catholics, while James II he portrays as much misunderstood, even minimizing his cowardice at the Boyne itself. Evelyn and M'Connell go through the long siege of Londonderry with its starvation and misery, and are present at the major battles. Particularly effective is the account of Sarsfield's sortie from Limerick after the first siege and before the second, guided and helped by the Rapparees, through the wild hills of nearby Tipperary to Ballyneaty to blow up an enemy siege train.

IV

Though debilitating illness with intermittent racking pain had been sapping his strength even in these early years, John Banim began at once to write the second series of *Tales by the O'Hara Family* (3 vols., 1826; No. 18). Visited in London by Michael in the summer of 1826, he seemed forty rather than twenty-eight; his hair was white and his step feeble. But by the end of the summer the two novels for the new collection had been completed. To the first and longest, *The Nowlans*, which occupied two of the three volumes of the second series when it appeared later in the year, Michael's explorations of the Tipperary hills near Limerick for *The Boyne Water* made a considerable contribution. It was there that Michael had spent a night in the cabin of a well-to-do farmer with a pretty daughter and a bedridden son, who did not make an appearance and about whom the family was anxious. From this milieu and these fragmentary circumstances John took the inspiration for the opening of *The Nowlans*: he made the sick son a priest and told his remarkable story.

Fully as melodramatic as anything the O'Haras had yet published, *The Nowlans*—set in the Slieve Felim Hills of Western Tipperary (spelled "Llieuve Ieullem" in the story: near Keeper Mountain) not far from the River Shannon and perhaps twelve or fifteen miles from Limerick—tells of a family like the Doolings in *Crohoore*: well-to-do farmers. Daniel Nowlan has married a woman of Protestant origins and vaunted Ascendancy connections but of humble origin, who has become a Catholic. Nowlan's elder brother, Aby, has inherited all their father's considerable wealth. Stupid, profligate, and irresponsible, he is squandering his substance in dissipation, toadying to the least worthy among the neighboring Protestant gentry, and living surrounded by a harem of mistresses and former mistresses and by numbers of his illegitimate children. Drawn from life, this figure is one of the most convincing of all the rich variety of Banim's Irishmen. Aby shows an interest in his nephew John Nowlan, Daniel's son, and—in the hope that John may be made his uncle's heir—John's parents interrupt the boy's training for the priesthood and send him to live with Aby.

In these surroundings, whatever priestly calling he may have had is deeply damaged by his youthful passion for his illegitimate cousin Maggy, who makes passionate love to him. He is not seduced; but although he leaves Aby's, resumes his training, and takes his vows, he is still vulnerable to temptation. He falls in love, as an adult this time, with Letitia Adams, the charming niece of a liberal-minded Protestant local landowner, elopes with her, and marries her. His sister, Peggy, is trapped into marriage with Letitia's brother, Frank, who—quite improbably, it may seem to modern readers—is a deep-dyed villain and a professional robber. The tragic dénouements of these two affairs form the main theme of *The Nowlans*.

This sensational theme of a renegade (and only belatedly repentant) priest made *The Nowlans* a highly original story. Into the unhappiness of John and Letty Nowlan, poverty-stricken, living in Dublin lodgings in the house of a wretchedly underpaid official with middle-class Protestant standards and pride, Banim put some of his own experiences. The setting and the personalities are those of Banim's Dublin student days spent in a suburb called Phibsborough with a family named Wheeler who were acquaintances of his father's. Elsewhere in the novel Banim touches upon those Evangelicals whom Eyre Crowe had put into his story *The Old and the New Light* (No. 15). Here they are mostly English, "sent from a Bible Society in London to investigate the progress of their benevolent efforts among the peasantry of Ireland," but they have a dreadful native Irish collaborator, an ex-priest named Horragan, who cares only for money and rich food and who preaches the new ideas in Irish. The caricature that Banim draws of Horragan is positively Dickensian. It is also rabidly hostile, and is allegedly based on the Reverend Mortimer O'Sullivan (1791–1859).

The Nowlans exhibits a pre-Victorian, Regency frankness in sexual matters, describing John Nowlan's embraces with his cousin Maggy, who later becomes proprietress of a bawdyhouse in Dublin, far more graphically than was usual in 1826. The wicked Frank Adams, who has been one of Maggy's lovers, wants to get rid of Peggy Nowlan by getting her into Maggy's hands, and promises Maggy that "for a season or so, there won't be a nicer article in your shop." One of the novel's most vivid aspects is Letty's inability, as a Protestant, to understand the pangs of conscience that John, as a Catholic priest, feels for having violated his vows and marrying her:

> Letty might suppose they were married; he knew they were not married; he knew they never could be: and though he indulged her illusion, partly in furtherance of his plan to sacrifice every thing to her happiness . . . he stood a renegade, a giver of dreadful scandal, a blasphemer, an outcast, and a marked sheep, she led with him a life of partaken sin and was, in fact, no more than his mistress. Do what he might, he could not prevent that. Immolate himself as he might, he believed he dared never call her his wife; and his blood curdled at the thought.[9]

Equally melodramatic, the other story of the new collection, *Peter of the Castle*, turns upon an entire series of uncertain identities, the truth being revealed only at the end. There is little about the tale that is peculiarly Irish except for the village wedding party and the awe and respect in which the inhabitants hold the local bandit. Banim deliberately declined to identify the exact locale of the story.

Declaring that Ireland's sad history and present misery made it a natural scene for romantic literature and adding that its people moved with astonishing speed from pleasure to despair with "a volatility of heart equal to the French volatility of manner," a reviewer of the new *Tales* hailed them as better not only than the earlier series but than those of Miss Edgeworth, Lady Morgan, or Maturin. Ease of manner, a natural way of telling his story, a straightforward attitude towards horror, and a fine treatment of humorous scenes: these were some of Banim's strengths. Not only was he good at "painting" manners; he excelled "in dealing with the passions in the fulness of their power," more like the old dramatists Webster or Ford than any author of "our time." Obviously a specialist in Gothic romance, the reviewer compared poor Peggy Nowlan's dangers on a trip to Dublin to some of the most famous scenes of suspense in old favorites. But Banim was too gloomy. He was in the same class as Scott "as regards impressiveness," but below him because of "the want of lightness and relief." If he could add these, he would give "Ireland a share in the honours which have been well-nigh monopolized by Scotland." Other critics were even more positive, the *Literary Gazette* declaring that "the author is truly a man of talent and genius," the *Edinburgh Review* that "he is one of the most masterly painters of national character that has yet appeared in Ireland," and the *Literary Chronicle* expressing the "highest opinion of his exalted talents."[10]

V

The year 1827 brought renewed illness to John Banim, who was able to do little new work beyond the revision of the second series of *Tales* for a new edition, with "the too highly coloured scenes of ardent passion . . . altered and amended." Michael, on the other hand, was busy with a full-length three-volume novel, on which he worked at intervals all through 1827. John read most of it that summer, and gave it his approval: he was trying to be altogether impartial, he wrote Michael, but he was sure that Michael "need not apprehend failure." Colburn accepted the novel, the last portion of which was delayed while Michael visited John in England between August and November. He found his brother dreadfully altered for the worse. No doubt John edited Michael's novel, but one cannot regard it as in any substantial measure John's work.[11]

Michael called it *The Croppy* (3 vols., 1828; No. 19), the term used by the extreme Protestants in Ireland, the Orangemen, for Catholics in general, deriving from the cropped haircut adopted by some of the United Irishmen in imitation of the French Revolutionary fashion. It became a generalized term of contempt in Orangemen's mouths as the 1790's wore on and the great uprising of 1798 approached. "Croppies lie down" was a favorite song of Orange military forces. The novel deals with the uprising not in Ulster and Dublin—as does Eyre Evans Crowe's story *The Northerns of 1798*, published the next year in his *Yesterday in Ireland* (No. 15)—but in its chief center in southern Ireland, County Wexford (Leinster) around the towns of Enniscorthy, Wexford, and New Ross. After the mass arrest by the Dublin government of the provincial leaders of the United Irishmen, betrayed into their hands by informers, and the outbreak of insurrection in Counties Kildare, Carlow, and Wicklow, the disorders spread into Wexford, where until recent months prosperity had ruled and the relationships between Protestant landlords and Catholic tenants and middle-class farmers and townsmen had been good. But the undisciplined yeomanry, Orange atrocities, and the deliberately spread rumor that a wholesale massacre of Catholics was imminent touched off an uprising more furious than any other in the south, wholly to the surprise of the inept Dublin government and its military arm.

The bloody disorders in this region, just across the county border from Michael Banim's native Kilkenny, were only thirty years in the past. The fashionable floweriness of his language in describing the beauties of the landscape and the happy lives of the gentry on the banks of the Slaney River, and the stilted highflown conversations he imagined between Eliza Hartley, daughter of a Baronet of highly conciliatory tendencies, and her two suitors only heighten the grimness of the explosion when it finally takes place. Shawn-a-Gow, the blacksmith, whose innocent son is killed before his eyes by the soldiery—but who has been forging pikes for his fellow rebels all along—personifies the determination of the persecuted Catholics. The terrors of the rebellion merge into the complexities of a standard Gothic plot in which Eliza is caught up. Nanny the Knitter, the old woman whose second profession is matchmaking for money, and Rattling Bill Nale, the juggler and manipulator of dice at fairs and military reviews, who betrays both sides for profit, are perhaps the best drawn of Banim's group of Irish characters.

Father Rourke, the militant priest who leads a party of the insurgents and who is hanged at the end on the bridge at Wexford, seems to have been modelled on Father Philip Roche, who suffered the same fate, and not, as has been suggested, on Father John Murphy of

Boulavogue.[12] Eliza's father, Sir Thomas Hartley, a United Irishman in his youth, who is now reluctant to lead the rebels, is under great pressure to take command. He protests against Orange atrocities, is eventually arrested and tried, and (so it seems) summarily executed. He was to some degree surely inspired by Bagenal Harvey, a major figure in the Wexford uprising. Sir Thomas explains himself:

> Never can I cease to wish ardently, and, I hope, purely, for the independence and happiness of my country. . . . As a Volunteer officer, in the first epoch of Ireland's glory [i.e., 1782–1783], I was an enthusiast. Fifteen years have since sobered down my mind, and yet I see no reason to criticise my more youthful views and feelings. It was the only period, during a lapse of six centuries, that Ireland's sons, pausing in their dissensions, united for her good, and therefore seemed capable of serving her.

But the good old days of the early 1780's have gone. Now Sir Thomas recoils "from the cruel devastations of a civil war." The excesses of the French Revolution have disillusioned him. The "lower orders" of each faith, he is sure, will now massacre all members of the other. "I shrink from the vortex!"[13]

A mass review of the yeomanry, just before the violence starts, is skillfully used to give the reader a survey of the widely varying human beings that make up the government's forces. Some who enlisted are willing to put on a red coat and learn "the theory of a soldier's trade," but shrink from action of any sort. One even steadfastly refuses to load his musket: "Me! . . . is it me?

—not I, upon my word and credit; how do I know but I might hurt some one?" Perhaps unfortunately, such pacific amateurs were in a great minority. A wicked young baronet, concealing an earlier marriage, uses the crisis to push his suit with his new sweetheart's family: "a dreadful convulsion is at hand: a bloody extirpation of all Protestants is meditated by the Papists of the country; property, rank, distinction, society—every thing may be swept away: oh! in that coming day of anarchy, amid that hurricane of vulgar and fierce passions, Heaven help the weak and unprotected!"[14]

Characteristic of both sides is the animus displayed by a recruiter for the United Irishmen, who explains to a prospective candidate

> the way we'll scourge them bloody dogs out iv our land, at the same time that we hender them from killin' us; an' he b'lieves every word I say,—no praise to him for the same;—an' I whips out my book, an' makes a man of him, an' gives him the sign; an' he talks to a friend about id, an' makes a man of him too; an' they go and get pikes made, an' hide 'em till the time comes.

As for the explanation of a Protestant United Irishman—

> It is a mistake that every Protestant is an Orangeman, or an enemy to Roman Catholics. . . . the originators of our confederacy were to a man Protestants; its present heads are chiefly Protestants. . . . I am a Protestant, myself. And, indeed, what means our title "United Irishmen," if it does not describe a combination of every sect for our country's good?

this is now hopelessly out of date and meaningless in Wexford at the moment of danger. In Shawn-a-Gow's smithy, the rebel agitator (a desperate villain and liar) reads out the oath that he solemnly declares the Protestants to be taking, "I do solemnly swear, that I will be thrue to the King and Government . . . and that I will exterminate . . . as far as I am able . . . the Catholics of Ireland, and that I will wade ankle deep in Papist blood." And yet, ironically enough, the counteroath which he administers is still the original oath of the United Irishmen that pledged "a brotherhood of affection among Irishmen of every religious persuasion" for "equal, full, and adequate representation of all the people of Ireland,"[15] an oath in the spirit of the American Revolution, which has now altogether lost its true meaning.

Father Rourke, the fighting priest who leads a band of insurrectionists, admits that he does not know whether the story of the Orangemen's oath is true or not; it does not matter, he says, because the Orangemen "act as if it were true—act as if literal extermination of the [Catholic] people was their wish and object." And at one moment, in his ornate and clumsy prose, Michael Banim generalizes from the heart about the Irish character: at the moment when they are most destructive, the Irish peasants are most given to laughter:

> Windows were shattered, and furniture was dashed to pieces and flung out through them into the street; and mingled with the shout of fury came the shout of merriment: the wildest act of destruction, in accordance with the hidden character of the Irish peasant, often producing the heartiest laugh:—hidden we have called that character, and it is so;—its minor

> traits, indeed, such as appear, or are put forward, in every-day intercourse, any one may catch; but owing to a long habit of abstraction, or rather banishment from all interchange of social thought or feeling with those ranking above him, the real moral elements that form every kind of character—the springings of the heart, and the mental combinations, no matter how rude, which end in impulse—those secrets of his inner heart, the Irish peasant keeps concealed to the present hour, as well from the oppressors he hates, as from the friends who, if they knew him better, could better serve him.[16]

Said the *Literary Chronicle*, "Delighted as we have been with all the previous productions of these gifted authors, it was reserved for the 'Croppy' alone to impress us with any idea of their full extent of their genius and capabilities. It is impossible to conceive a scene, or actors, better suited to the purpose of such writers, than Ireland and the unquiet spirits of 1798; and equally difficult to imagine in what other quarter they could have received the justice awarded to them in this. The story itself glows with the very essence of romance and excitation."[17]

VI

While Michael Banim was visiting John in England between August and November of 1827, engaged on the final volume of *The Croppy*, reading aloud each night for John's criticism what he had written that day, and "adopting his suggestions as I went on," John also showed him the draft of a new novel of his own:

> I read in MS. at the same time, the rough copy of a tale, which he had put together between whiles and in the lapses between his attacks of pain. This was done without the knowledge of the doctors. He could not submit to the sentence of positive idleness: the tale I allude to was published the year following, under the title of "The Anglo-Irish." It was of a different character from the "O'Hara Tales," and was not announced as proceeding from the same authors.
>
> I cannot say how the "Anglo-Irish" was received —I believe indifferently. The full power of the writer's mind was not brought to bear on it; unhappily, there was a physical inability to strain the brain to its tension at the time it was written.[18]

The absence of the familiar "O'Hara Family" signature on the title page, and the "different character" of the novel, to which Michael Banim refers, did arouse some speculation as to the identity of the author.

Some people thought that the novel was by Lady Morgan's husband, the physician Sir Thomas Morgan, who had written many essays and whom Colburn had pressed in 1826 to try his hand at an Irish novel. Sir Thomas wrote off to his lady, "Colburn wants me to write a political novel. For God's sake make me out a canvas, and I shall try it." Probably he spoke to friends about his project and the rumor spread. So, when *The Anglo-Irish of the Nineteenth Century* (3 vols., 1828; No. 20) appeared anonymously in 1828, some jumped to the conclusion that Morgan had written it.[19] But Michael Banim's statement that he read it in John Banim's own manuscript is in itself decisive.

Despite its lack of the sustained power that characterizes John Banim at his best, *The Anglo-Irish* is by no means to be dismissed as the inferior product of a sick and tired man. Nor was it received "indifferently," as Michael Banim suggests. When it appeared, published anonymously in three volumes by Colburn in 1828, the *Morning Chronicle* said of it, "The incidents of Irish history, and the character, notions, feelings and habits engendered by the unprecedented situation of the people, combine to form a source of interest as fertile and as various as that from which the great Novelist of the North has created his Scotch historical romances," while the *Scotsman* was even more fulsome:

> This novel will be much read. Its great topic—the policy of England towards Ireland—the question, What ought now to be done with the Irish Catholics? is uppermost at present in the public mind, and is momentous if not engrossing; its great staple—the feelings of the English and the Irish towards each other, or rather of the provincializing Anglo-Irish, or Orange, faction, towards their half countrymen— would have been interesting at any time, from its requiring at once a portraiture of manners and an analysis of motives; but it is doubly so now, from the feelings of which it consists, and the manner in which they are dealt with, involving the quiet and prosperity of an empire; and to these attractions we must add likewise the introduction on the canvas of well-known public characters; and, beyond all, and without which the rest would lose all its natural zest, the shrewdness, knowledge of the world, scenic power, and general talents of the author. Who he is we do not pretend to know.[20]

When a modern reader turns to the novel today, he will find much to sustain these opinions, and he will find it all the more puzzling that Professor Flanagan, in the course of discussing John Banim's writings, not only fails to mention *The Anglo-Irish* but even omits it completely from what purports to be his complete list of Banim's works.

What we see in *The Anglo-Irish* is not so much the impact of illness and fatigue—the plot is not much more mechanical or the episodes more improbable than those of the fiction written at the height of Banim's powers—as the impact of Banim's disillusionment with his own past hopes for conciliation and understanding between Englishmen and Irishmen. Whereas previously he had been careful to balance the extreme anti-Catholic and anti-Protestant views of his most violently partisan characters with moderate and conciliatory views put into the mouths of his heroes and heroines—even in the seventeenth century—now, for the first time, he has clearly lost hope and has turned bitter. The loathing mouthed in the 1680's and early 1690's by George Walker and Father O'Haggarty in *The Boyne Water* for all members of the other sect has in *The Anglo-Irish* become the common currency of the small talk of English and Ascendancy gentlefolk on the one hand and of Irish peasants on the other.

Contempt and hatred for the Irish Catholics, mingled with fears of violence and a leaning towards brutal repression, characterize even the casual conversation of the gentry in London and in Dublin. Throughout *The Anglo-Irish*, Banim puts these views into the mouths of his most important characters with such a deadpan seriousness that only a careful reader who has the advantage of knowing Banim's genuine opinions can be absolutely sure he does not mean them seriously. Long pages of the novel, then, are simply slashing and sustained satire, no doubt reporting accurately enough what Banim heard every day in London. As the Clare election of 1828 approached and with it the inevitability of Catholic Emancipation (unsatisfactory as the details of the Bill would be), Banim had so far lost hope that he could no longer suppress his true feelings. Nonetheless, he did not publish them under the familiar "O'Hara Family" pseudonym, long since a transparent disguise for the best-known Irish novelist in England.

The hero of *The Anglo-Irish* is the Honorable Gerald Blount, younger son of Lord Clangore, an Irish peer, who dies at the opening of the novel, when Gerald and his elder brother are still schoolboys. The time (Banim never did properly work out his chronology for this novel) is about 1814. The three guardians of the brothers are "the Minister" (Lord Castlereagh himself), a leading general, also of Irish origin, and a quiet Ascendancy Irish landowner, Mr. Knightly, who actually lives in Ireland. In a long-sustained conference between these guardians and their two wards, the themes of the novel are enunciated. The two grandees batter Mr. Knightly with questions: When *will* the Irish grow any quieter, the "unhappy, misguided creatures. . . . What with Whiteboys and Right-boys, United-men, Shanavests, Caravats, Threshers, Carders, and now, Rockites," it is clear that the Irish "never can be peaceable so long as they remain what they are." They are turbulent, ferocious, they thirst for human life: how can "English gentlemen, or Irish gentlemen of English descent, . . . think of settling in the country?"

There can be no change, the two Englishmen smugly and sadly agree, until "English views, interests, industry—English character, in fact—" replace Irish "views, interests, and indolence." All the people must become "English-Irish." Mr. Knightly seems to assent, and the boys themselves resolve that until there is security in Ireland they can never visit their own large Irish estates, from which, of course, their income is derived. In fact, the guardians agree, with Mr. Knightly demurring so subtly that his ideas are never voiced, that the Irish must be taught another severe military lesson: conquer them thoroughly at last: that is what "our distinguished countryman, now immortalizing himself on the peninsula"—the Duke of Wellington, of course—recommends.[21]

Violently anti-Irish without ever having seen Ireland, young Gerald swears to be "English-Irish." Everything he sees—an incident in which an Irish schoolboy responds with unseemly violence to English bullying at school, a brawl amongst Irish laborers in London, the foul conditions in St. Giles's, a London slum area inhabited chiefly by Irish, the well-deserved teasing he himself receives at the hands of Knightly's daughter, a charming young Irish girl and friend of his sister—contributes to making Gerald as anti-Irish as a self-proclaimed "English-Irishman" can be. At Cambridge, he meets Irish undergraduates—Protestants, of course—but his prejudices are only confirmed: "Cannot these men sit quieter ... and talk a little less loud, and, in a word, do as others do?" Why don't they stop worrying about their social position? How they "blunder and squabble amongst themselves about the great bone of contention, Catholic Emancipation." And if these Irishmen abroad are so unruly, "what, upon his own soil, must be the genuine Hibernian—papist, politician, and with an O to his name?"²² When his Irish acquaintances get roaring drunk and play dangerous tricks upon one of their number, Gerald is more convinced than ever. In his young manhood, ready to embark on a political career, he is, we realize, an absentee—like Maria Edgeworth's Glenthorn in *Ennui* (No. 3) or Colambre in *The Absentee* (No. 4), though not so bored as the first or so eagerly well-intentioned as the second—and the purpose of the book is to get him to Ireland so that he may begin to understand things for himself. Meanwhile, many an English reader would perhaps have been content to accept the views of Castlereagh, Wellington, and the rest that what Ireland needed most was more bloodshed.

There is one saving grace: Gerald is already in favor of Catholic Emancipation—for the wrong reasons, it is true: his theory, much in vogue at the time, being that if the Catholics were emancipated, Catholicism would wither away of itself when faced by the natural superiority of Protestantism. Until he goes to Ireland, he is indifferent to the reports of "Captain Rock's" increased activity, of famines, and of his brother's own agent's harshness. "No rents," complains his brother, Clangore, "no lease premiums; no renewal-premiums. In some instances, [the agent] in vain ejects the cotters and small farmers, who will not pay him a shilling; for either the ground remains unlet, or Captain Rock shoots, burns, or drives away, a new tenant."²³ In London, Gerald soon meets "the Secretary," a sardonic portrait of John Wilson Croker, scribbling away during one of his own dinner parties on a savage review of Lady Morgan,²⁴ and hears the current literary gossip, including a sarcastic remark about the Reverend George Croly—another of the Irish Protestant literary circle that included Maginn and Croker—whose latest novel is predicting the imminent "destruction of Popery, root and branch."[25] At dinner, some blame the sorry state of Ireland upon Sir Walter Raleigh's introduction of the potato.

Others (the Evangelicals) blame the Catholic priests as teachers of evil: "let us say to the people of Ireland, in plain language, 'We wish to change your religious belief, because we know it keeps you poor, ignorant, miserable, and most of all, because it is a blasphemy.'" An open challenge to the priests, mostly as ignorant as their flocks, but some of them deadly enemies trained by the "calculating, evading, cruel" Jesuits, would wipe out their faith in a decade. Irish Catholic children must be sent to schools where they may "hear the words of the book of life." So Gerald is soon induced to subscribe to the Evangelicals' Bible society. In *The Anglo-Irish* it is represented by O'Hanlon, like Horragan in *The Nowlans* a renegade priest who has become "a stout biblical." A visiting Scot says that he does not know Ireland well but all one needs to do is "make her people a moral, and an industrious, and a calculating people." So the chit-chat rambles over all the views and prejudices about Ireland then reigning in society, and Banim gives Croker the last word, when he tells Gerald that it is "All stuff and nonsense.... By virtue of certain old black-letter enactments, these Catholics are, this moment, eligible to political power, without ceasing to be Catholics: but such is the legal ignorance on both sides, that neither Catholic nor Protestant sees or admits the fact."

Castlereagh's trickiness on the issue is lampooned, as he refuses to admit that the English Government (Pitt) had actually once promised political equality to Catholics to get Catholic support for the Act of Union early in 1801. In Parliament, Henry Grattan, "the grey-headed veteran" of the Catholic cause, eloquently puts the Catholics' claims on the highest moral grounds. He is greeted by cheers, and that ends the matter. The basic difficulty, as the intelligent English cynic, Gunning (probably a portrait of a contemporary figure), tells Gerald, is the inveterate and ineradicable anti-Catholic sentiment of the English:

> Englishmen know that they enjoy their present independence; their liberty to read, and think, and speak, without a book-censor, or an inquisitor; to go to church or stay at home of a rainy Sunday; to pass a shovel-hat in the street without being afraid of it,—these, and other comforts, they know they possess, chiefly because Romanists have been and are kept down. And do you think they will set Romanists up again, upon the remotest chance of losing any one of their pleasant privileges?[26]

But all of these exchanges of views are preliminary to Gerald's actual visit to Ireland, which comes about by accident: he is shipwrecked on the coast. Here he falls at once into the hands of the followers of "Captain Rock," from whom he receives good treatment, but promptly escapes. He finds that the stagecoach driver taking him to Dublin has much to tell him about the English: "It's not the best o' you, I'm thinking, ye send over here to us, for samples, to agent us, and steward us, and lawyer us, and then make little of us after making nothing at all of us," says this man, who is in fact a former tenant on the

Clangore estates, evicted by the rackrenting Scotch agent Bignell, against whom a major Rockite plot is brewing.

Says the coachman, Michael Farrell:

> My father took a waste of three hundred acres, or thereaway, from the Irish lord,—he was Irish then,—that owned 'em; and by dint of hard work and careful looking-after, made 'em a good farum at the end o' twenty-five or thirty years. By course, he got 'em at a low rent; but at a short lase too; and he knew that when the lase would drop, he wasn't to expect a new one, on the same terms.

Ready to meet any reasonable demand, he nonetheless found—Lord Clangore now having become an absentee—that the agent now asked "just as much rent . . . as we all knew wouldn't lave us a good mouthful o' praties after paying it." So the steward came forward and paid the new rent, because he intended "to split the farum into little takes, and re-let it, to twenty or thirty poor divvles, at another rack-rent."[27] The result for the Farrells was disaster. Michael had joined the Rockites, and Gerald Blount realizes that a desperate appeal from Michael was one of those he had himself received in England and dismissed without paying any attention. His Irish education has begun.

It is continued for a time in Dublin, where he hears a debate between O'Connell and Banim's own friend of earlier days, Richard Lalor Sheil, both mentioned by name and vividly portrayed, as is Sir Harcourt Lees, the Orange clergyman-baronet (also in Crowe's *The Old Light and the New Light*, No. 15), and other notable Dubliners of the period. The hatred and fear of the Irish peasant that he heard in London Gerald now hears again in Dublin: a prominent Dublin Protestant (who is also a dishonest bankrupt) remarks that the Irish "are a half-savage race who hate us, our religion, our superior station, and our English descent, just as the Caffers and Hottentots hate the members and subjects of our paternal Colonial Government at the Cape." They will not take advantage of the kind efforts to help them by establishing schools, to which "they will not send their wild little children, merely because their bigoted priests object to our Bible without note or comment," although this proves how idolatrous and blasphemous their own priests are!

The real trouble, says another Ascendancy gentleman, is the rise of a new class of Irish Catholic professional men and landowners. This has altered the former proper subservience of the lower "caste" and now the Irish Catholics even threaten to take their betters to law. Unbelievable as it seems,

> the son of a fellow whom, thirty or forty years ago, you might have paid with a horsewhipping, or with setting your dogs at his heels, if he presumed to teaze you with a complaint of high rent, or a complaint against your land-steward ... will now threaten to indict you for a common assault at the quarter-sessions, when you only lay your whip across his shoulders. ...

The remedy? Educate them, convert them, keep them down, make them tidy, set them all to drain the bogs, and especially "thin them," by shipping them off to the colonies, forbidding marriage among them, or, best of all, letting them rebel and killing them off. The climactic toast of this enlightening evening is "The Pope in the pillory, the pillory in hell, pelted with priests by the devil,"[28] which is cheered to the echo. In *The Anglo-Irish* there is precious little left of John Banim's advocacy of conciliation.

The final volume of the novel, filled with further adventures amongst the Rockites, closes with the discomfiture of the agent, Bignell, and with Gerald's decision to settle down and become an Irish landlord. He succeeds to the Earldom and marries the daughter of his tolerant, decent godfather, Mr. Knightly, who has always been deeply sympathetic with the Irish Catholic cause. All this is somewhat stagy and mechanical, reflecting Banim's increasing fatigue as he tried to bring his violent, disillusioned novel to an end. He did so abruptly, promising that Gerald's later fortunes would be the subject of a sequel. He never wrote it, but there was no need for it. John Banim had got off his mind the pent-up furious resentments that were obsessing him.

VII

A temporary remission of his illness and, no doubt, the passage of the Catholic Emancipation Bill (April, 1829) while his next book was in progress somewhat mitigated John Banim's feelings. This book appeared as *The Denounced* (3 vols., 1830; No. 21), under the familiar "O'Hara Family" pseudonym, actually dedicated to the Duke of Wellington, who had been castigated in *The Anglo-Irish*. It consists of two novels, *The Last Baron of Crana*, set in the decades immediately after the Battle Aughrim (1691) and so in some sense a sequel to *The*

Boyne Water, although none of the same characters reappear; and *The Conformists*, set in the later years of George II, between 1750 and 1760. Both stories of the cruel workings of the penal laws, they show signs of John Banim's increasing inability to write full-length novels: prosiness, a certain incoherence, and—in *The Last Baron of Crana*, at least—a degree of mystification about the identity of the characters that sometimes approaches the ludicrous. Moreover, the careful and precise use of local color characteristic of *The Boyne Water* has now vanished, and the setting is left blurred or indefinite: in *The Last Baron of Crana*, largely somewhere in Ulster, apparently not far from Coleraine (Derry) and in a still more vaguely identified region of southern Ireland; in *The Conformists*, possibly the town and neighborhood of Kilkenny itself, although this is never specified.

One thing is clear: in these two novels John Banim was pulling his punches. In his introduction, he tells us why: intending to write of the abuses of penal days, he was nonetheless concerned "how far such allusions might affect, without the will or seeking of the writer, a question *at that time debated*, and it seemed certain, according to the opinions of competent friends, that if no prejudice interfered with the indispensable task, harm could scarce be done." In other words, if Banim treated his subject fairly, his work would not prejudice the passage of the Catholic Emancipation Bill. But, he continues, while the tales were in progress "the question alluded to *became unexpectedly decided*": that is to say, the Bill was passed. Then Banim began to fear that his stories might be criticized as "opening old wounds afresh." So, after the passage of the Bill ("the late great decision"), he "carefully and anxiously reviewed them, remodelled them,—in fact, rewrote them."

It is clear to the modern reader that this process did the novels no good. By curbing his indignation at the operation of the penal laws, Banim further enfeebled his stories. He assures us that the "Lately Made Free" will only rejoice at being emancipated from the shackles that bound their ancestors, whereas those who have disapproved of Emancipation ("the slave's enfranchisement") may at last cease to regret that "the last festering links" of the "old rusty chain of disability" have been broken.[29] But to us he seems to have robbed his own stories of some of the powerful impact they might have had if he had not edited them.

What the modern reader will appreciate and remember in *The Last Baron of Crana* is the warmth of the friendship between ancient enemies, as Miles Pendergast, a Protestant Ulsterman, fulfills the pledge made on the battlefield to his dying opponent Redmond O'Burke, a Catholic of the south, that he will care for O'Burke's only son. The sinister and corrupt working out of the penal laws is shown in the danger to which Burke exposes himself by harboring in his house a small nest of papists, whom he allows to worship in their own faith. The Rapparees appear, of course, this time as righters of Catholic wrongs, Robin Hoods on the Ulster highways, led by the semi-legendary Randall Oge O'Hagan, who is not what he appears to be. There is a fine scene of a bull-baiting, in which the great Irish wolfhound, symbol of ancient Gaelic might, outdoes a vicious English bulldog. And the savage prejudices of Protestant Ulstermen are reenforced from the pulpit by the (historical) Bishop of Meath, Dr. Dopping (1643–1697), a fanatical anti-Catholic.

In *The Conformists*, peace has descended; there is no foreign threat to support the Catholics, and yet the penal laws remain in all their rigor. Moreover, we are dealing now not with last Barons and other grand people but with simple village Catholics of the south, denied the right to worship freely or to educate their children. There is more pathos in the arrest of the admittedly rather slow-witted Daniel D'Arcy for trying to get instruction from a hedge schoolmaster than in all the dangers encountered by the relatively unconvincing grand gentry of *The Last Baron of Crana*.

Dan's father, the once-prosperous farmer Hugh D'Arcy, has been brought to the edge of ruin by the harsh operation of the penal laws that forbade Catholics to hold land by any lease running for more than thirty-five years and that deprived a Catholic at once of any farm that produced an annual profit one-third larger than the amount of annual rent. "The first individual of the established creed who should discover the rate of profit" could immediately seize the land.

> Catholic farmers, seeing themselves deprived of long and advantageous holdings, and even of the profits which they might hope to amass under short tenures, ceased to be agriculturalists, and commenced graziers. [In fact this was possible only for very large landowners, most of them Protestants.] Lands were no longer drained and enclosed; good houses were no longer built on them, or those previously standing repaired; pasturage wasted the fields, which were virtually forbidden to be cultivated; and the real yeomen of Ireland sunk in the scale of social importance, and along with becoming poor, grew indolent and apathetic in pursuits which required little industry and less labour. [The shift to grazing actually took

> place because the markets were better for meat and wool than for agriculture. Banim's heart is in the right place but his history and economics are weak here.][30]

Although the Catholic Hugh D'Arcy has been a kind and considerate landlord, his best tenants will not renew their leases, but prefer to emigrate; their successors cannot pay enough rent to keep him going, and themselves often run off. The declassing of the yeomen is vividly portrayed in the decision of young Daniel to drop his efforts at education and cultivate the fields himself. Amidst the grinding injustice of the times, the happy ending of *The Conformists* seems contrived and mechanical.

VIII

These two were John Banim's last sustained works of fiction about Ireland. His next novel, *The Smuggler* (3 vols., 1831), dealt wholly with English scenes, being set in the region near Eastbourne, where he had been living in 1829, and involving him in a disagreeable dispute with his publishers, Colburn having merged with Bentley in a new firm. Banim moved to France in late 1829; his health grew steadily worse. All he could manage was a series of shorter stories, published in the various *Annuals* of the period. These were collections of prose and verse by various authors, sometimes elaborately illustrated and prettily bound for gifts at Christmas. Not until 1838 did a collection of these appear as *The Bit O'Writin'* (3 vols.; No. 24).

Meanwhile Michael wrote *The Ghost-Hunter and his Family* (1833; No. 22), published in the Library of Romance, edited by Leitch Ritchie, a series of cheap one-volume novels designed to break the stranglehold of the expensive two- and three-volume novels on the market. The personages of *The Ghost-Hunter* were modelled directly on John and Michael's maternal grandparents and on their mother's brother and sister. She had often told her sons about her family, and the idea of writing the story was suggested by John in a letter of November 10, 1828. "My dear Michael," he had written, "if health permitted, I could use these people, and bring their real and unimagined qualities into play, with credit to the Irish character, all Papist as it is, sweetly, primitively, and amiably."[31]

Michael also wrote *The Mayor of Wind-Gap* (No. 23), a pleasant and flowery story, published as the first of two novels by "The O'Hara Family" in three volumes in 1835. It is the second novel, however, *Canvassing*, that seizes our interest. Its anonymous author was a newly co-opted "O'Hara," Miss Harriet Martin (1801–1891). She was the second daughter of the second marriage of Richard Martin (1754–1834), M.P. for Galway, the famous "Humanity Dick," portrayed in 1825 as "King" M'Loughlin in Eyre Crowe's short novel *Connemara* (No. 14). Owner of vast estates in Connemara, totalling about one-third of the entire county of Galway in area but sparsely inhabited, and possessor of a splendid and almost inaccessible castle at Ballynahinch, Martin was a famous duellist, a beloved and kind landlord, and a pioneer in the movement for ending cruelty to animals. Saluted in verse by Thomas Moore and Thomas Hood and portrayed in fiction not only by Crowe but as "Uncle

Godfrey" by Charles Lever in his *Charles O'Malley* (1841), the famous and picturesque Dick Martin[32] is most lovingly represented in his own daughter's lively and unjustly neglected novel, *Canvassing*, in which he appears as "Mr. Wilmot," proprietor of Castle Wilmot in Connemara, "good-natured, careless, and extravagant."[33]

In this Galway election he is not himself running for office, but has promised his interest to young Lord Warringdon, an English noble, instructing all Wilmot tenants (the local Catholic forty-shilling freeholders enfranchised in the years before Catholic Emancipation raised the minimum value of a voter's holding to £10.) to vote for Warringdon, whose election manifesto is so written as to suit everyone, "those who cry out for Catholic Emancipation, and those who insist on keeping up the Protestant ascendancy." But there is a contest, and against its background is played out an elaborate and brilliantly written comedy of matchmaking, in which Lady Anne Wilmot procures husbands for both her daughters by supremely clever tactics. Duels are a matter of daily occurrence in what one of the Wilmot girls (the clever one, as Harriet Martin was the clever Martin) calls "this merry, murderous country of ours." There are fine genre scenes among the servants; there is a most sophisticated and handsome Catholic priest, mistaken as a rival for one of the Wilmot girls by Lord Warringdon, who has never met anybody like him; there are the local social-climbing Irish middle classes, anxious to ape English society in every detail; there is a duel between a stupid Englishman and a hot-headed Irishman, who become fast friends immediately afterwards, though both are wounded.

But above all, there is Mr. Wilmot, drawn by his own daughter: "Who is there we'd think of comparing with Mr. Wilmot, in regard to fire-ating; he's the wondher of Ireland, not to talk of the Province [Connaught]." The election, with its drunken disorders and its scandalous irregularities, provides one climax: Pat Conny must be reminded "he was only to be Pat Conny the first time he voted, but Dennis Sleevan the second time, in regard of poor Dennis not being convanient just then, because he was berried last week";[34] and Martin Donovan, whose lease has expired, must be reminded to put a live flea inside the document so he can swear the lease "has life in it." The other climax is provided by Lady Anne's success in securing the husbands for her daughters. Here most nineteenth-century novelists would have stopped.

But in a sort of epilogue, far more awkward in style, and yet imbued with a convincing sincerity, the reader is taken into the households of both the married daughters only a few years after their weddings. Both marriages are disastrous failures. And in the end, even the brilliantly successful Lady Anne admits it would have been better had she done nothing to make the matches but had run the risk that her daughters might remain spinsters. In the clever and witty Maria Wilmot, who puts the dinner table in a roar of laughter and who frightens the men until a man comes along so insensitive that he marries her as it were for a joke, Harriet Martin at thirty-four may have been commenting on her own spinsterhood, destined to last ninety long years: she was too intelligent and too bright, her contemporaries agreed, to attract a suitable husband. But she did write this one admirable forgotten novel, as good in its own way for the early century as in their time would be the best novels written later in the century by her own distant relative Violet Martin ("Martin Ross") (1862–1915) in collaboration with Edith Oenone Somerville (1858–1949).

IX

The Banim brothers' best work was now done. One family tragedy after another, combined with the steady deterioration of his health, reduced John Banim by the mid-1830's virtually to misery. Public appeals and subscriptions provided the money needed to bring him home to Ireland and buy for his last years a small house near Kilkenny on the Dublin road. In 1838, after he had been living there for three years, a collection was published of the shorter fiction written in earlier years. Appearing in three volumes as *The Bit O'Writin' and Other Stories* (No. 24) as by "The O'Hara Family," it included eighteen stories. Most of them are laid in Ireland, and go back to anecdotes or longer tales heard in his youth. They often have the pungent Irish phraseology that marked his best work: a sullen man in a pub is called "as serious as a pig getting a sun-dial by heart." But by far the best is the longest: the title story. Here, without the slightest tone of patronizing, an illiterate Irishman, a former sailor in the British navy, makes his claim on the government for prize money due to him. How he gets it despite the kind efforts of his semiliterate friends, and what he does with it once he has it, form a cheerful Irish comic tale.[35] The collection is our final Banim reprint in this series.

After it was published, John gave Michael some collaboration on the final three-volume "O'Hara" story, *Father Connell* (3 vols., 1842), published in the year of John's death and notable for its affectionate portrait of their own parish priest, Father Richard O'Donnell, who in later years became Dean of Ossory. Yeats admired it. But as a piece of literature the novel now seems too flat and long-winded to deserve republication here. The same is true of Michael Banim's last effort, more than twenty years later still, at a novel of his own, *The Town of the Cascades* (2 vols., 1864), a cautionary tale about the perils of drink. It has always had admirers, but like the various shorter stories that Michael wrote after John died, it should perhaps not be resuscitated.[36]

Into the brief space of a decade or so, between 1825 and 1835, then, the two brothers Banim crammed the nine single novels or collections of novels here reprinted as their best work. Far more of the best stories than is traditionally recognized (despite John's cheerful and grateful acknowledgments) were by Michael, who has seldom received credit. With the striking exception of the angry and disillusioned *Anglo-Irish*, so badly needing revival, all of the Banims' work—whether historical in the manner of Scott or set in their own day and reporting on Irish life—was written, as John declared in a letter putting forth his claims to consideration by the "affluent protectors of literature," with a "uniform political tendency, viz. the formation of a good and affectionate feeling between England and Ireland." And this was true, although—as he himself said later, replying to a generous testimonial from his fellow townsmen of Kilkenny after he returned to Ireland in 1835—his work was inspired "by a devoted love of our country, and by an indignant wish to convince her slanderers, and in some slight degree at least to soften the hearts of her oppressors."[37] This tension, at times scarcely bearable, between natural indignation at the English and the Irish Protestants and a persistent conviction that conciliation held the only hope for the future animated the entire work of "The O'Hara Family," Ireland's first true native voices in fiction.

Robert Lee Wolff

Notes

1. Michael Sadleir, *Nineteenth-Century Fiction* (London: Constable; and Berkeley and Los Angeles: University of California Press, 1951), has an accurate bibliographical description of the first editions of the Banims' works. There is no mention of the Banims in J. Finneran, ed., *Anglo-Irish Literature. A Review of Research* (New York: Modern Language Association of America, 1976). The entry in *The New Cambridge Bibliography of English Literature*, III, 2nd edition (Cambridge: University Press, 1969), lists the Banims' works and the scholarly work about them down to about 1967. There has been nothing since the discussion in Thomas Flanagan, *The Irish Novelists, 1800–1850* (New York: Columbia University Press, 1959), Chapters 11 and 12, which is far from satisfactory. Patrick Joseph Murray, *The Life of John Banim, the Irish Novelist* (London: William Lay, 1857; No. 25) is valuable for the many quotations in extenso from John Banim's letters to Michael Banim and from the correspondence between John Banim and Gerald Griffin. For Harriet Martin, see above and below, text and notes.

2. Flanagan, p. 175. This Flanagan "documents" with a single footnote (p. 175 n. 10) intended to "set forth" the publication history of the Banim novels. It altogether omits two of these, misdates a second, and gives incorrectly the contents of a third.

3. Murray, *Life*, letters of May 2 and July 10, 1824, pp. 125, 139.

4. *Tales* (1825), I, 104, 191.

5. *Tales* (1825), III, 39–40.

6. Murray, *Life*, pp. 154–155.

7. Flanagan, p. 189.

8. *The Boyne Water* (1826), III, 435–436.

9. *Tales, Second Series* (1826), I, 268, 239; II, 53–54.

10. *New Monthly Magazine* XIX (1827), 23–25; other reviews quoted in an advertisement in a publisher's catalogue at the end of Volume I of *The Croppy* (1828).

11. Murray, *Life*, pp. 190, 191–193. Flanagan says only that Michael "collaborated" on the book.

12. Thomas Pakenham, *The Year of Liberty. The Great Irish Rebellion of 1798* (London: Hodder and Stoughton, 1969), p. 267 for Father Roche; pp. 147 ff. for Father Murphy of Boulavogue. Flanagan wrongly says (p. 200) that Rourke in *The Croppy* was patterned upon Murphy.

13. *The Croppy* (1828), I, 272–276.

14. *Ibid.*, I, 161, 253.

15. *Ibid.*, II, 11, 13, 27–30.

16. *Ibid.*, II, 85; III, 7.

17. Advertisement in publisher's catalogue at the end of Volume I of *The Denounced* (1830).

18. Murray, *Life*, pp. 193–194.

19. Lionel Stevenson, *The Wild Irish Girl* (London: Chapman and Hall, 1936), pp. 254–255.

20. Criticisms quoted from publisher's catalogue at the end of Volume III of (John Carne) Anonymous, *Stratton Hill* (London: Colburn, 1829), for the *Morning Chronicle*; for the *Scotsman*, advertisement at the end of Volume I of (Eyre Crowe) Anonymous, *Yesterday in Ireland* (1829).

21. *The Anglo-Irish*, I, 19–27.

22. *Ibid.*, I, 82–83.

23. *Ibid.*, I, 99–100.

24. For Lady Morgan's feud with Croker see my introduction to her novels included in this series.

25. Croly's novel, which Banim (I, 146–147) calls "The Angel of the World," saying that it was dedicated to Canning, was actually called *Salathiel. A Story of the Past, the Present, and the Future* (3 vols.; London: Colburn, 1828), and was dedicated to the Duke of Newcastle. It dealt with the Wandering Jew.

26. *The Anglo-Irish*, I, 156, 161, 237, 205, 169, 191.

27. *Ibid.*, II, 99–100, 101–103.

28. *Ibid.*, II, 262–263, 267, 272.

29. *The Denounced* (1830), I, (v)-viii.

30. *Ibid.*, III, 35, 35–36.

31. Murray, *Life*, pp. 205–206.

32. Shevawn Lynam, *Humanity Dick* (London: Hamish Hamilton, 1975), is a good new biography of Harriet Martin's father. It mentions *Canvassing* only briefly (p. 276). The date of Harriet's death is given as an addendum to the chart in Archer E.S. Martin, *Genealogy of the Martin Family of Ballinahinch Castle in the County of Galway, Ireland* (privately printed; Winnipeg: The Stovel Company, 1891). Murray, *Life*, p. 217, unequivocally attributes *Canvassing* ("admirable story") to Miss Martin, and so did Michael Banim in a preface written in 1865 for a new edi-

tion of the two tales published in one volume by James Duffy. Michael added that he could not explain why the story was published as "by the O'Hara Family." See Sadleir, *Nineteenth-Century Fiction*, I, 25, under No. 147a. It is said by Miss Lynam that Michael Banim and Miss Martin met in Paris.

33. *The Mayor of Wind-Gap and Canvassing* (1835), II, 37.

34. *Ibid.*, III, 35, 18, 175, 179.

35. *The Bit O'Writin' and Other Stories*, II, 281–282, from the story called "Ill Got, Ill Gone." Of the eighteen stories, the earlier appearance of the following eleven in the various Annuals of the time can be traced (in the order of their appearance in the three-volume book edition here reprinted). In Volume II: "The Hall of the Castle" from *The Keepsake*, 1830; "The Half-Brothers" from *The Keepsake*, 1829; "Twice Lost but Saved" from *The Keepsake*, 1831; "The Faithful Servant" from *The Keepsake*, 1830; "The Roman Merchant" from *The Amulet*, 1831. In Volume III: "The Church-Yard Watch" from *Friendship's Offering*, 1832; "The Last of the Storm" from *The Literary Souvenir*, 1830; "The Rival Dreamers" from *The Gem*, 1829; "The Substitute" from *Friendship's Offering*, 1832; "The White Bristol" from *Friendship's Offering*, 1831; "The Publican's Dream" from *Friendship's Offering*, 1829. All of these references except one ("The Half-Brothers") can be found in Andrew Boyle, *An Index to the Annuals, 1820–1850* (all published, Worcester: Andrew Boyle, Ltd., 1967), I, 16.

36. (Banim, John and Michael) The O'Hara Family, *Father Connell* (3 vols.; London: T.C. Newby and T.W. Boone, 1842); Banim, Michael, Survivor of the O'Hara Family, *The Town of the Cascades* (2 vols.; London: Chapman and Hall, 1864).

37. Murray, *Life*, pp. 220 (letter of November 28, 1832) and 254 (letter of September, 1835).

THE LIFE

OF

JOHN BANIM.

THE LIFE

OF

JOHN BANIM,

The Irish Novelist,

AUTHOR OF "DAMON AND PYTHIAS," &c. AND ONE OF THE WRITERS OF
"TALES BY THE O'HARA FAMILY."

WITH

EXTRACTS FROM HIS CORRESPONDENCE,

GENERAL AND LITERARY.

BY

PATRICK JOSEPH MURRAY.

LONDON:
WILLIAM LAY, KING WILLIAM STREET, STRAND.
1857.

LONDON:
R. CLAY, PRINTER, BREAD STREET HILL.

TO

RICHARD ARMSTRONG, Esq. Q.C.

IN MEMORY OF

HAPPY DAYS AND PLEASANT NIGHTS,

THIS MEMORIAL OF JOHN BANIM IS DEDICATED,

BY, ONCE HIS PUPIL,

AND FOR EVER HIS FRIEND,

PATRICK JOSEPH MURRAY.

BIOGRAPHY OF JOHN BANIM.

CHAPTER I.

INTRODUCTION—BIRTH—SCHOOL DAYS—YOUTH—FIRST LOVE.

It has been said that the lives of literary men in England are, in general, devoid of incidents either interesting or exciting, and yet, in all the long catalogue of human joys and sorrows, of combats against the world, and of triumphs over difficulties almost insurmountable, of instances where the indomitable will has raised its possessor to the enjoyment of every object sought, and to the full fruition of every hope long cherished, where can such glorious examples be found as in the pages of literary biography? It is true that many a noble intellect has been shattered in the pursuit of literary fame; it is true that ghastly forms of martyred genius flit across the scene, and that, from the lowest depths of the deep hearts of Poets, the cry of gnawing hunger, and the wail of helpless, hopeless sorrow arises, with an anguish more frightful than that of Philoctetes, more awful that that of Lear. Truly, literature has had its martyrs—Nash, the creature of genius, of famine, and despair, tells us: " I sat up late and rose early, contended with the cold and conversed with scarcity, and all my labours turned to loss—

> 'Why is't damnation to despair and die
> When life is my true happiness' disease?'"

Churchyard, who wore out life on the food and in the rags of a beggar, had written on his grave, " Poverty and Poetry his tomb doth enclose." Stowe, after the labour of forty-five years, was a strolling mendicant through the country of whose antiquities he had been the learned chronicler. Otway, when he had endured all the woes of want, was choked by the hungry eagerness with which he tried to devour a loaf, the price of which he had begged. The saddest picture of all, in the martyrology of genius, is Chatterton—

> "the marvellous boy;
> The sleepless soul that perish'd in his pride"—

writing home to his mother those brave letters in which he promises to become great and famous, because, " by abstinence and perseverance, a man may accomplish whatever he pleases;" and then, after enduring days of starvation, and refusing a dinner from his landlady, the poor staymaker, he dies by his own hand of poison, and is buried amongst the rank graves of beggars in Shoe-lane workhouse. Literary biography has its kind good hearts too, doing deeds that shine in the face of heaven—its "noble silent men, scattered here and there; silently thinking; silently working; whom no morning newspaper makes mention of." Look at Goldsmith giving to the relief of want, whilst himself existing on pennies. Look at Samuel Johnson crowding his house with the needy. Look at him walking all night around St. James's Square, because otherwise his companion, Richard Savage, would sleep upon a cobbler's bulk. Look again, he is returning home late at night, his dim eyes serve him but poorly to see his way, and in his rolling, shambling walk, he stumbles over some object lying on the footpath; he stoops—it is a woman, half dead with cold, disease, and want. He takes her on his back, carries her to his lodgings, places her in his own bed, sends for a physician, and finding that she is a poor fallen outcast, prays, and teaches her to pray, and upon her recovery places her where poverty cannot again drive her from virtue. When Harte dined with Cave, meat was taken behind a screen placed at the end of the room; and there sat Johnson, too ragged and too proud to appear at table. But he heard them praise his Life of Savage—and the same man, so poor and so proud, some few years afterwards flung back to the clever puppy Chesterfield his praises of the Dictionary. Well has Thomas Carlyle written, "Old Samuel Johnson, the greatest soul in England in his day—Corsica Boswell flaunted at public shows with printed ribbons round his hat; but the great old Samuel stayed at home. The world-wide soul wrapt up in its thoughts, in its sorrows, what could paradings and ribbons in the hat do for it?" Truly nothing. For it, honour and rectitude did all. These are the facts and incidents which give to literary biography its charms.

Think of Kirke White, poor murdered child of song and sorrow; of John Keats, by his solitary hearth, a gloom-rapt soul, to whom

"The bare heath of life presents no bloom;"

of Gerald Griffin, so worn and wan before his time, starving by day, and awakened at night by the dread pulsation of his throbbing heart, to sigh lest day and its toil had come once more; and, most woful of all,

Sir Walter and Southey—so bright in intellect, and so dauntless in labour once, but so crushed and broken at the close of life—come before us, all teaching great truths in the moral of their lives, and proving, too, that old Burton judged rightly when, in " The Anatomy of Melancholy," he quaintly wrote, that the Destinies of old " put poverty upon Mercury as a punishment ; since when, poetry and beggary are Gemini, twin-born brats, inseparable companions. Mercury can help them to knowledge, but not to money."

It is not by reason alone of its fascinating details that literary biography should be prized and estimated. The author, more than any other man, rises by his own merits, or sinks through his own faults. Even in the days when the lot of the man of genius was, but too often,

"Toil, envy, want, the Patron, and the jail,"

the want and the jail were frequently attributable to his own misconduct ; but, in this our age, when from literature have sprung the glories of the Church, the Bench, the Senate, and the Bar, genius need no longer dress in rags, or live in poverty—its Patron is the Public ; and for him who is entering on the journey of life, the best guide will be the biography of some literary man of the time. He will there discover how, by honourable conduct and by persevering application, all the honours of the kingdom can be obtained—and how, on the other hand, the brightest gifts of genius are useless, if desecrated by idleness or by misapplication. He will learn, also, to doubt the truth of one who has written :

" Let no man be bred to literature alone, for, as has been far less truly said of another occupation, it will not be bread to him. Fallacious hopes, bitter disappointments, uncertain rewards, vile impositions, and censure and slander from the oppressors, are their lot, as sure as ever they put pen to paper for publication, or risk their peace of mind on the black, black sea of printer's ink. With a fortune to sustain, or a profession to stand by, it may still be bad enough; but without one or the other it is as foolish as alchemy, as desperate as suicide." *

The facts show to the reader how interesting and how useful a study literary biography becomes when rightly pursued; and we have endeavoured to render our Biography of John Banim as faithful a memoir as facts could make it, and to give it, through his own letters, somewhat the character of an autobiography.

There is a charm about biography which is immediately felt and acknowledged by all; but autobiography is still more attractive, being the record of the heart, the feeling and the actions of him who is the subject of his own pen.

Great old Samuel Johnson said, that if any man were to note down the facts of his daily existence, the diary *should* prove interesting, and for our parts we believe, most firmly, that he was right; we even consider that an indifferently executed autobiography is more interesting than an ordinarily compiled biography. Who would not rather read Horace's own account of his school days, of his boyhood, and of his every-day life, than the most erudite and accurate biographical sketch composed by his annotators? When he writes of himself he is before us, as in the years when he, the freedman's son, was brought to Rome by a father, noble in the nobility of manhood, and was sent to learn all that the Roman Knight could know. We see him as when he went attended by slaves, and dressed as if his estate

* Jerdan's Autobiography, Vol. I. p. 39.

had been princely. When he relates the moral lessons given him by his father, and adds, to the noble born Mecænas—

"Nil me pœniteat sanum patris hujus"—

the old man is present before us, living, breathing, and respected. When he describes his home life, that exquisite picture of Epicurean—*real* Epicurean—existence, we see him plainly, jogging upon the bob-tailed mule, or inquiring the price of bread and herbs, or loitering in the Circus, or lounging in the Forum, or listening to the fortune-tellers; and we return with him at night to the supper of onions, pulse, and pancakes, served by the three slaves; and observing the two cups, and the tumbler, upon the white stone slab, we think him a Roman "right gay fellow," and grasping his hand, in fancy, we cry, in his own line—

"Nil ego contulerim jucundo sanus amico;"

and we hear him say, as his eyes sparkle,

"Hic me consolor victurum suaviús, ac si
Quæstor avus, pater atque meus, patruusque fuisset."

And turn now to Montaigne. Who could tell, as he himself tells, the history of his early life? Who could place so well before us his father, Pierre Eyquem, *Ecuyer*, the brave and loyal soldier who had seen service beyond the mountains; who mixed his language with "illustrations out of modern authors, especially Spanish?" The man is before us, carrying the canes loaded with lead, and with them exercising his arms for throwing the stone. We see him walking with leaden-soled shoes, that he might be afterwards the lighter for leaping and running. The old man and his son are before us, when Michael writes: "Of his vaulting he has left little miracles behind him; and I have seen him, when past three-score, laugh at our agilities, throw himself in his furred gown into the saddle, make the tour of a table upon his thumbs, and scarce ever mount the stairs, up to his chamber, without taking three or four steps at a time."

Who could tell as well as Montaigne the plan of education marked out for him by his father; his being, before he could articulate, committed to the care of a German, who was ignorant of French, but who spoke Latin fluently; the scheme of education working so well, that George Buchanan—"that great Scotch poet," who was his tutor in the College of Guienne, where Michael played the chief parts in the Latin tragedies of Buchanan, Guerente, and Muret—told him that he must write a treatise upon Education, founded on the plan of that carried out by Montaigne's father, Buchanan being then tutor to that Count de Brissac who afterwards proved so valiant and so brave a gentleman? Who but Montaigne could lead us onward, through all his charming, babbling book, where he, his habits, his errors, and fine, noble, too truthful disposition steal out in every page, till we agree in his opinion, "Je n'ay pas plus faict mon livre, que mon livre m'a faict,—livre consubstantiel à son autheur?" Who but Robert Southey could tell us so charmingly of his own early life, as in the first pages of his Memoir we read from his own pen? Boswell's inimitable work, with all its life-like sketches, is not so interesting as the few personal incidents stated by Johnson himself. Who does not wish that Sydney Smith had continued that preface to his works, which he begins with the words, "When I first went into the

Church, I had a living in the middle of Salisbury Plain?" In these books, the writers are our friends; their minds, their actions, their hopes and fears are before us; and when the work is biography, we like it better the nearer it approaches to autobiography, by the insertion of the private letters of him who forms the subject. Thus Robert Southey thought, when about to edit the poems, and to compose a memoir, of Kirke White, he wrote to Neville White: "The most valuable materials which could be entrusted to me would be his letters,—the more that could be said of him in his own words the better." Letters give the chief charm to the biography of Byron, and of Scott. In the Sonnets of Shakespeare, those assumed to refer to himself are the most admired; and it has been well observed of Petrarch, that "his correspondence and verses together afford the progressive interest of a narrative in which the poet is always identified with the man."

It is true that genius has often been its own doomster. Debauchery and improvidence have, alas! been lures to lead the grandest souls to ruin; and fancies which in the dawn of fame blazed bright in beauty, have set in black clouds of gross and earthly passion. But there are other sufferers who have perished in the contest with the world, and who, in mental anguish and in bodily pain, attempted to accomplish the great deeds of which in youth they dreamed those dreams that come only in the days when—

> "All we met was fair and good,
> And all was good that time could bring,
> And all the secret of the spring
> Moved in the chambers of the blood."

These are the real martyrs of genius who, commencing

life in strength and hope, with that hope whose rosy light tints every rugged pathway in the far-off steeps that must be passed ere the gorgeous dream-land of golden fame can be reached—commencing life, too, with that power which ever dwells in the deep heart of youth, making to-day but the training ground for a future, when, amongst the clashing of minds, in the jarring struggle with the world, triumph shall crown him a victor—hope on for ever.

Such a man as this was John Banim: a bright-hearted, true-souled Irishman. He began his way of toil in trusting daring; side by side with a loving, unchanging wife, he would try the power of his mind, the readiness of his intellect, and the versatility of his genius; and had Omniscient Wisdom spared him health, as fully as it bestowed upon him energy of soul and ability of mind, he would have been the Scott of Ireland. But all his life long he laboured amidst the frowns of Fortune or the tortures of disease. He wrote in the intervals of anguish, frequently too during its paroxysms, and closed his life a mind-wreck, drifting away upon the lone black sea of pain and sorrow. But herein it is that his life deserves a record: its home love, its beautiful affection for her whom the Germans so thoughtfully call "the house-mother:" his never-flagging hope; his patient endurance; his triumphs; his efforts after excellence, form many important teachings for him who would enter the world a candidate for literary fame.

Banim was in heart and soul a man; and in toiling onward in his self-chosen profession, amidst all his griefs was ever a hero, disdaining to be, while the soul of a man dwelt in manhood's frame—

> "An infant crying in the night:
> An infant crying for the light
> And with no language **but a cry.**"

" Work" was his motto, and of the great psalm of life he made the anthem,

Laborare Est Orare.

Like Southey, he was always hoping, and always working; and the glory of his toil was not in the present work, but in that which should be accomplished in future times. Like Scott, he loved the humorous side of things, and when not in heroics was most at ease. His letters are more hearty than those of Moore; and the self-reliant independence of one who would be successful by his own efforts, is plain and evident in all his communications with the household at home. From the first letter to the last, now before us, these feelings are fully expressed; and much as we have read, much as we know, of literary men and their habits, we believe that of those who are the supports of the periodical Press, there is no man whom a Christian, a gentleman, or a brother *littérateur* would prefer to have called friend, before John Banim.

In the year 1792 there resided in the city of Kilkenny a young, hard-working man, named Michael Banim. A natural love of out-door exercise and field sports had sprung up in his breast, and had been strengthened by all the influences that extend to young men who reside in a county, the sporting habits of whose gentry are even less remarkable than those exhibited by the members of the once famous Kilkenny Hunt. Michael

Banim united pleasure with business, pushing his way in the world as a trader in all the necessaries of a sportsman's and angler's outfit,—dealing in everything, from a fowling-piece of John Rigby's to one of Martin Kelly's fishing-rods. He was a farmer too, and kept a pair of well-bred horses.

From the days when Venator, in "The Complete Angler," kissed the pretty milkmaid who sang so sweetly (one could wish, with Sir Thomas Overbury, " that she may die in the spring, and, being dead, may have good store of flowers stuck round about her winding-sheet"), and for which the grave Piscator reproves him with a "Come, scholar! let Maudlin alone : do not you offer to spoil her voice," to the time when young Squire Thornhill stole away the heart of poor Olivia Primrose—sportsmen have been the victims of bright eyes, and have made fond husbands too, notwithstanding the calumny of the jilted lover in Locksley Hall, who declares of his sporting rival :—

" He will hold thee, when his passion shall have spent its novel force,
Something better than his dog, a little dearer than his horse."

And so Michael Banim fell beneath the power of the god who "rules the court, the camp, the grove," and was married, in the year 1792, to Joannah Carroll.

She was of honest, respectable parentage, and of her character and personal appearance her eldest son, Michael, has given, in describing Rose Brady, the heroine of " The Ghost Hunter and His Family," the following sketch :—

"She could not be called beautiful, for her nose was neither Roman nor Grecian; nay, as we wish to speak candidly in all cases, we must confess that it was rather broad at the base, and perhaps about the sixteenth of an inch too wide. But then her lips were cherry-red, and beautifully formed; her forehead was as smooth as polished ivory; her cheeks were round and peachy, and, in colour, 'like to the Catherine pear, the side that's next the sun;' her chin was full, marbly, and a little dimpled; and as for teeth, Rose might be excused for unnecessarily displaying them, had she had the vanity to do so. The eye is the gem of the countenance; and Rose could boast two dark hazel ones, beaming with good-nature or with affection, full of sense and intellect, and sometimes shooting forth a sly humour. She was not tall, but her figure was nicely moulded. Richardson, while enumerating the perfections of his Clarissa, (poor, poor Clarissa!) relates that her attire always bore the gloss of newness. We claim the same praise for our humble little heroine, and we add that whatever she wore seemed of the exact colour, kind, and pattern, which became her best.

"She was as cheerfully industrious as a bee in the garden. Almost from her childhood she had been accustomed to earn something for herself; and by assiduity and prudence in her occupations, she was enabled not only to contribute to the comforts of the family, but to 'put money in her purse:' and that purse, a capacious one of gold-flowered silk, lay in a deep corner of the chest in her bedroom, and into it guinea after guinea found their way, until Rose had laid up her own dower."

She possessed a mind of very superior order, and a

store of good sense, and womanly, wifely patience; and these, with health and trust in Heaven, were her only marriage portion.

Michael Banim was a man of hasty temper, but with a fund of deep and genuine feeling at heart; and here his wife's gentle affection was the quiet soother of all care; and soon he was a man well to do in the world, respected by his superiors in rank, and—best test of all of one's real worth—respected by his neighbours and by his equals.

In August, 1796, there was born to him a son named Michael, who is still living, and whom, in the course of this biography, we shall have frequent occasion to mention. His second son, John Banim, was born on the 3d day of April, 1798.

John grew up a plain-looking child, with great staring eyes; and his only characteristic was a kind, loving disposition, which endeared him to all the humble household. He was petted by his mother, and her kindness, in conjunction with his own love of those about him, rendered his early years but one united train of childish joys.

His mother, as we have stated, petted, and as a matter of course, indulged him: the best place at table, and the nicest dainties of the dinner, even in mere childhood, were his; and although Mrs. Banim did not spoil her boy so excessively as did Quick the actor his little girl, who, because she wished to dabble her feet in the gravy of a saddle of mutton, was permitted to sit astride upon the joint, yet little John Banim merely escaped the socially atrocious character of an *enfant terrible*.

His father was a man of some information, for his

position and time; his mother was a woman of good mental powers, increased and strengthened by a love for reading. Thus both the parents of the future novelist were capable of understanding and appreciating the advantages of education, and in his fourth year their son John was sent to a school kept by Mrs. Alice Moore; where it was possible to learn the "Horn Book," and some fair share of the rudiments of reading, provided the words were not too long, and were those in ordinary use.

Here however, John did not continue a scholar. Like the more famous Academy and Lyceum, Alice Moore's school was held upon the ground-floor; and this circumstance so much excited the indignation of little Banim, that he rushed to his home from the cottage seminary, after an hour's tuition, declaring to his mother that he could not stay in a school where "there wasn't a bit of paper on the walls, or a step of stairs in the house." Mrs. Banim thought this outburst but the childish indication of an aspiring mind, and did not force her little boy to return, but sent him to the school of a Miss Lamb, who appears to have taught him the very merest branches of learning. She was, like many other schoolmistresses—women who are supported by parents simply because they act as a species of upper nurses, keeping the children from harm and home—good-humoured, quiet, and fat. With Miss Lamb, John remained until he could, as she used afterwards to boast, "turn the primer."

In his fifth year he was removed from Miss Lamb's to a school at that period well known in Kilkenny and its vicinity as "The English Academy, Kilkenny." Its master, Mr. George Charles Buchanan, was an oddity; and if ever man lived for whom the apology offered by Sir Walter for one of his characters should be freely admitted as a plea in bar of all deprecation, George Charles Buchanan could claim its fullest benefit, for truly "the man was mortal, and was born a schoolmaster."

Banim was, as we have observed, adoringly fond of his mother. With a child's love he ever feared to lose her, and about the period of his entrance into Mr. Buchanan's school his chief grief was lest a notorious highwayman of the time, named "Farrel the Robber," should steal away his mother whilst he was absent. This phantom haunted all his hours of play; and if, for a time, he forgot his mother's fancied danger, upon recollecting the fact he deserted his playmates, and ran to the house to assure himself of her presence and safety. She, in her turn, used to watch for him; and as the eager little face was pressed to the window, she smiled upon it those smiles which gave a balm to many a sorrow in after years.

A young, warm soul like this could not confine itself to one object of affection, and John's love for his elder brother Michael was, even in these years, tender and devoted. The second day after John's introduction to Mr. Buchanan's establishment, Michael was placed upon his knees in the centre of the school-room, in punishment for some fault. John inquired the reason, and finding that it was but the preliminary to a more severe punishment, rushed to his brother's side, and threw his arms around the offender's neck. The master ordered him to his seat—he but clung the closer; and threats were unavailing to induce him to abandon the culprit. Bribes were tried; five shillings were offered—he was unpurchaseable ; two crown pieces, bright and shining, were clinked before him, but all was unavailing ; and at length, as the reward of his consistent affection, his brother was forgiven. John led him in triumph to his place, and having seen him safely seated, burst, for the first time that day, into tears.

Michael Banim, the father, was, as we have written, a man of strong and violent temper. He punished his children at one time for trifles ; at another he permitted more serious offences to pass unreproved, being ever guided by the feeling of the moment, which was excited by various circumstances unconnected with the particular fault before him. Mrs. Banim rarely punished, yet a reproving word from her lips was more dreaded by her children than blows and violent threats from the hand and tongue of their father. Indeed so great a feeling of terror did his mother's anger excite in the mind of John, that once, when he had watched her through a keyhole flog his brother for some offence with a whip which he had frequently seen his father use for a like purpose, he became so much terrified at the unusual occurrence, that he ran to the barrack-gate, and entreated the sentry to come and save his brother, whom his mother was about to murder.

These are but the traits of childhood, which friends treasure up in memory, to make a story for the winter fireside ; and yet they show the spirit of a future man, who in years of well won, honourably worn reputation, looks back to those days of childish griefs and joys, with swelling heart, because they were the days of home and love.

Mr. Buchanan's Academy was not exactly suited to a

boy of Banim's disposition. The master was a clever man, but professed to teach all subjects, commencing with what he called "oratorical reading," and ending with the modern languages. He was an excellent instructor for a more advanced pupil, and of himself and his school "The O'Hara Family" have given the following exceedingly graphic account, in the novel "Father Connell:"—

"Through the partition separating his bedchamber from the school-room the head of the seminary had bored a good many holes, nearly an inch in diameter, some straight forward, some slantingly, to enable himself to peer into every corner of the study, before entering it each morning; and this is to be kept in mind. At either end of the long apartment was a large square window, framed with stone, and indeed stone also in its principal divisions. Overhead ran enormous beams of old oak, and in the spaces between them were monotonous flights, all in a row, and equally distant from each other, of monotonous angels, in stucco—the usual children's heads, with goose wings shooting from under their ears; and sometimes one or two of these angels became fallen angels, flapping down, on clipped wings, either upon the middle of the floor, or else upon the boys' heads, as they sat to their desks, and confusing them and their books and slates with fragments of stucco and mortar, rotten laths, and rusty nails. In a kind of recess, on the side of the school-room opposite to the boys' double desks, was an old table, flanked by a form, at which, at certain hours of the day, sat some half-dozen young girls, from six to ten years, who came up from the quaint old parlour below, under the care of the master's daughter, who therein superintended their education in inferior matters, to be occasionally delivered into his hands for more excelling instruction. The principal of this celebrated seminary wrote himself down in full, and in a precise round hand, James Charles Buchmahon, and his establishment as 'the English Academy;' principal, we have called him—despotic monarch we should have called him; for he never had had more than one assistant, and the head of that one he broke before they had been many weeks together. And never were absolute monarchy and deep searching scrutiny more distinctly stamped and carved on any countenance, than upon that of James Charles Buchmahon, master of the English Academy. And that countenance was long and of a soiled sallow colour; and the puckering of his brows and eyelids awful; and the unblinking steadiness of his bluish grey eyes insufferable; and the cold-blooded resoluteness of his marbly lips unrelaxable. At the time we speak of him, James Charles Buchmahon might have been between fifty and sixty; but he wore well. He was tall, with a good figure and remarkably well-turned limbs; 'and he had the gift to know it,' for in order not to hide a point of the beauty of those limbs from the world, he always arrayed them in very tight fitting pantaloons, which reached down to his ankles. His coat and waistcoat were invariably black. A very small white muslin cravat, and a frill sticking out quite straight from his breast, occupied the space from his chin to his waist. And James Charles Buchmahon's hat was of cream colour beaver, high crowned and broad brimmed; and he ever carried either a formidable walking-stick of stout oak, or else a substitute for it, made of five or six peeled switches, cunningly twisted together, and at one end loaded with lead."

From this establishment, after an attendance of five years, Banim was removed to a seminary kept by the Rev. Mr. Magrath, at that period considered the best Roman Catholic school in Ireland; where he continued a pupil for about twelve months, and was then sent to the academy of a well-known teacher, named Terence Doyle.

Although not a very idle boy, Banim loved to study in his own way, and at his own time; and his chiefest pleasure was to steal away from school, and lying under a hedge, or beneath the shelter of a haycock, to pore over some prized volume of "romance or fairy fable." Hans Andersen, in all his dreamy youth, never longed to hear the lore of fairy-land more earnestly than did little John Banim, and his ready memory enabled him to retain the subject of each narrative of wonder. From admiration however, the future novelist soon aspired to imitation; and in his sixth year, having listened in silent delight to a fairy fiction of more than usual interest, he resolved to write a story, his own sole composition.

He was not sufficiently tall to write conveniently at a table, even when seated, and having placed the paper upon his bed-room floor, he lay down beside it and commenced the construction of his plot. During three months he devoted nearly all his hours of play to the completion of his task; and when at length he had concluded, the writing was so execrable that he alone could decipher it. In this dilemma he obtained the assistance of his brother Michael, and of a schoolfellow —they acted as amanuenses, relieving each other when weary of writing from John's dictation. When the tale was fully transcribed, it was stitched in a blue cover, and John determined that it should be printed. But here the important question of expense arose to mind, and after long deliberation the youthful author thought of resorting to a subscription publication. Accordingly the manuscript was shown to several of his father's friends, and in the course of a week the subscribers amounted to thirty, at a payment of one shilling each. Disappointment was again the lot of our little genius; for in all Kilkenny he could not induce a printer to undertake the issuing of his story. This was a heavy blow to his hopes; but honourable, even as a child, he no sooner found that he could not publish the tale than he waited upon his subscribers for the purpose of restoring to them their shillings. All received him kindly, and refused the money, telling him that they were quite satisfied with reading the manuscript.

His literary efforts did not end with his fairy story. We have seen a romance in two thick manuscript volumes, written in his tenth year; and have looked through several manuscript poems, particularly one extending to over a thousand lines, entitled "Hibernia," written about the same period.

This early authorship is not unusual amongst those who have afterwards distinguished themselves in literature, as most students of literary history are aware. Cato and Hobbes, Bacon and Descartes, Boyle and Alfieri, Cowley and Pope, with a hundred others, were, in childhood as in manhood, philosophers, or poets, or painters. Like these last, Banim longed to be a poet, even in early days; and amid his stolen rambles in the summer fields felt all that joy in Nature, which

Byron so nobly expressed, when he makes the boy Tasso cry:—

> "From my very birth
> My soul was drunk with love, which did pervade
> And mingle with whate'er I saw on earth;
> Of objects all inanimate I made
> Idols, and out of wild and lonely flowers,
> And rocks whereby they grew, a paradise,
> Where I did lay me down within the shade
> Of waving trees, and dream'd uncounted hours,
> Though I was chid for wandering."

The poetic faculty, indeed, appears generally to have developed itself in early life; and whilst Tasso, Ariosto, and Lope de Vega were, even in school days, poets or romance writers, Boccaccio tells us,—and the analogy of his case with that of Banim is striking,—" Before seven years of age, when as yet I had met with no stories, was without a master, and hardly knew my letters, I had a natural talent for fiction, and produced some little tales."

But neither in the biography of Boccaccio, nor of any other man of genius, can we discover efforts so ardent and persevering to secure self-improvement as those exhibited, even in childhood, by Banim. Whilst in his ninth year, he began a strange birth-day observance. About a week before his birth-day he commenced the arrangement and perusal of all the verses, and pieces in prose, composed during the preceding year. When all had been read, and duly criticised, he generally found that one set was puerile,—he himself being but a child,—another set was turgid, a third portion was dull, a fourth lot was forced or unnatural; and the boy Banim was as fastidious in self-criticism as, in grave manhood, were Gibbon, Buffon, or Campbell. The evening of the birth-day having arrived, the condemned manuscripts were gathered in a pile, to which a lighted match was applied, and as the blaze mounted high the little author danced gleefully around the holocaust.

He felt no regret in thus destroying his compositions. He was resolved that the productions of his intellect in the succeeding year should be superior to those of the past, and fancied that the pieces condemned to the flames would but disgrace the more finished efforts of the months to come.

Banim, from early youth, had all that adoration of Poetry which is the characteristic of genius; and his love for

"The pleasing cadence of a line,
Struck by the concert of the sacred nine,"

was only equalled by his admiration of a poet. A good example of his self-estimate, and of this poetic feeling, was exhibited in his tenth year. The private theatre of Kilkenny was then open, and Banim was admitted to witness one of the performances. He was delighted with all he saw. Everything around was so unusual: the audience all in full dress, a brilliantly lighted house, the glittering costume of the actors, the beauty of the scenery, all rendered the spot a fairy realm for the child-poet.

He did not, however, attend so much for the purpose of seeing the play, as for that of observing his idol, Thomas Moore, who was one of the performers. He was then in the first glory of his success, and formed the theme of general conversation. On the occasion of Banim's visit to the theatre, Moore recited his own

"Monologue on National Music." It was encored, and Banim was the loudest of those demanding the repetition. The beauty of the poetry struck the fancy of the child, and so profound was the impression created by it upon his memory, that he, the following morning, repeated the entire with almost perfect accuracy, and with the gestures and inflections employed by Moore in its delivery. After having breakfasted, he was observed to dress himself in his best clothes, and the family saw him leave the shop, and, with a roll of papers under his arm, walk towards the house in which Moore lodged: he was about to introduce himself to Moore as a brother poet, and the roll of papers was the manuscript verses by which he meant to prove his right to the "honourable name." Moore, remembering probably the trembling anxiety with which he had, in his fourteenth year, sent "the attempts of a youthful muse" to the editor of "The Anthologia Hibernica," and the "honour and glory" which he enjoyed when he found himself, shortly afterwards, called "our esteemed correspondent T. M.," * received his odd little visitor kindly. He read a few of the verses, inquired as to his progress at school, advised him to be attentive and diligent, and closed the interview by asking, if there was anything he could do to oblige "his brother poet." To be called his "brother poet" was quite sufficient for Banim; but the offer of obliging him was too flattering to be slighted, so, after some consideration, he told the good-natured bard that there was nothing in the world he should like so much as a season ticket to the private theatre, where he could see

* See Moore's "Journal and Correspondence," vol. i. p. 22; and "Irish Quarterly Review," vol. ii. No. vi. p. 385.

Mr. Moore on the nights of performance. This request was at once granted, and, for the remainder of the theatrical season, little John Banim was happy as his heart could desire,—the same ticket which opened the theatre to him was, he considered, a tribute to his poetic ability. And how the boy's soul would have swelled could he then have known that but twenty-two years later his own fame would be so fully acknowledged that this same great poet, whom he was now so anxious to please, would, when in Kilkenny, call upon old Michael Banim, and, finding that he was from home, write, as a card, and leave for the old man, these words—"Mr. Thomas Moore called to pay his respects to the father of the author of 'The O'Hara Family!'" *

Literary pursuits, however, were not the only ones by which Banim's attention was engaged: he frequently devoted his play hours to mechanical inventions. He formed a complicated machine which was to realize that dream of philosophy—perpetual motion. Having read "Rasselas," he fancied that the philosopher of the happy valley must have been a very unskilful artificer. He accordingly, of wicker-work and brown paper, formed three pairs of wings, and fastened one wing to each wrist of his brother, and of his younger sister; having mounted with his two companions upon a manure heap, he fastened the remaining pair of wings to his own wrists, and all three, jumping from their eminence, found themselves, in place of soaring to the clouds, deposited in the "verdant mud" which formed their lake. His next attempt was the construction of sky-rockets, intended to mount to a most extraordinary height, but

* Moore's "Journal and Correspondence," vol. vi. p. 136.

which only blazed along the ground, burning the pyrotechnist, and almost destroying the house.

This last exploit developed a very remarkable trait in his character. His father was so much offended by the danger to which the family and the building had been exposed, that in one of his outbreaks of passion he ordered the child to leave the house, and seek his fortune in the world. John took his cap, and went forth. It was a winter night, dark and cold, with a roaring wind abroad. Away the boy went. Mrs. Banim was silent, knowing that remonstrance could conduce to no end, save that of increasing her husband's anger; and even he seemed anxious, but was too passionate to recal the offender. A quarter of an hour elapsed, and a sturdy knock was heard at the door: it was opened, and John reappeared. He approached his father, and taking off his cap, said, "As I am to go, I'll thank you, sir, for the sixpence I lent you the other day;"—this was the last remaining sixpence of the thirty shillings subscribed for the unprinted fairy tale; and with it he was as willing, though a child, to commence his way in the world, with as bold a heart, as self-reliant a confidence, as when, in later years, he went forth with his young wife to venture upon the troubled tide of literature. The sixpence was repaid him, but, in addition, a second was given, and he was ordered to bed, his father having forgotten all his anger in the surprise of the moment.

These were Banim's characteristics, and these are the histories of his life, in early school days.

When he had continued for about twelve months at Mr. Doyle's academy, he was removed, in his thirteenth year, to that seminary which can show upon its register the names of many men illustrious in literature—

Kilkenny College. Of this college Banim has left us the following account, in his tale, "The Fetches:"—

"Kilkenny College was the most famous as well as the most ancient preparatory school of Ireland. It commenced as an appendage to the magnificent cathedral of St. Canice, for the preservation of which, after Cromwell's spoliation, we are indebted to the classic Pococke, and was then situated, according to Stanihurst, 'in the weste of the churchyard' of that edifice, and had for its founder Pierce or Peter Butler, Earl of Ormond and Ossory. And 'out of this schoole,' continues Stanihurst, 'have sprouted such proper impes, through the painful diligence, and laboursome industrie of that famous lettered man, Mr. Peter White, as generally the whole weale publicke of Ireland, and especially the southern parts of that island, are greatly thereby furthered.' We have a sure clue to the date of its first erection, by the same writer mentioning that fact as ' of late ;' and also by his proceeding to inform us that (under Mr. Peter White, the original master) 'it was my happie hap (God and my parents be thanked) to have been one of his crue; and I take it to stande with my dutie, sith I may not stretch mine abilitie in requiting his good turns, yet to manifest my good will in remembering his pains. And certes I will acknowledge myself so much bound, and beholden to him and his, as for his sake, I reverence the meanest stone cemented in the walls of that famous schoole.' In 1684, the first Duke of Ormond, then' Lord Lieutenant of Ireland, granted a new charter to Kilkenny College, vesting in himself and his heirs male the appointment of masters, and the office and dignity of patrons and governors of the establishment. The statutes passed by him on this occasion, no less than twenty-five in number, are each of formidable length, regulating everything, from the master's morals, religion, and salary, to the punishment to be inflicted upon an urchin for 'cutting or defacing the desks or forms, walls or windows of the school.' Under this new arrangement the college also changed its situation from 'the weste of the churchyard' of St. Canice, to a large building at the other extremity of the town of Kilkenny, which together with a fine park, and the rectories and tithes of several parishes, near and distant, the patron granted, in trust, for its uses and advantage. But during the short and inauspicious Irish reign of James II., that soon after ensued, this endowment was frustrated. The first master, appointed by the Duke of Ormond, fled on account of his politics; and 'King James,' says Harris, ' by a charter dated the 21st of February, 1689, upon the ruins of this school, erected and endowed a royal college, consisting of a rector, eight professors, and two scholars in the name of more, to be called the Royal College of St. Canice, Kilkenny, of the foundation of King James:' and then followed 'Articles conclus du consentement unanime des regents des ecoles de Kilkenny, sous le protection de l'illustrissime et reverendissime l'evesque d'Ossory,' as curious, at least, as the state laws previously passed for the same establishment under hand and seal of the representative of majesty. William triumphed, however; James sought the retirement of St. Germains, Ireland once more rested beneath the reflux of Protestantism, and Kilkenny College, in common with every other public institution, reassumed its Protestant charter and arrangement, and to this day continues to enjoy both, with, we should perhaps mention, only one difference from the whole economy proposed by the first Duke of Ormond; and that is, remarkably enough, a lapse of the right of presentation to the school by the Ormond family, in consequence of the attainder of the Duke in 1715, and the vesture of said right in the provost and fellows of Trinity, Dublin. It has been seen that Stanihurst was a 'proper impe' of the old establishment; Harris, by his own acknowledgment, too, was also educated in Kilkenny College, under the first master nominated by the Duke of Ormond; as also were, subsequently, Thomas Prior, George Berkeley, Bishop of Cloyne, and other celebrated characters; among whom, if our recollection does not fail us, we believe we may rank Swift. In fact, it was after its return to the hands of Protestant masters and governors that this seminary rose to the height of its fame, and that young Irish noblemen and gentlemen crowded its classes for the most approved preparation for university honours. It might be called the then Eton of the sister country. We find it necessary to observe that the building to which the title 'College of Kilkenny' now applies is not the same endowed by the Duke of Ormond. The Irish tourist is at present shown, from an opposite bank of the Nore, a large square modern house, three stories high, dashed or plastered, and flaunting with gay and ample windows; and this, he is informed, is the college. Turning its back, in suitable abstraction, upon the hum and bustle of the small though populous city, it faces towards the green country, an extensive lawn spreading before it, and the placid river running hard by, and is, altogether, appropriately and beautifully situated. But the original edifice, that existed at the time of our story, was pushed farther back, faced into the street of the town, and was a grey, reverend pile of irregular and rather straggling design, or, we should perhaps say, of no design at all, having, partly, a monastic physiognomy, and partly that of a dwelling-house, and bearing, to its present gay successor, about the same likeness that the levee skirts of Anne's time bear to the smart swallow-tail of the last summer but one. We surmise that, at a more remote period, it belonged to the old and beautiful Augustinian Abbey of St. John, of which the main building was not more than three hundred yards distant, and which was richly endowed ' for the salvation of his soul and those of his predecessors and successors' (as Ledwich abstracts its charter) by William Marshall the elder, Earl of Pembroke, in 1220. The entrance to the school-room was immediately from the street, through huge oak folding-doors, arching at top to suit the arched stone doorway, and gained by two grand flights of steps at each side, that formed a spacious platform before the entrance, and allowed under them a passage by which visitors approached the college. To the left was another gateway where carriages had egress. The whole front of the building was of cut stone, with Gothic windows composed of numerous small panes of glass, separately leaded, and each of diamond form; giving the appearance of a side or back rather than of a front, on account of its grotesque gables, chimneys, and spouts, the last of which jetted into the street, to the no small annoyance in rainy weather of the neighbours and the passengers; while from the platform before the school-room entrance, the lads of the college contrived, in all weathers, further annoyances of every description. But in the past, as well as the present time, the lawn of the college was devoted to the exercise and sports of the students, and had, for its left hand boundary, 'the dark walk,'—a shrubbery so called to this day, though its appearance, and indeed identity, are changed,—and for its right the crystal Nore, of which the opposite banks were flanked by a wall some forty feet high; and over this wall—its foundations on a level with the top—towered in uncouth grandeur, amid throngs of luxuriant trees, the old family castle of the all but regal Ormonds. Close by the dark walk, at the left of the lawn, there ran too, as there at present runs, an artificial, but deep, rapid, and sufficiently broad stream, conjectured to have been an aqueduct formed by the old monks of St. John's Abbey, that while it discharged its immediate agency of setting in motion the waterwheels of more than one grist-mill on its course, served, at the same time, to cut off the college grounds from the adjacent gardens of the poorer class of people who inhabited the near outlet."

At the period of Banim's entrance the Rev. Andrew O'Callaghan was master. He was a man of learning and ability, but our young poet disapproved of one portion of his system of instruction — the complaint was, that Mr. O'Callaghan preferred a strict, grammatical translation in prose, to the most flowing and spirited metrical version his pupil could produce.

Whilst at the Kilkenny College, Banim evinced a very remarkable talent for drawing and painting; and having selected the profession of an artist as that to which he wished to devote his life, he was, in the year 1813, removed from his last school, the College of Kilkenny, and sent to Dublin, where he became a pupil in the drawing academy of the Royal Dublin Society. He continued a pupil in this academy during the two succeeding years, and was a regular and industrious student. He had the honour to receive the highest prize in the gift of the committee, for his drawings placed in the first exhibition held after his year of entrance.

During his two years of pupilage he lodged and boarded in Phibsborough, in the house of a Mr. Oliver Wheeler, an old friend of his father. Of Wheeler's habits, appearance, his household, and mode of life, Banim gave the following sketch, in "The Nowlans," when describing the poor abode of John and Letty Nowlan:—

"The old man, who had some petty situation of thirty or forty pounds a-year in some public office, was upwards of seventy-five years, tall, shrivelled, stooped in the neck, ill-set on his limbs, and with a peculiar drag of one leg, which, from certain reasons, and taken with other things, rendered him very disagreeable to John. He was obliged to be up every morning at seven, in order to reach his office, or place of occupation, by eight; and he might be heard creeping about the lower part of the house, making the parlour and kitchen fires, to save his daughter and niece so much trouble; cooking his own solitary breakfast, his fat wife lying in bed; and then cautiously shutting the hall-door after him, as, rubbing his hands, he tried to bustle off in a brisk, youthful pace, to his important day's work. His voice could never be heard in the house: if ever a man of a house lived under petticoat law, it was he. The coarse, masculine, guttural tones of his spouse often rose, indeed, to some pitch; but his, never. In other respects, too, he showed utter pusillanimity of spirit. He would never appear to John, in answer to a summons for arranging any misunderstanding (and several there soon arose) between him or poor Letty, and the daughter or niece; his wife always represented him; and he would run to hide behind a door, or into the yard, if he heard John's foot on the stairs during these domestic commotions; nay, even when all was at peace, his habitual poverty of nerve urged him to shun a single *rencontre* with his lodger: or, perhaps, he still dreaded to be called to account for anything his wife or daughter had said; and whenever he was caught by John in the passage, or the yard, his fidgets, as he lisped and mumbled, and continually tapped his chest with one hand, ever complaining of his asthma, called up sentiments of irresistible disgust. His sole attempts at manhood we have indicated, in describing the way he used to step out to his day's labour every morning. But rarer proofs of this still farcical and contemptible humour came under John's eye. As he and his ancient fellow-labourer before described (a contrast to him, by the way, being square-built, erect in his body, cross in his temper, and loud and independent in his tones) used to fumble about in the yard of an evening, chopping or sawing sticks and rotten boards, and mending the little sheds with them, or for ever watering the roots of the sad laburnum-tree, there was a would-be briskness in his every motion (he knew his wife was always looking at him out of the parlour window), an energy in the way he grasped his saw, adze, or hammer, or his watering-pot, and jerked them from hand to hand, or upon a bench, when he had done with them; all of which plainly bespoke his ambition not to pass ' for so very old a man, neither; certainly to give an idea that he was a miracle for his age. Every Sunday he appeared caparisoned for church in a complete shining suit of black, taken out of a press, and in a hat, also shining, extracted from one of his wife's early bandboxes; the clothes and the hat some ten years in his, or rather in her possession, and thus displayed once a week during that period, yet both looking as if sent home the Saturday night before; and indeed, considering that they had encountered scarce three months of careful wear altogether, namely, the wear of about two hours every seventh day for ten years, it was not, after all, so surprising they should look so new. Sometimes his wife allowed him to invite to a Sunday dinner five or six old men like himself, all clad in shining black too; and when John saw them come crawling towards the house, or, joined with their host, crawling and stalking about the yard, he felt an odd sensation of disgust, such as he thought might be aroused by the sight of so many old shining black beetles; the insects that, of all that crept, were his antipathy and loathing. His wife has been called fat: she was so, to excess; so much so, that she waddled under her own fardel—herself: but she was strong and sturdy too; and her waddle did not lessen the length and stamp of her stride, when, upon occasions that required a show of authority, she came out to scold, or, as her niece called it, to 'ballyrag,' in the kitchen, at her hand-maidens, or in the hall, at her poor lodgers upstairs. Then the little house shook from top to bottom under her heavy and indignant step, as well as with the echoes of her coarse man's voice, half smothered amid the fat of her throat, and the sputterings of her great pursy lips. And poor Letty also shook, from top to toe, on these occasions, and flew for shelter to John's arms. When not called upon thus to enforce law in any refractory branch of her garrison, Mrs. Grimes spent the day in a vast indolent armchair, reading pathetic novels of the last age, or casting up her accounts, to reassure herself, over and over again, of the pounds, shillings, and pence, laid up during the last month or week, and how half a farthing might be split for six months to come. Every day, by twelve o'clock, she was dressed 'like any lady' (still according to her niece) to receive her cronies, or strike with importance the tax-collectors or landlord's agent, none of whom had ever to call a second time; and that was her constant boast: but even there, shut up in her parlour, the old female despot was fully as much dreaded as if her voice and her stride sounded every moment through the house, or as much as if she had lain there screwed down in her coffin, and that, at the least turn of a hand, herself or her ghost might come out to roar for a strict reckoning. Her daughter and niece (the latter an orphan) supplied the place of a servant maid, in lieu of the eating, drinking, sleeping, such as it was, that came to their lot. They were of a size, and that size very little; of an age, and that more than thirty; but from their stunted growth, hard, liny shape, and nondescript expression of features, might pass for ten years younger, or ten years older, as the spectator fancied. They gave no idea of flesh and blood. They never looked as if they were warm, or soft to the touch. One would as soon think of flirting with them, as with the old wooden effigies to be found in the niches of old cathedrals. They imparted no notion, much less sensation of sex. But they were as active as bees, and as strong as little horses; and as despotic and cruel, if they dared, and whenever they dared, as the old tyrant herself. From the moment they arose in the morning, thump, thump, thump, went their little heels, through the passage, to the kitchen, up stairs and down stairs, or into the parlour, to see after the fires the old man had lighted; to make up the beds; to prepare breakfast; to put everything to rights; to sweep, to brush, to shake carpets, to clean shoes, knives, and forks; to rub, scrub, polish, and beautify, for ever and ever; the daughter always leading the niece; and the whole of this gone through in a sturdy, important, vain-glorious manner; accompanied by slapping of doors, every two minutes, and (ever since Letty had refused to go down to the parlour to join an evening party) by loud, rude talking, and boisterous laughing, just to show that they did not care a farthing for the kind of conceited poor lodgers they had got in the house. The housekeeping of the establishment was peculiarly loathsome to John. The baker had never sent in a loaf, bun, roll, biscuit, or muffin, since the day, now some fifteen years ago, when Mrs. Grimes came to reside in the neighbourhood: and even the home-made bread was of the coarsest possible quality, and often used a fortnight after it had been baked. Each day the dairyman left one halfpenny worth of milk at the door. They made their own precious mould candles, or burnt such nefarious oil in the kitchen lamp, or, upon a gala night, in the passage, as poisoned and fumigated the whole house. The morning tea-leaves were preserved and boiled for evening. No eggs, no fresh butter, ever appeared. The fires, after having been once made up in the morning, were slaked with a compost of coal-dust and yellow clay, which, shaped into balls, also formed stuffing between the bars. Upon a Saturday evening, the old man sneaked out to drive hard bargains for some of the odds and ends left in the butcher's stall after the day's sale; and these, conveyed home by stealth, furnished, by means of salting and hanging up in a cool place, savoury dinners for the week. Upon a washing-day, starch was made out of potatoes, to save a farthing. No charity was in the house, nor in a heart in the house. In the faces of all professed beggars the street-door was slammed without a word, but with a scowl calculated to wither up the wretched suitor; and with respect to such as strove to hide the profession under barrel-organs, flutes, flageolets, hurdy-gurdies, or the big drum and pandean pipes, their tune was indeed listened to, but never requited. Yet the family was a pious family. Mr. and Mrs. Grimes sallied out to church every Sunday, and sat at the parlour-window every Sunday evening (while their daughter and niece went, in turn, to have a rest, as they said), a huge old Bible open before them, and visible to all passers by, that the neighbours might remark, 'There's a fine old couple!' John, however, thought it odd that, after all this, his cold mutton or his cold beef used to come up to him, out of the safe (a pretty 'safe,' truly), rather diminished since he had last the pleasure of seeing it; and one Sunday evening, after listening for half an hour to the daughter's shrill voice reading the Bible before supper, when, on particular business, he somewhat suddenly entered the parlour, he was still more surprised to find the good family seated round the ham (a rare temptation, no doubt, in their system of housekeeping) which that day had formed part of his dinner. But nothing irked him half so much as the ostentatious triumph over starvation, the provoking assumption of comfort, nay, elegance, as it were, and the audacious independence which resulted from the whole economy. He felt it, as before hinted, to be the most irritating specimen of poverty. Old Grimes's glossy Sunday coat, perpetually the same, was worse than the clouted gaberdine of a roving beggar. Every burnished thing around him seemed to shine with a beggarly polish. The whole house and its inhabitants had an air of looking better than they really were, or ought to be; and the meanness, the sturdiness, the avarice, the hardheartedness, that produced this polish and this air, he considered as loathsome as the noise, the thumping about, the loud talking, and the endless fagging of the two little skinny Helots was brazen and vexatious."

We have given these, and former extracts, from Banim's works, as they prove how strongly the everyday events of his early life became impressed upon his mind; and how he, like Sir Walter, Galt, and Moir, drew from the world around him the materials of which the scenes and characters of his novels were composed. Thus situated, the poor boy worked out his lonely time. But even here the depressing effects of his abode could not repress his ardent industry, or overcome his love of literature; and whilst residing at Oliver Wheeler's, he first "saw himself in print." The piece was a metrical criticism on the Exhibition of Irish Artists, and was entitled "A Dialogue in the Exhibition Room."

We shall now introduce some extracts from his letters written during his residence in Dublin. In each of these, as in all those which we shall insert, addressed by him to his friends at home, there is a love of all that surrounded the hearth which recals those beautiful letters written by Moore to the dear friends in Aungier Street, and which show a heart that not fame, not other and brighter hopes than those of youth, could soil or taint.

Banim's first letter is addressed to his mother, and describes his mode of life:—

"DUBLIN, *December* 23, 1813.

"MY DEAREST MOTHER,—Your anxious love could not wish me better than I am, or with better prospects before me. I have the countenance of all, and the friendship of many of the first artists and amateurs in my profession. I meet with warm encouragement, and hope of success from every one.

"If with the assistance of heaven, and I know your prayers will aid me, I can persevere in my studies, and endeavour to trace the footsteps of eminent painters, what have I to fear, or you to make you sorrowful or apprehensive?

"I am as contented and happy, as any one in my position could be. I am grinding my colours every second day, from seven in the morning until night; every intermediate day is spent in the gallery and in drawing from the figure."

The two following letters are addressed to his father. In the first he writes of his lonely Christmas; in the second he tells of his every-day occupations, and in the refusal of the " nice blue coat," as a present, because he could himself afford to buy one we can trace the spirit which he evinced when requiring repayment of the sixpence which he had lent his father; and though not quite sixteen years old when this letter was written, it proves that then, as in later years, he was ever anxious to be the support, rather than the incumbrance, of his family :—

"Dublin, *December* 25, 1813.

" My dear Father,—I write to you on the festival of Christmas, the first from my birth that I have spent from home.

" There is nothing in the intercourse with strangers to recompense one for the absence from our kindred : but I must not murmur against what cannot be avoided.

" The festival of Christmas reminds me that I am solitary. There is no equivalent for the peace and blessings I have hitherto enjoyed at our Christmas hearth."

"Dublin, *March* 23, 1814.

" My dear Father,—It would be the dearest wish of my heart, could I have the inexpressible pleasure of embracing you all at Easter. Solitary and retired as I live, it would indeed be a treat to my feelings : but necessity interferes to prevent this indulgence. Sunday excepted, I have scarely a moment unemployed. In the morning early I attend my tuition : then either painting a portrait at home, or studying the antique in the gallery, employs me until six ; my dinner is scarcely swallowed, when I am off again, either to the figure academy, or the anatomical lectures, opened for the benefit of artists by the Irish Institution. I am scarcely ever home again until ten, and then generally fall asleep soon. Notwithstanding my conviction of its imprudence, I am greatly tempted to yield to the overflowing impulses of my heart, and anticipate my summer visit by an Easter one.

"You state your intention, my dear father, of sending me a nice blue coat. Providence has thrown a few guineas in my way lately, and I have the prospect of a few more. Let me decline your offer, therefore. I will positively treat myself to a new coat and other etceteras, the fruits of my own earning."

Two years of the dreary life here recorded passed by, and at length Banim returned to Kilkenny, intending to commence life as an artist and teacher of drawing; and although he had received but two years' tuition in his art, he was fortunate in securing very satisfactory and encouraging employment.

He was just eighteen years of age, about the middle height, and of good figure. His face was oval, and though not handsome, his high broad forehead, and his dark-hued eyes, teeming with life and spirit, saved him from the designation—ugly. And now the common fate was his. Tennyson sings of youth—

"In the spring a young man's fancy lightly turns to thoughts of love;"—

and our poet-painter was no exception to the rule. He was the admirer of every pretty girl in Kilkenny, and between rhyming, painting, flirting, and book-lending, his entire time was fully occupied.

One evening, whilst he was sitting at tea with his mother, the good woman abruptly said to him,—

"John."

"Well, mother?" was the response.

"Whom do you love, John?" she continued.

"Well, mother," he replied, "upon my word there are so many of them that I am afraid I can't particularise; but let me see,"—and, counting his fingers, he added, "there is Mary—, and there's Anne—, and there's Kate, and there's Jane."

"John, John," cried his mother, smiling at the confession; "you know well that is not the answer I taught you to give to the question—long ago you knew it and would say, 'I love God above all things, and my neighbour as myself for the love of God.' I see, John, your boyish days are over." Truly, the boyish days were over, the catechism was forgotten, self was forgotten, and the dream of youth was upon him.

At one of the schools which he attended, as the teacher of drawing, was a young girl, named Anne D——, a boarder in the establishment, and a pupil of Banim's. She was a fair, bright-eyed girl, in the full, fresh beauty of seventeen, artless, innocent, and pure-minded. The young teacher—the poet and the painter—forgot the grave moral of the history of the tutor Abelard and the pupil Eloise; and, day by day, a deep whole heart passion grew within his breast, and each attendance at the school served but to strengthen his affection. He dared not tell her of his love; but love, when the youth is only in his nineteenth year, and the maiden in her eighteenth, cannot long lie hidden, and soon each read, in the eyes of each, that tale of passion which was to end but in the death of one, in the long and lingering agony of the other.

When Banim found that this girl loved him, he seemed another being. He concealed his affection from all: he told his brother that his mornings were devoted to sketching the landscapes around Kilkenny; but these early morning hours were the trysting times when he and Anne D—— roamed along the quiet banks of the Nore, or strolled through the fields, accompanied by an under governess, who aided the young lovers, and devised means by which the absence of her charge might escape detection.

For both it was a happy dream; for them—

"Love took up the glass of Time, and turn'd it in his glowing
  hands;
Every moment, lightly shaken, ran itself in golden sands.
Love took up the harp of Life, and smote on all the chords
  with might;
Smote the chord of Self, that, trembling, pass'd in music out
  of sight."

Mornings of love, days of love-musing, nights of dreaming love, rarely continue unnoticed by those who are intimate with the lover; and Banim's brother having discovered this secret of his morning's walks, was made his confidant in the confession, "I love Anne D—— as boy never loved girl before."

That his love was true and deep cannot be doubted; and as the expression of feeling, rather than as a proof of his poetic ability, we insert the following pieces, written at this period:—

"My Anna is tall, and my Anna is fair,
  Dark brown is her eye, and jet black is her hair,—
  She is straight as the poplar that springs in the dale,
  Her eye-beam is such as the glories that sail

Over the bosom of midsummer heaven,
When angels disport in the sunbeam of even.
The bright rose of summer indeed does not streak
With full ruddy blush the warm snow of her cheek;
For love thought it pity to scatter or spread
With ill-judging craft all his treasure of red,
But gave it to glow in a spot so divine
That the essence of all in a kiss might be mine."

The following is a scrap from a long effusion:—

"It is the blushing time of roses,
 I feel the fragrance it discloses;
 Love laughs before my beaming eye
 Through grove and garden, earth and sky;
 In every path, o'er dale, o'er hill,
 I meet that babe of beauty still."

"TO ANNA.

"Yes, Love hath lent his smile of pleasure
 To gild the morning of my days,
 Oh! every sod my footsteps measure
 Through fortune's doubtful, devious maze—
   Every path of toil they press
   That beam shall bless—
 That holy beam shall brighten up
 The foulest draught of sorrow's cup—
 That holy beam shall light the shade
 Of life when all her fancies fade,
 And on the way, to me so dark,
 Leading to fame's magnetic altar,
 Oh! even there that angel spark
 Shall brightly guide my ardent gaze;
 My heart shall sparkle to a blaze,
      And never falter.
 I thank thee, high and holy pow'r,
 That thus upon my natal hour
 Thy blessed bounty hath bestowed
 More than to mortal life is owed;
 If thy dispensing hand had given
 All other joy this side of heaven;

The monarch's crown, the hero's crest,
All honours, riches, gems, the best,
And Anna's love away the while,
I'd change them all for Anna's smile."

Banim's nature was impetuous, and, having assured himself of his mistress's affection, he resolved to wait upon her father and demand her hand. A year had passed since he first loved her, and he would not be satisfied until he called her his wife. He was not twenty years of age, his profession was not more than sufficient to support him, his friends were reduced in circumstances, owing to the inability of some persons to repay certain sums of money lent by old Michael Banim; but all prudential considerations were despised by the lover, and so he went forth, accompanied by a friend, to seek the consent of Anne's father.

Anne D—— was the natural daughter of a gentleman residing in a neighbouring county. He was a surly, rude-tempered old man, and replied to Banim's request of his daughter's hand with sneers and scoffing. The young lover retorted the insulting expressions used; both parties were violent, and recriminations were ended by the order of the old man that Banim should at once leave the house. He returned to Kilkenny, dispirited and heart-sick; he had never permitted himself to contemplate a rejection of his suit, and when he, the same evening, obtained an interview with Anne D——, it was one of tears and sorrow—it was the last time he ever spoke to her, save clandestinely.

The doors of the school in which Anne resided were closed against him; all communication was barred between them, and by stratagem alone could he tell her how deeply and how truly she was still beloved. All means of addressing her were tried, and those who watched Anne and her fellow-pupils as, on Sunday evenings, they left the church, might have observed a figure clothed as a countrywoman, in long grey cloak and full deep hood, stealing close to Anne's side: this was Banim disguised; and it was on these occasions that he contrived to press his mistress's hand, whilst he placed within it a poem, or a letter, telling her to love and hope. In this manner, and by transmitting notes in his sister's school basket, he was enabled to communicate with her.

Anne's father induced a female relative of the girl to call upon her at the school, and by a pretended sympathy, endeavour to discover if her love for Banim were real and deep. The plan succeeded; Anne told the whole story of her heart. It was considered that absence alone could cure her girlish folly, and her father arranged that she should be secretly removed from school, and placed in the house of one of her mother's family. She was removed; but Banim discovered the day and hour at which she was to leave, and the route by which she was to travel. He found that the chaise, bearing Anne and her female protector, was to pass by his father's door—he took his place by the threshold, and as the carriage rolled by, he rushed, bare-headed, before the vehicle: to avoid the danger of overturning him, the horses were suddenly and violently checked, Anne leaned from the window, pale and terrified and sobbing bitterly; the lovers' eyes met but for a moment, the carriage moved quickly onward, and John Banim never more, in life, saw Anne D——.

He re-entered the house, and uttered no cry, but sat

in stony sorrow. A small parcel was placed in his hand, it was addressed to him, the hand-writing was that of Anne, he tore it eagerly open,—it contained his own miniature which he had painted for her, and which for months she had worn concealed in her bosom; the parcel also contained his letters and verses. He examined the miniature closely; it bore no secret line: he pored over the papers in hope that they might conceal some covert intimation that this return of all his offerings was not Anne's own free act,—but all was as he himself had written, not one line or word to tell him she was faithful. He paused a moment looking upon the miniature, and then, dashing it to the ground, crushed it to atoms beneath his feet,—tore the letters and verses into fragments; and as he scattered them away, as the memory of all his hopes and joys came back upon him when he thought of their vows and promises, he cried, bitterly and fiercely, " Curse her! curse her! to abandon me and break my heart!" and burst into angry tears.

No commiseration could soothe him; no attention could win a smile, or word of pleasure from his lips. His constant complaint was, that Anne had abandoned him, although no earthly power could induce him to forget or abandon her. Now she was false, false as only heartless woman can be; and in his despair he wrote such lines as the following:—

> " Thou that in youthful folly's bower
> Wouldst lavish thus an idle hour;
> Thou that wouldst fondly hope to win
> The love a woman's heart within—
> Go, heart of hope, to pleasure's sleep,
> But let it be nor long nor deep—

> Go, taste the bloom of woman's lip,
> But only taste, and lightly sip—
> Go, if it suit thy sparkling soul,
> On passion's frantic wave to roll:
> Partake of ev'ry boasted feeling
> Of all that's worth a lover's stealing;
> But give thy lightest leisure hour
> Alone to love's delusive power;
> Pledge not thy faith a hair beyond
> The sigh of sense or passion fond.
> Let not one vital cord of thine
> Round faithless woman's heart entwine.
> No youthful hope shall perish then,
> As fickle woman roams amain;
> No fainting pulse, no brimming eye
> Shall note the wanton trifler fly;
> No riven heart-string there shall break,
> When woman spurns her bondage weak;
> And not a withering pang shall wait
> To blast thy hopes and gloom thy fate."

But Anne was not faithless, and to the last hour of his life Banim regretted his doubt of her affection; he learned but too late that

" ——Love is love for evermore."

The house to which Anne D—— had been removed was situated about twenty-five miles from Kilkenny, and the affection that still lingered in Banim's heart induced him to open a new correspondence with her. He sent the letters by trusty messengers; he knew that they had been deposited in places with which Anne was acquainted; he wrote again and again, in all the fervour of his earlier love: but to none of his letters was there a reply. Anne was not faithless; she received one only letter, and that the first, all gloomy and half upbraiding; she was detected in the act of reading it, and the succeeding letters were intercepted.

Anne made no complaint. She thought of the past-by days of joy, of the mornings when, out by the sunny river, she had heard the tale of love, as only youth in its spring can breathe it, whilst around the path of the poet-painter and his fair bright idol,

"The summer murmur'd with her leafy lips,"

and pining for the loss of all her heart held dear, her cheek grew pale, her step lost all its bounding lightness, her eyes shone with that terrible brilliancy which shows the wasting of life, and then it was plain that the fiend, Consumption, had seized her. She never struggled against the disease; she was removed from the school in Kilkenny in the month of September, and whilst Banim was condemning her as a heartless mistress, she was expiring, with his love the sole treasure of her life; and in the November following her removal from school, a period of less than two months, Anne D—— was dead.

Banim was informed of the melancholy catastrophe the day succeeding that of her decease; and then came the full tide of sorrow upon his heart, for in hearing she was dead he heard also that her love for him had been the cause of all her griefs, and in her agony his name had been the last upon her lips.

When he discovered that she was no more, he merely said to his brother, who was appalled by the pain displayed in his features, "Anne D—— is dead!" and retiring to his bed-room, remained in solitude and silence.

He rose early the following morning; it was cold November weather, the rain was falling, and a gloom was in the sky and upon the earth. Banim left his home, wishing once more to look upon the victim who had been so dear in life, but who now, in death, was dearer than ever. He was too poor to hire a chaise; he borrowed a horse, but he could not endure the slow, steady pace of the animal, and when about a mile from Kilkenny sent it back by a country child, and continued his way on foot.

He never knew by what route, or how he traversed the twenty-five dreary miles which lay between him and the corpse of his beloved, but night had closed around the dripping weary man as he reached the farmhouse where the body of Anne D—— lay. None of her relatives were present as he entered, and but few friends sat around. He stood beside the dead one's head, and the long black lashes of the closed eyes resting upon the pallid cheek, the shrunken features, and the worn look of her whom he had once thought so beautiful, from whom he had so recently parted in all the glory of her youth, terrified him, and he gazed upon her but shed no tear. His face of agony attracted the attention of those persons who had gathered by the coffin, and as he stood beside its head, one of Anne's half-sisters recognised him, called him the murderer of her sister, and demanded that he should be thrust from the room.

At first Banim felt indignant at this cruel conduct, but suddenly he thought that if Anne had never loved him she might be then living happily; had she never met him she might be joyous and in health—but now she was a wreck of hope, of peace, of life; and scarcely daring to look upon her, he tottered from the room. He had eaten nothing since the preceding day; he felt no hunger, but entering an out-house, sank upon the wet straw of a car-shed, and there, in a stupor of grief, continued until he heard the funeral guests assembling.

He rose, re-entered the house, and being permitted to stand beside the coffin, saw the face of his Anne for the last time, as the coffin-lid hid it for ever. He followed the body to the churchyard, stood by as the earth was piled up, and when all had departed, cast himself upon the fresh green mound that marked the grave of his first love. He never could recollect where the night succeeding this day of woe was passed, but the following morning his brother met him about ten miles from home. Leaning upon the arm extended to him, he trailed his limbs along until he reached his father's house. With his brother's help he ascended to his room, and though from the time when they had met upon the road no word had been spoken by either, yet when entering his apartment he appeared to recognise it; the feeling of consciousness was but momentary, and he sank upon his bed powerless and senseless, prostrated in mind and body.

During the twelve months succeeding this day, Banim merely existed. The whole system seemed shattered. His head ached so violently that, in his paroxysms of pain, his body rocked with an involuntary motion so violently, that as his head rested upon his mother's breast, it required all the latter's strength to curb the violent swaying of the sufferer. "It seemed," he said, "as if the brain were surging through the skull from rear to front, and from front to rear, alternately." He lost all anxiety for his profession or for literature, no occupation could interest him, he could rarely be induced to leave the house, and when he did go abroad he quickly became wearied; he seldom spoke, and thus his first love laid the seeds of that frightful suffering which, during the greater portion of his existence, rendered him one of the most miserable of men. The three nights of suffering and exposure to which at Anne D——'s decease he was subjected, broke down the stamina of life, and left him, at twenty years of age, a victim to spinal disease, which, but a few years later, reduced him to a crippled body, whilst gifted with a mind active as ever genius possessed: his fate indeed was harder than that of Tantalus.

The first symptom of returning health evinced by the sufferer was the composition of some verses. They show the weary spirit that would free itself from all recollections of the past, and would—

> "Pluck from the memory a rooted sorrow;
> Raze out the written troubles of the brain."

Sorrow, however, at nineteen, cannot be very deeply seated, and he must be melodramatic indeed who fancies that in plucking it from his bosom his heart may form its root; and thus, as time rolled on, Banim found that the world had its joys still, even after all his woes; and so for him once more arose the bright blue days,—

> "Full of the sun, loud with a thousand larks."

Then it was that, as the clouds passed away, the darkened spirit cast off its veil of grief, and he wrote such verses as these detached fragments:—

> "I saw her, God of goodness great!
> I saw her in her winding-sheet;
> And I saw her mingle then
> With her mother earth again,
> I saw her—and I could not save—
> Sink into her early grave.
>
> It cannot last. The fever of affliction
> But feeds on thought. And all the balm

> Designed by preaching patience for the sufferer's pang
> Changes to poison on his parched lip.
>
> Avoid me, Memory, we are friends no more.
> It is an awful hour, the midnight moon
> Looks from her land of loneliness upon me,
> Yet in the silent night I fear no foe,
> I fear no stalking spectre as I fear thee, Memory."

We here close the first part of this biography of John Banim. We have told the story of his life to his twenty-first year. It shows him to have been swayed by all the passions and weakness that dictate the actions of other men, but it shows too the energy which marked his later years. A boy, he left his home for Dublin; two years in the metropolis had not corrupted him: like Southey he was too pure a worshipper of beauty and of goodness to be vicious, even if faith and early training had not spread their shields above him; and so, a boy, he returned to his father's roof.

CHAPTER II.

RESTORED HEALTH—LIFE IN KILKENNY—REMOVAL TO DUBLIN—ABANDONMENT OF ART AND ADOPTION OF LITERATURE AS A PROFESSION—LIFE IN DUBLIN—LETTERS—OBTAINS CHARTER FOR ROYAL IRISH ACADEMY, AND IS THANKED BY VOTE OF IRISH ARTISTS—LETTERS—PUBLISHES "THE CELT'S PARADISE," AND DEDICATES IT TO THE LATE LORD CLONCURRY—EXTRACTS—CONTEMPLATES REMOVING TO LONDON—LETTERS—PLAY OF "DAMON AND PYTHIAS" ACTED AT COVENT GARDEN: ITS SUCCESS—EXTRACTS—LETTERS—VISIT TO KILKENNY AFTER FIRST LITERARY SUCCESS—FIRST IDEA OF NOVEL WRITING—PUBLISHES A PAMPHLET ON THE ERECTION OF A TESTIMONIAL COMMEMORATIVE OF THE VISIT OF GEORGE IV. TO IRELAND—EXTRACTS—LETTERS.

THE Christmas of 1818 had passed before Banim's health apparently recovered the shock which it had received during the days and nights of anguish and exposure, endured whilst he watched by the death bed and by the grave of Anne D——. We have written "apparently recovered," for, in fact, the results of that woful time were the evils of his after years, and ended but with his life.

With returning health came all the buoyant spirit of youth and hope, and Banim entered into all the pleasures and convivialities of his native town. Those who can remember what country towns in Ireland were about six-and-thirty years ago, will understand the dangerous position in which these tastes and connexions placed him who exhibited ability and social powers of even a lesser degree than those of Banim. He formed no low, or mean, or vulgar acquaintances, but in the round of pleasure which formed his chief solace he found himself the companion of those who were his superiors in birth and fortune. They were not drunkards, but they loved the midnight meeting around the supper table; as the glasses twinkled the fancy grew bright, quips and drollery gave a fascinating charm to each for each, and Banim might truly apply to himself a passage of Charles Lamb's, "We dealt about the wit, or what passes for it, after midnight, jovially. Of the quality called fancy I certainly possessed a larger share than my companions:" and thus he became careless of tuitions, and all but neglected his duty to the few schools and pupils who still continued to employ him. Debts now began to accumulate; credit failed, and Banim, disgusted by his course of life, resolved, after a few months' experience of its evils, to abandon all its temptations and false pleasures. This was not difficult; at all periods of his existence he was temperate, and in joining the convivial parties of his fellow townsmen he sought only a relief in society from the pains of memory and the woes of solitude.

Although inattentive in these times to professional engagements, he had not been completely idle; he had painted a few portraits, and had become a contributor to a local newspaper, "The Leinster Gazette," of which he became the editor. This latter employment he considered a very important one, as it was a walk, however humble, in the great path of literature. It gave him, he thought, a position as a literary character; and indeed he is not the first distinguished man whose genius developed itself in the columns of a provincial journal. Debts and difficulties, however, gathered around him, and with many another man, he found that small, like great "pleasant vices" entail long, painful, and harassing repentant regrets. Insignificant as his debts were in amount, they formed a terrible obstacle to the peaceful pursuit of his profession. He had begun to lament his five months of dissipation; he was then and ever sensitive in regard to money matters, and thus he became morbidly eager in his anxiety to discharge every monetary claim against him.

With restored health he had recovered his courage and love of literature. He believed that as an artist he could not succeed unless he devoted time to perfecting his taste and skill, and time he was not satisfied to spend in the acquisition. He had pleased himself by his literary efforts published in the local journal, and he fancied that by other and better considered labours he could please the world of readers. He was not formed by nature to lag or hesitate when he had once formed a project: he determined to abandon the profession of an artist for that of an author. It was a poor chance, in truth; but when did genius or courage (and what is genius but the noblest courage?) doubt? And Banim resolved to leave Kilkenny and try his fortune in Dublin. He knew that great difficulties should be overcome before his merit could be appreciated or even known: he possessed few friends in the city, and they were chiefly amongst the artists, the late Thomas J. Mulvany being the most remarkable and most likely to aid him. But these considerations were unheeded. He wished to be out in the great world, amongst the clash and jarring of minds and interests, where the strong bold will and the ready mind, or the flashing wit, could win golden fame, and hold it safe and surely. He longed to be away from the scenes of his lost hopes, his past-by joys, his present sorrows, and he would dare or seek difficulties that he might find a greater glory in their surmounting; thus resembling that bright image of young genius, as Virgil has described it in the character of Ascanius—

"Optat aprum, aut fulvum descendere monte leonem."

Early in the year 1820 Banim left his father's house for Dublin, and from this period we may date his life as a literary man. Mulvany had known him whilst he was a pupil in the School of Art, of the Royal Dublin Society, in the year 1813, and now received him kindly, and aided him by his counsel and interest.

At this time the Dublin artists were endeavouring to obtain a Charter of Incorporation, and a Government grant in aid of the profession in Ireland. Banim loved the old memories of his art pupilage, and he gave all the assistance in his power to strengthen the claims and demands of its Irish members. At the period of which we write, reporting for the public journals was not so highly valued as at present; whilst "leaders" and their writers were much more important than in our day. Banim had become a contributor to two or three of the more important papers, and he was thus enabled to serve the interests of his former professional brethren through his position on the newspaper press. His services were not denied by the artists, and when, in the year 1820, the Charter of Incorporation was obtained, they presented him an address and a considerable sum of money, as a testimony of their appreciation of his successful efforts to support their interests, and the advancement of art in Ireland.

His life in Dublin was a hard and disheartening struggle with disappointments, and his wants were many, and yet such as make the poor proud man of genius, who would be successful, a silent long-suffering martyr. The debts contracted during his wild days in Kilkenny were a source of anxiety from which he could not easily escape. He was ever anxious to repay this money, and, as we shall hereafter find, he set aside the first sums received from the publishers to defray these charges. The debts, and the thoughts of the times in which they were contracted, ever haunted his memory as relics of a period of awful agony and disappointment. But this desire to forget the past extended but to that painful epoch of his unhappy love; whilst the thought of home, the true-hearted affection for all who dwelt there, were as bright and pure as in the days of his residence in Phibsborough, when a student in the art school of the Royal Dublin Society. He loved ever and always the scenes of childhood's joys and sorrows, and when he had been some months in Dublin, we find that he thus wrote to his brother, describing his feelings for home :—

"DUBLIN, *May 10th*, 1820.

"MY DEAR MICHAEL,—The health that I enjoy is wonderful to myself,—do not be so fearful on my account. You that stay at home and are very happy have many superfluous apprehensions about a younger son or brother who roves about a little. Be assured of this, my dear and only friends, almost the sole thing that sends the blood to my heart or the tear to my eye is the recollection now and then that I am parted from you; but this gives me greater strength for the struggle to get back,—and back I will return, if God spares me life, and we will spend and end our days together."

He had, about the date of this letter, begun to think that he possessed sufficient ability to enable him to work his way in the great world of London. He had found that Dublin gives but small hope to him who depends on literature alone as the means of support; and though his friend Mulvany, and the late Joseph Kirk, were willing to aid him in all his prospective successes, he was dissatisfied with himself and with his position. He was a poor man, but, like Griffin, a bold daring one, who would not wait upon fortune as a suitor. He told his brother, Michael, that he had determined to seek his bread in London. Michael remonstrated; reminding him that many men of greater talent and experience than he possessed had gone to the wonderful city and launched upon its vast troubled sea the ventures of their lives, and that wreck and ruin had been their fate, after weary struggles of unavailing energy, and of unflagging, patient, mental toil.

But the brave heart, self-reliant and conscious, would not doubt of success, and but rested until means could be secured to defray the expenses of the journey and outfit. When that true genius, Chatterton, wrote home to his only friend, his mother, that "by abstinence and perseverance a man may accomplish whatever he pleases;" when great Samuel Johnson came up to town, and learned gratefully from the Irish artist whom he has called Ofellus, in his "Art of Living in London," how to exist respectably on ten-pence a day; when poor Gerald Griffin, pure bright soul of genius, went forth, a boy, to gain the fame for which his breast so panted; not he, not any one of these, felt more deeply or more truly the whole-heart devotion to literature than did Banim when writing the following letter, in reply to his brother's cautions and warnings. We read in the whole range of literary biography nothing more pathetic than these words in the succeeding letter: "I know not how long I could fast; even that I may be called on to try. I have been the best part of two days without tasting food, of late;" and then comes the grim addition, "often have I gone to whistle for my dinner."

The letter to which we have last referred is as follows:—

"DUBLIN, *May* 18*th*, 1820.

"MY DEAR MICHAEL,—You speak very gloomily on the uncertainty of my means if I go to London. Don't let your fear affect you so keenly. I have not found a crock of gold, nor has a prize in the lottery turned up for me: but with heaven's help I shall not want means. No man of ordinary talents wants them in London, with proper conduct and half the introductions I hold. Say I possess no talent,—this you will not say, it would not be what you feel. I have a consciousness of possessing some powers; and situated as I am, it is not vanity to say so. I have health, hope, energy, and good humour, and I trust in the Lord God for the rest.

"I know not how long I could fast; even this I may

be called on to try. I have been the best part of two days without tasting food of late. Often have I gone to whistle for my dinner, and once I walked about the town during the night for the want of a bed. I see you start at this. I can assure you, without affectation, it has amused me, and I thrive on it. I am fatter and better looking than when you saw me. At the present time I am comparatively rich, and go as high as ten-pence for my dinner, and a goodly plate of beef and vegetables it is."

This sad letter is but the plain statement of Banim's condition in the early period of his connexion with the Dublin press. In addition to his employments upon the metropolitan journals, he obtained some slight assistance to his funds from occasional contributions to the provincial papers. He wrote some very clever, but ephemeral articles for a now forgotten paper, "The Limerick Evening Post." These contributions were on all subjects of the day, particularly theatrical topics, and bore the signature, A TRAVELLER.

Amidst the toiling of his every-day life the old love for poetry and poetical composition was ardent and true, as in the time when he aspired to be the "brother poet" of Moore; and he devoted his leisure hours to the composition and construction of poems and dramas. He had been introduced to Charles Philips; at that period a man of note and of rising fame in Ireland. Philips had just published his poem, "The Emerald Isle," and his "Specimens of Irish Eloquence;" and having obtained for himself the reputation of taste and ability, was willing to assist, by his counsel and interest, any worthy literary man who needed either.

He found in Banim a young ardent genius; he examined some of his poetical compositions, he advised and suggested, and his wishes were acceded to most cheerfully and readily. By Philips's advice Banim abandoned for a time his proposed removal to London, and applied himself closely to the completion of a poem which he had commenced, and which he called "Ossian's Paradise." Philips showed some portions of the poem to Sheil, and to Mr. William Curran,* and the latter gentleman having read some passages to the late Lord Cloncurry, his Lordship expressed his willingness, in accordance with Banim's request, to accept the dedication of the work. These, however, were not the only personages who expressed opinions favourable to Banim's ability. The manuscript was shown to Sir Walter, who, with his never failing kindness to young authors, read the extracts submitted to him, and expressed his approbation of the composition.

Thus at length Banim seemed about to achieve that position in literature for which he longed as eagerly as he who cried—

> "For poesy my heart and pulses beat,
> For poesy my blood runs red and fleet,
> As Moses' serpent the Egyptians swallow'd,
> One passion eats the rest."

His life was now full of hope, and he thus wrote to his father:—

"DUBLIN, *October 12th,* 1820.

"MY DEAR FATHER,—When difficulties pressed most on me, I determined to wage war with them manfully;

* Now Ex-Commissioner of Insolvents.

I called on my own mind, and put its friendship for me to the proof. In the midst of occasionally using my pencil, of newspaper scribbling and reporting, and surrounded by privation, and almost every evil but bad health, I manufactured some hundreds of verses, with notes appending, which I called 'Ossian's Paradise.'

"I handed Ossian's Paradise to a friend, an eminent poet, a celebrated orator and lawyer; he showed it to a friend of his, a Mr. C———n, who introduced it to Lord Cloncurry;—it pleased both. It was subsequently submitted to the greatest writer of the day, Scott; his judgment was:—'It is a poem possessing imagination in a high degree, often much beauty of language, with a considerable command of numbers and metre.' This opinion was accompanied by a candid criticism on particular portions, with a view to its success when published.

"Ossian's Paradise is to be published by Mr. Warren, of Bond-street, London. I am to receive £20 within a month, with fifty copies to dispose of on my own account. If it runs to a second edition, £10 more; these terms my friend before mentioned, Mr. Shiel, thinks advantageous.

"My dear father, do not blame me for not communicating this matter in its progress. I will explain my motive. My failures hitherto had given to all of you at home quite enough of uneasiness, and I wished to have a rational probability of success in view before I should excite your interest: if I had failed, I had determined to be silent on the affair to you, my mother, and Michael, and to all the world besides.

"Do me the favour, my dear Sir, of requesting Michael to read this letter for my old schoolmaster

Mr. Buchanan; and fill your glass in the evening to the success of Ossian's Paradise, when you three are seated round the little octagon table in your own sanctum sanctorum; and my own dearest mother, perhaps she may have cause to think more respectably than was her wont of my rhyming propensities."

These were the real truths of his position and hopes, and to some cautions of his brother, Michael, against indulging in too sanguine expectations of success, he thus replies:—

"DUBLIN, *October 17th*, 1820.

"MY DEAR BROTHER,—I am not erecting a structure on the doubtful success of Ossian's Paradise.

"The panting desire for fame is corrected, I will not say extinguished in me. I have before now allowed the vivacity of hope, or the restlessness of suspense, to torture and distract me; but this shall not be again. I have held out my hand to grasp my object over and over: I have never yet touched it. Disappointment with me became as systematically attendant on exertion, as shadow upon substance; so much so, that I could not get a glimpse of the one without looking hard for the other; so I will not reckon on success in this instance beforehand.

"I will tell you what I intend doing. I am strongly encouraged, by persons whose judgment I ought to respect, to prepare a second poem. I regard the present as an opportunity not to be neglected, and I am, and will continue to be, at work accordingly. Of course, I give up for the present my journey to London.

"While I occupy myself with this second poem, I have to make out £1 per week; every shilling of Ossian's money being destined to liquidate my debts, as far as it will go."

The reply to this letter was satisfactory; and in a subsequent one he thus explains why he has resolved to become an author, and why he has selected literature as a means of placing himself in a position of comparative independence, at least, of his creditors:—

"DUBLIN, *October 27th,* 1820.

"MY DEAR MICHAEL,—You are quite right in supposing I do not calculate at present with a view to the remote future; in fact, my dear brother, you will see I cannot do so. My only speculation just now is, and ought to be, the payment of the last shilling I owe; and this must be done by any means that are the readiest, and are honourable. But what are readiest means? I see none, I am unconscious of any other within my reach, but the pen. This may be a fallacious assistant, most probably so. But I am rationally encouraged, so far at least as to make indifference to the opportunity criminal."

Like Hazlitt, Banim had now finally, at the prompting of genius, relinquished the brush for the pen, and some months before Ossian's Paradise appeared, he commenced the composition of a second poem. With the old love of home still, as ever, around his heart, he thus writes to his father, and the mingling of poetry and clothes reminds one of Moore's early London letters. He writes:—

"DUBLIN, *November* 30*th*, 1820.

"MY DEAR FATHER,—I am employed for another and larger work, which, in case of the success of the present, Mr. Warren promises to give me a fair price for. I am not flattered into anything like sanguine hope. I will continue to do my best: if I succeed, I will thank God; if I fail, it may be for the better, and I will thank Him then also.

"In remembering me to my dearest mother and to Joanna, say that I thank them for their present; they have knitted me a fine lot of stockings indeed,—they fit me excellently well, and to all appearance they are everlasting."

He had, whilst dwelling in his country home, formed the usual ideal of a poet, and fancied that genius was all inspiration, that poetry sprang up, spontaneous, from the brain, requiring little care or culture. His ideal had been the conventional one of those who contribute to the "Poet's Corner" of provincial newspapers; but a few months spent in the world and amongst books, taught him, that poetry, like every other pursuit of mankind, requires patient, thoughtful application; and that he who would

"Fling a poem, like a comet, out,"

must be careful lest his planet flame but as a fire-work meteor. We shall hereafter find how anxiously he had considered the materials by which a novel can and should be formed. In the following letter he half gravely, half humorously, describes the qualities requisite to constitute the poet and the philosopher. The letter is addressed to Michael Banim:—

"DUBLIN, *December 28th*, 1820.

"MY DEAR MICHAEL,—Poetry is a different thing altogether from what I considered it to be some time ago. A good poem is not the fire flash of inspiration, it is rather the steady sober light of a large pile of solid, inflammable materials, first collected with choice and patience, and then fired with a steady and skilful hand. From what you recollect of my verbose effusions, you will judge how little I knew of the craft.

"You confound the poet and the philosopher; they are different beings.

"RECEIPT TO MAKE A PHILOSOPHER.

" To make a philosopher, take a subdued and austere understanding, a knowledge of all the theories and facts on all the subjects, things, systems, matters, and essences in the world; and over, and under, and round about the world; in the body of man; in the mind, soul, spirit, and heart of man; in his brain, and in his motions, actions and formations—of all compounds, simples, and intelligences in the air, sky, and space above the earth, and in the waters under the earth, and in the eternities above the air, sky and space, or below the waters.

"Take a consummate and intimate acquaintance with all the histories of all the nations that have ever existed and do exist; of all the languages ever spoken by man, in every age and nation; accompany these mere acquirements, with an understanding prepared to appreciate—a judgment capable of enumerating, arranging, comparing, discriminating, combining, separating, and deducing. To generate and mature your accompaniments, keep the mind, for God knows how long before, exclusively exercised in the most rigid, practical, and matter-of-fact habits, and this done, you have your philosopher. Now for—

"A RECEIPT TO MAKE A POET.

"Let the mind, by early practice and associations, attain, first, a quick susceptibility of the beauties of nature in her material works and in her immaterial complex operations; in the heart and passions of man, as produced by extrinsic circumstances. Keep the fancy and imagination always up, always ready to be fixed by the slightest touch from a beautiful scene, a pathetic expression of feeling, an impressive situation, an heroic character, or a romantic association. Let the individual in preparation feel strongly that trees, rocks, flowers, and sky and water are beautiful; but you need not teach him why, and by what combined operations and remote contingencies, they are so. Let him feel the effect; be not anxious he should understand the cause. Thus qualified to receive his assorted materials, next cultivate his taste on the best poetical models; thus he may learn how to select, refuse, and combine. After this, initiate him into a thorough knowledge of rhetoric, that he may acquire the simplest and shortest way of expressing his feelings. All this done, shake him well, and continue to shake him, that the proper ferment and excitation may always be kept up. And here is your poet.

"N.B.—If you give him his meals regularly, he will become indolent and dull.

"If the understanding be exclusively cultivated, can the imagination soar? The poet and the philosopher are necessarily dissimilar creatures. Perhaps a little, only a little, of the one mingled with the composition of the other, might make both of them the more perfect. In building his structure, the philosopher must use the square and compass, the proper order of architecture must be observed throughout; and from the quoin stone to the pinnacle, every thing must be uniform, and solid, and infrangible.

" With the poet originality must stand for method; diversity for order.—And throughout the whole of his fairy palace, inside and outside, the line of beauty must play and curve with easy and unaffected grace and vivacity."

Our poet was now happy in his rational hope of success; the poem, however, did not appear until the month of February, 1821. Some short time previous to the period of its publication, Banim, by, we believe, Sheil's advice, altered the proposed title from "Ossian's Paradise" to "The Celt's Paradise," and under the latter title the poem was issued. The dedication was as follows:—"To the Right Hon. Lord Cloncurry; as a small Tribute of the Author's Admiration of his Lordship's Public Spirit and Love of Country, the following Poem is most Respectfully Inscribed."

This poem is now all but unknown, and a copy is rarely to be found, even at the book-stands or literary auctions. Yet it possesses passages of considerable poetic vigour, and of great beauty. Saint Patrick and Ossian the bard, are represented as discoursing chiefly on subjects of Irish mythology, and the latter thus describes the Celt's Paradise :—

" The summer there
Is cloudless, calm, and ever fair.
I saw it once! my waking blood
At that one thought rolls back the flood

> Of age and sorrow, and swells up
> Like old wine sparkling o'er its cup.
> I'll tell thee of the time I spent
> Beneath that cloudless firmament,
> And thou shalt judge if aught could be
> So pure a Paradise to me,
> If by my own frail spirit led
> Its smile I had not forfeited.
> Give me the old Clarshech I hung
> On my loved tree, so long unstrung,
> E'en to its master's measure free,
> It may refuse its minstrelsy:
> But give it—and the song tho' cold
> May kindle at a thought of old,
> Of younger days—and now and then
> It may be strong and bright again.
> Hear a song of age's daring,
> The sighings of the harp of Erin !
> When thou, the warbler of the West,
> Wakest from thy long, long rest !

In this Paradise the highest place is thus assigned to the patriot, and patriot poet :

> "All were happy ; but some felt
> A holier joy, and others dwelt
> In higher glory. I saw one
> Who, for the good deeds he had done
> On earth, was here a worshipped king,
> Triumphant o'er all suffering.
> On the utmost verge of his own shore,
> One foot amid the breakers' roar,
> Another on the rocky strand,
> He met the invading foe,—his hand
> Grasped its good sword. He was alone
> And they were thousands; and when flown
> His strength at last, he could but throw
> Between his country and the foe
> His heart,—and, through it bid them smite
> At hers.
>   He fell, but in the light
> Of Paradise the hero's deed

Found fittest eulogy and meed;
The gaping death-gash on his side
Was turned to glory; far and wide,
As a bright star, it beamed; and he
Walked on in immortality,
Worshipped and wondered at : the brave,
Unconscious, to his virtue gave
Honour and fame and praise,—the old
Blessed him as he passed by, and told
His name in reverence.
          And thousands rushed,
Forgetful of themselves, to gaze,
And give, in looking, their heart's praise
To him, of heroes the highest and best,
Whose death-wound was turned to a star on his breast.
With him walked one in converse high,
        Music and song
At his birth informed his tongue,
And fired his soul; and with them came
The throb for freedom; but the name
Of his own land had passed away,
And fettered amid her waves she lay,
Like a strong man on his hill,—the bard
In all her breezes only heard
The sigh of her past fame,—no strain
Rose o'er her desolated plain
To mourn her glories gone, or call
The blush of shame for her early fall
Up to her cold destroyer's cheek,
Or on his heart in thunders break,
  But the bard caught up his harp, and woke
His Country's Song! and as it broke
Forth in its pride, unmoved he met
From despot tongues their chide or threat,
Their lordly frown or luring smile,
That strove to silence, or beguile
To silence, a song so high and bold,
So true and fearless; for it told
Her tale in every strain! The wrong
And outrage she had suffered long
Went forth among the nations; till
The eyes of men began to fill

> With sorrow for her sorrows, and
> Even in that cold and careless land
> That wrought her woe, one manly sigh
> Was heard at last in sympathy
> With all her sufferings; and for this
> Thro' our world of light and bliss
> He walked immortal, side by side
> With him, the hero, who had died
> The highest death a man can die
> For his native land and her liberty!
> And equal reverence to the bard
> All creatures gave; and his reward
> Was equal glory,—a blessed song
> Went with them as they passed along;
> It was over and round them on their way,
> And ever it said through the cloudless day,
> 'Joy to the hero who dared and died
> For his country's honour, and fame, and pride;
> And joy to the bard whose song brought fame
> And pride to his fallen country's name!'"

The "Celt's Paradise" has its Eve, a thing of aërial beauty, "who moved in light of her own making." Had "The Loves of the Angels," or "Heaven and Earth," been published before the appearance of Banim's poem, he could not escape the charge of plagiarism, but as "The Celt's Paradise" was issued some months before these works, the coincidence is less striking than that which so plainly appears between these two fine compositions.

Ossian thus describes the first appearance of the fair spirit :—

> "I sat in the tall tree's trembling shade,
> And the moss of its trunk my pillow made.
> My eyes could not their watching keep,
> My soul was sinking in its sleep,
> And wild and wavering thoughts came on,
> Of deeds imagined, actions done,

And vain hopes mingling with the true,
And real things a man may do.
A sigh came o'er me soft and warm!
I started—but nor shade nor form,
Appeared thro' half-seen gloom around,
To utter such a silver sound.
It might be the sob of the summer air,
Which glowed so rich and sultry there—
Again I slumbered—again the sigh
Of woman's fondness fluttered nigh—
And while I listened, gentle lips,
Gently met mine—and, touched, and trembled,—
As if beneath the moon's eclipse
Alone, love's feeling long dissembled,
Might dare to own in bashful kisses,
Its maiden flame and modest blisses.

    Fondly I raised my arms and prest,—
They closed upon my lonely breast.
Back from their kiss the young lips started,
Sighed one rich sigh—and touched and parted—
I thought of the huntress young and fair,
Whose gifted glance had left me there,
And I said in the strength of my young heart's sigh,
While the tear of passion brimmed mine eye,—
——' Lady of Kisses !—Lip of love !—
From the air around or sky above,
Come and bless my desolate arms
With the richness of thy charms."

The charms of his spirit-mistress are thus described, but she seems to possess too largely the graces of a houri :—

"And shining and soft was her virgin form,
In full blown beauty wild and warm!
I know not if aught of earthly blood
Mingled with the magic flood,
That fed her veins—but you might see
A rich vein wandering sportively,
Beneath the bright transparent skin,
That kept its sparkling essence in.

'Twas an earthly shape, but polish'd too high
For an earthly touch or an earthly eye—
'Twas an earthly shape!—What else could be
Moulded or made to rapture me?
What other form could loveliness take,
To bid my doating eye-balls ache,
And boil my blood and fire my brain
In agonies of blissful pain!—
Nay, Saint, I pass thy word of scorn—
Thyself hath sung this very morn
Of beautiful and blushing things,
With golden hair and snowy wings,
Fair beyond minstrel's fancyings,
Who, moulded like to forms of earth,
Even in thy own heaven have birth,
Tho' basking in such holy light,
Hath made them look more soft and white—
I tell thee there she sat with me,
Fairer than earthly woman may be—
And she floated before my fainting glance,
Like the shapes of air that softly dance
Round the glorious evening sun,
In the joy that his daily task is done.
Her eye was large and soft and dark,
Floating in fondness—often a spark
Of mild and chastened light shone through,
And it was even as a drop of dew
Half seen within a darkened bower,
In the morning misty hour,
And you might know that underneath
All of her that did look or breathe,
There was a spirit pure and chaste,
As ice upon the unsunn'd waste,
Or silver waters under ground,
That the searching day has never found."

The following lines, descriptive of the lovers' life in Paradise, are very musical and fanciful:—

" Or we wandered among shining streams,
That like the bard's delicious dreams,

Ever flow thro' beds of flowers,
And golden vales, and blushing bowers.
And all in playfulness we gaze,
With sportive and well feigned amaze
On the water—and start, and blush
To see ourselves there, and we rush
And plunge together, as if to save
Each other from that innocent wave,
Then with it go and glide along,
In echoing laughter, mirth, and song.
Or alone we sat by the foamy fountain,
In the solitude of the silent mountain,
And I plucked a water-flower from its flow,
And wreathed it with leaves on the mountain that grow.
And when on her head it was a crown,
At her feet I knelt me down,
And called her the lady and the queen
Of that wild and desolate scene.
Or often—for our pure nature gave
That triumph o'er the gloomy grave—
Often our spirits winged away,
Disembodied through the day,
And into aught they would possess,
Breathed themselves in gentleness;
And so became the breeze or dew,
Or shrub, or flower of any hue.

" Then sometimes my love was the tall young tree,
That grows on the mountain lonelily,
And I was the wooing eglantine,
Around her slender shape to twine,
And climb till I kissed the topmost bough,
That blossomed on her fragrant brow;
Or she was the softly opening flower,
Among a thousand in her bower,
And I was the bee that passed all by,
'Till I saw my own flower blushing nigh,
And then in her bleeding bosom I lay,
And sipt its sweets and flew away.
Or still she was that rose, and I
Came down as a soft wind from the sky,

> And sadly I sighed thro' fields and bowers,
> Till I found at last my flower of flowers,
> And then beneath her folds I crept,
> And there in perfumed sweetness slept.
> Or a crystal drop was on her leaf,
> And I playfully called it the tear of grief,
> And then I was the loving light,
> To kiss away its essence bright!
> Or she kept her own immortal form,
> And I came as the breezes wild and warm
> Of which she breathed. I was a sigh
> Within her heart, alternately
> Coming and going, or as she lay
> Reclining, I stole in amorous play,
> And fluttered all over her gentle frame,
> As if to fan its virgin flame!"

This poem, we need scarce remark, is not at all worthy of that reputation which Banim afterwards attained; but it exhibits undoubted proof of poetic ability, and is distinguished by an intensity of feeling very perceptible in his plays and in his novel "The Nowlans."

The poem would have reached a second edition, but, unfortunately, Warren, the publisher, became bankrupt; and all Banim's bright hopes and expectations were, for the time, crushed.

He does not seem, however, to have permitted this disappointment to check his ardour in the pursuit of literary fame. He had succeeded in gaining a price (and not a low one for a poet unknown to the public and the trade) for his work, and he saw in this success the first dawning of his future fame. He continued to occupy his unemployed hours in writing plays and poems. He composed, amid all his wants and necessities, a very long and elaborate poem, and a tragedy, entitled "Turgesius;" but, as we shall presently find, the latter was rejected by the theatres—the former was condemned by Banim himself; and both were eventually committed to the flames.

He had occasionally his hours of relaxation, and these were generally spent with his friend Mulvany. One of their favourite amusements was to walk observingly through the streets, and guess, from the general appearance of the passers by, the trades to which they belonged. Each of the friends prided himself on his discernment; and years afterwards Banim used to look back to those walks with all the grave joys of pleasant memory; and loved to tell how, when they differed as to the trade of the passengers under discussion, they watched his features, endeavouring to discover if he were good-humoured enough to reply civilly to such questions as, "Are you a tailor?" or, "Are you a shoe-maker?" and how, of twenty persons named tailors by him, only two were discovered to be of other trades.

His fortunes were now about to brighten; and of his hopes and fears, of his studies and pursuits, at this period, he gave the following account, in a letter addressed to his father:—

"DUBLIN, *March* 10, 1821.

"MY DEAR FATHER,—I have made it a point not to trouble you with any of my humble speculations, until they should arrive at something of a reasonable prospect of success; therefore I did not write any account of the matter, which I now sit down to detail.

"You recollect my old tragedy, bearing the magniloquent name of 'Turgesius,' which you at home thought so highly of, and which, if you remember, Mr. Buchanan pronounced to be 'most honourable to him, as emanating from a young gentleman, while a pupil of his English academy.' Through a friend, this was forwarded to Mr. Elliston, manager of Drury Lane Theatre, by whom, my friend's good opinion notwithstanding, it was rejected, with some softening praise to be sure — but rejected it was.

"After that, 'Ossian's Paradise,' (the title of which, by the way, I have changed, and now call it 'The Celt's Paradise') occupied exclusively my leisure hours. When this was put into train for publication, in the end of October, I sat down to refit old 'Turgesius' for another trial—this took me three weeks of what time I could spare, and then, at the instance of the friend before hinted at, I sent him to Mr. Harris, of Covent Garden, who also returned it, with, to be sure, a polite note, but still—rejecting him.

"Well, had I been made for fretting, this might have caused me to fret. I did not, however: I got the manager's note about 7 o'clock in the evening; I tied a cord about the hopeless tragedy—all condemned criminals are manacled, you know—and I flung it into perpetual exile, into the bottom of a lumber box.

"Before I went to bed I made the first arrangement for a new tragedy; Pliny's letters supplied me with the raw material; his anecdote of Damon and Pythias gave me the idea to be wrought out. The last refusal of my old play came to hand in the middle of December; I was then, and had been for some time, engaged in compiling for a new poem: this employment I immediately set aside, and fell to work on Damon and Pythias.

"It took me three weeks to study and design my subject, and collect the necessary local knowledge of the persons and of the scene of action, and, in five weeks after, I completed the first copy of the play, which I then named 'The Test.' In less than a fortnight after I put the finish to it, and I have now the pleasure of announcing to you at home, who are so anxious about me, that I have received the strongest assurance of its being acted at Covent Garden immediately, or soon after Easter.

"I am slow to encourage, in you or myself, sanguine hope of success; but a presentiment which I cannot force from me, says that this play will do, and produce fame and more tangible good.

"It will have the aid of an actor who, in my mind as well as in the estimation of all who have seen him, is of very first-rate eminence—I mean Macready.*

"I should mention that to Mr. Sheil I owe my introduction to the theatre, and he has kindly undertaken to bestow on me and my bantling all the care and solicitude of a father. He will assist in correcting and arranging for the stage; and this is valuable in the extreme, he being the most successful dramatist of the day.

"This object being so far accomplished, I have now turned again to compile for my poem, and as some of the scenery and localities which I propose to make use of, are situate in the immediate vicinity of Limerick, I intend, with God's help, to go down there on Thursday evening, and remain for two months: by that time I shall have made important progress in the poem, and the fate of the play will have been decided.

---

* Macready knew, from the first reading of the play, that it was exactly suited to his powers; and it possessed an equally great attraction for him in the fact, that no female character divided the interest of his part.

"My dear dear mother will pray for me; beg of her to have good hopes of me. As to my venture, whether the play lives or dies, tell her I will persevere, and if God blesses me with life and health, I will succeed at last."

The play here mentioned has been frequently called the joint composition of Banim and Sheil. In the preface to the original edition, Banim states that the play owed much to the generous aid of Mr. Sheil; but the aid consisted in that very important assistance to a young dramatist—an introduction and recommendation to a manager. Sheil was a powerful friend at this period, in a case requiring such help as Banim needed. His own "Adelaide," "Bellamira," "Apostate," and, above all, "Evadne," had placed him high in the opinion of the stage authorities, and with his recommendation Banim was enabled to catch, and by his own genius to keep, the attention of the rulers of Covent Garden Theatre. Those who knew Sheil best are able to state, and do state, that he was at this time, as at all others, a fast and steady supporter of those who possessed the claim of merit or friendship, upon his services and good offices.

"Damon and Pythias" was produced at Covent Garden Theatre on the 28th day of May, 1821, the author being in his twenty-fourth year. It was performed at a time when the public taste was somewhat improved, and when the noble language of great Shakespeare was introduced once more upon the stage, excluding the alterations of Tate, and, as Charles Knight has it, "the joinery of Cibber." Our fellow-countryman, Macready, was, at that time, as in later years, the reformer of the stage; and not two months before the representation of "Damon and Pythias," he had, at Covent Garden, played Richard, with "the original character and language of Shakespeare," to the Richmond of Abbott, Mrs. Bunn being the Queen Margaret, and Mrs. Vining the Lady Anne. These were rather favourable times in which to produce so grave and classical a drama as Banim's; yet he had great difficulties to surmount, and the dangers of depreciation by comparison were imminent. His play was performed on the 28th of May, but on the 9th, "Romeo and Juliet" was played; on the 11th, "The Provoked Husband;" and on the 15th, "The Tempest," with Macready for Prospero, Abbott for Ferdinand, William Farren for Stephano, Miss Foote for Ariel, and Miss Hallande for Miranda; and the latter was repeated on the 22d. "Damon and Pythias," therefore, was not a tragedy bursting upon the town at a time when the playgoers were easily overawed by the high-sounding name of *Tragedy;* and our young author was to depend for success upon the real merit of his work.

The cast of the play was as follows :—

DAMON	Macready.
PYTHIAS (*in love with Calanthe*)	Charles Kemble.
DIONYSIUS	Abbott.
DAMOCLES	Egerton.
NICIAS . (*father to Pythias*) .	Chapman.
CALANTHE (*in love with Pythias*)	Miss Dance.
HERMIONE.	Miss Foote.
ARRIA	Mrs. Conner.
DAMON'S SON	Master Morris.
PHILISTIAS.	Mr. Jeffries.
PROCLES	Mr. Comer.
LUCULLUS (*Damon's Freed Man*)	Mr. Conner.

The story on which the plot is founded is, as Banim informed his father in the letter last above given, in

Pliny. In Dodsley's "Old Plays" there is, however, a play entitled "Damon and Pythias," which Banim may have seen. The only material alteration from either play or story in the tragedy is, that Banim's Damon has only six hours given him in which he is to visit and bid a last farewell to his wife; in the play and story, one friend is permitted to depart for six months, the other friend remaining as a hostage. "Damon and Pythias" was performed seven times during the remainder of the season, which closed on the 7th of August.

This tragedy is quite neglected on the London Stage, but it is occasionally performed in the Theatre Royal, Dublin. Its original success as a stage piece was due to Sheil's advice, who kindly prepared it for green-room critics, and through his judicious management Banim was little vexed by those clippings and manglings which so agonizingly tortured the soul of Mr. Puff, when he discovered that Tilburina's "first meeting with Don Whiskerandos—his gallant behaviour in the sea fight—and the simile of the canary-bird," had been cut out.*

The success of the tragedy was the crowning glory of Banim's hopes at this period. All the London papers were unanimous in its praise; and referring to his fire-work and other boyish failures, and slyly retorting his brother Michael's cautions, he wrote to the latter, announcing his success—"at length, my dear Michael, one of my *sky-rockets* has gone off."

Macready and Charles Kemble played most gloriously; it was precisely the style of tragedy most approved by Macready—it possessed that isolation for himself which rendered Richelieu so marked a fa-

* See Appendix 2.

vourite with him, and not less so with the audiences; besides, "Damon and Pythias" had no *rôle* sufficiently prominent to detract from the interest which this great actor desired his own character should possess. Indeed, the only performer who failed in the representation of the tragedy was Miss Dance, who entirely misunderstood the conception of Calanthe.

Always desirous that the dear ones at home should rejoice and share in the pleasures of his success, Banim thus wrote to his father, and the true-hearted trust in the toil of the future, and the purest resolve to pay the few—but, to him, great—debts incurred in the wild days, are worthy of notice:—

"LIMERICK, *June 3rd*, 1821.

"MY DEAR FATHER,—If the papers have not already informed you of the fact, this letter goes to tell you, that at length, thanks to God, a trump has turned up for me. The play has been successful. I have got Mr. Sheil's letter, giving Macready's account. I have also read the Courier, Globe, and Morning Chronicle. There is no doubt of my success, so again I am a free man, my debts paid to the last farthing, and I am in possession once more of my seat by the old fireside, with my health better than ever it was to fit me for working on.

"The moment I receive even part of the proceeds, I will fly to Kilkenny; that, however, may be some weeks. Joanna is to weave a laurel crown for me; my poor mother shall place it on my brow, and we shall be as happy as happy can be."

This letter, it will be perceived, was written from Limerick. He had gone there for the purpose of making arrangements for a regular series of articles to be contributed to "The Limerick Evening Post," and, as has been already stated, to gather local knowledge. Whilst staying in Limerick, and visiting the remarkable and interesting localities of the city, Banim first discovered that the stirring era of the Great Revolution, and the position of Ireland at that period, were romantic and exciting in all the glowing colours of that greatest of romances—historic fact; and many of the incidents afterwards introduced into his novel "The Boyne Water" were suggested by local association, and treasured in his never failing memory. Having arranged his business in Limerick, Banim returned to Dublin.

Upon arriving in town, he found every party and grade of citizens in anxious expectation of the proposed visit of George the Fourth to Ireland. As all know, the King did then pay a visit to this country, remembered only as having incited Byron to compose "The Irish Avatar," and by the erection of an unmeaning granite pillar at Kingstown. Banim, after the departure of the King for England, in September, 1821, went, late in the same month, to rejoin the dear friends at home; and his first act was to pay, from the money received for "Damon and Pythias," the sums due to the creditors of former days.

This reunion was a happy one; he did not, whilst revisiting old scenes and reviving old memories— some sad and dreary—neglect the duties of his self-selected profession. Although devoted to literature, he still desired to see the arts supported and encouraged. With all literary men who have abandoned the pencil for the pen, like Hazlitt and Hood and

Lover, he was ever ready in assisting to secure the interests of his old associates and of their profession. When Banim found that the people of Ireland were about to erect a testimonial to commemorate the Royal Visit, (and this project, as all our projects of the same kind, ended but in failure,) he thought that the time was suitable for introducing to the public attention the requirements of Art in Ireland.

Accordingly, whilst still in Kilkenny, he commenced the composition of a letter which he completed before his return to Dublin. It was published in the month of January, 1822, by Milliken. It is in pamphlet shape, and extends to thirty-two pages. The title-page is as follows: "A Letter to the Committee appointed to appropriate a Fund for a National Testimonial, Commemorative of His Majesty's First Visit to Ireland. By John Banim, Esq.;" and the letter is dedicated, "To those of every Class who have contributed any Sum towards the Erection of a National Testimonial, Commemorative of His Majesty's First Visit to Ireland."

He commences by recounting the various plans proposed, and after showing that all professions, and all bodies in the city possess appropriate buildings in which to assemble—that all professions, save one, are enabled to claim some particular place of meeting as their own, for all their peculiar uses and purposes—he demands, "Where is your Temple of Art? Where is your Louvre or Somerset House?" He then instances the support given to Art by the great statesmen and rulers of other nations; but, assuming that it may be contended that in this country the professions of painting and sculpture are not of sufficient importance to justify the serious contemplation of an outlay of the fund collected, in erecting an Irish National Gallery and School of Art, he writes, referring to the great men who have been the patrons of Art, thus :—

"With the theorist who may think the immortal names we have glanced at were or are wrong in their large and national estimation of art; with the political huckster who picks his steps through every path of cultivated pursuit, leaning on Adam Smith as on a walking-stick; with him, to whose stunted apprehension this spacious and flowery world is but a sales-market or a counting-house; and mind and talent, in all their varied impulses and uncontrollable tendencies, predoomed exclusively to buy and sell, and barter and calculate;—with him to whose taste the pounds, shillings, and pence of a nation are the most glorious acquirements of a nation, and who is well prepared to run us up and down the politico-economical gamut on every note and key of 'increase and of supply,' 'demand and market,' —with such a theorist we have another appeal. If individuals of the order we have mentioned be wrong, let us ascertain the sense of the past and present civilized world on the importance of the Arts, generally.

"Egypt is a wilderness. We only remember that she was. But of our recollections of her old name, which is the most lively—the most interesting? which most arouses our sympathy, commands our respect, our veneration? Is it our recollection of her wealth, her grandeur, her arms, her commerce? No: it is her mind, and not her wealth; her philosophy, and not her arms; her arts, and not her commerce, which we remember with vivacity, which we admire, respect, emulate. We explore her waste places for one atom of her art; if found, we cherish it as a saint's relic or a parent's memento, and we point to it and say, 'This is a part of Egypt.'

"Her foster-child, Greece—old Greece, has left us a greater variety of models for admiration. Her laws, her arms, her poets, orators, heroes, either were more distinguished, or history has better defined and transmitted them to us. They invite our attention equally with her arts—but only equally. With her Lycurgus, her Homer, her Leonidas, we rank her Phidias, her Praxiteles, her Apelles; and while we burn at the recollection of her Marathon and Thermopylæ, we glow with as pure an ardour over the historical memory of her pictured Thunderer, or in the actual presence of her Farnese and Apollo. In Greece, a painter* was allowed to assume the regal purple and golden crown. In Greece, painters and statuaries were eligible to the highest offices of the state.† In Greece, it was the law that none but men of noble birth should profess the Art.‡ Pamphilus, the master of Apelles, was a statesman and a philosopher as well as an artist. By his influence the elementary principles of the Art were taught in the public schools of Greece, and its acquirement associated with a liberal education.§ When Emilius, after subduing all Macedonia, demanded of the Athenians their most renowned philosopher to educate his children, and their best painter to superintend the ornaments for his triumph, the Athenians sent Metrodorus to the Roman General, telling him, they had provided in one person all he had required of two.§ Metrodorus was an artist.

"From the political structure of ancient Rome, we must not expect much practical excellence in the Art. But that which the Romans either did not or could not rival, they knew how to admire and appreciate. Quinctilian, Pliny, Tacitus, are often the historians or eulogists of ancient Art; and Cicero himself plucks from the garland of the graphic muse some of his sweetest flowers of exemplification.

"The Augustan age of Britain does not present a character which stands more boldly forward than that of Reynolds. Those who do, and those who do not, understand his excellence, concur in estimating it as a high national honour and ornament. The more than Augustan age of Britain, her present age, displays a galaxy of talent, as various as it is consummately excellent. With the senate, the field, the cabinet—with science, philosophy, poetry, great and immortal names are connected. Yet, against any of them, the names of West and Lawrence may be fearlessly arrayed. They stand as high as any in national estimation. They are as often appealed to as evidence of national character. They are as much the boast of their country. Their fame is as widely diffused through polite

---

* Apelles. † Vide MOORE—F. Junius de Picturâ veterum.
‡ Pliny. § Turnbull—Rise and Decline of Art in ancient Greece and modern Italy.

nations. They are parallels to Britain's proudest names, and can be produced to the same extent.

"During thirty years, the profession of arms would seem to have been the only one pursued with enthusiasm in France, yet her Arts were not forgotten. In the hot career of her unrivalled success, elated and laurelled with triumph, France could pause, and hold out to Art the hand of patronage and protection. The genius of victory, gathering up all her trophies, often came to the genius of Art, and sued for her graphic immortality. Denon, David, Le Fevre, Le Theyre, were or are contemporaneous with every era of thirty years of political convulsion in France;—bright names, like bright stars, have risen around them in the national horizon, yet theirs have not been eclipsed.

"Italy has, at present, no name, no character, but that which her Arts reflect upon her. It is the only current which keeps her floating up to the level of nations. Italy, that was the war-school of the world—whose thought was intelligence—whose tongue was oratory—whose breath was patriotism—whose sword was victory—Italy is a province—an abject, trampled province. Her Tully, her Cato, her Scipio, her Augustus, her Brutus, are no more—Italy has only her Canova."

And so the life of a literary man of our day was entered upon. To Banim, as to all others, it was the cold, stern enchantress, the demon Mistress, that wins men's love, and then claims health, and energy, and buoyant youth's bright blooming hours, as smallest duties offered in her worship—and thus Banim, and Laman Blanchard, and Thomas Hood, have each been types of this class, and to each we may apply these lines of Charles Mackay:—

> "'Mid his writing,
> And inditing,
> Death had beckoned him away,
> Ere the sentence he had planned
> Found completion at his hand."

CHAPTER III.

FIRST PLAN OF "TALES BY THE O'HARA FAMILY"— MICHAEL BANIM'S SHARE IN THEM—THEIR DESIGN—JOHN BANIM'S MARRIAGE—REMOVAL TO LONDON—LETTERS—HINTS TO NOVELISTS —LITERARY STRUGGLES — LETTERS — ILLNESS— LITERARY EMPLOYMENT—ILLNESS OF MRS. BANIM—LOVE OF HOME—LETTERS —PLAYS—HIS OPINIONS OF LITERARY MEN—ACQUAINTANCE WITH WASHINGTON IRVING—CONNEXION WITH DRURY-LANE THEATRE —LETTERS—PROGRESS OF FIRST SERIES OF "TALES BY THE O'HARA FAMILY"—CONNEXION WITH ARNOLD AND THE ENGLISH OPERA HOUSE—OPINIONS OF KEAN, MISS KELLY, WASHINGTON IRVING AND OTHERS—LETTERS—ACQUAINTANCE WITH GERALD GRIFFIN — THEIR FRIENDSHIP — MISUNDERSTANDING BETWEEN THEM—LETTERS—ILLNESS—PUBLISHES "REVELATIONS OF THE DEAD-ALIVE;" EXTRACTS—OBTAINS PUBLISHER FOR "TALES BY THE O'HARA FAMILY"—LETTERS.

WHILST visiting his family, after the production of "Damon and Pythias," Banim frequently wandered away through the lovely scenery of the county Kilkenny; he generally resided, on these occasions, with some friend of his father, and was always accompanied by his brother Michael. Few counties in Ireland can present scenery more varied or picturesque than Kilkenny. Thomastown, Jerpoint, and Kells, possess monuments of older days, interesting and valuable to the antiquary: Inistiogue, and Woodstock, once the residence of the authoress of "Psyche," are glowing in all the pride of leafy loveliness; and every feature of sylvan beauty is enhanced by the proximity of the bright, pure, gentle-flowing Nore. Banim's favourite spot, amidst these scenes, is thus described in "The Fetches":—

"It rises from the edge of the Nore, at about thirteen miles from Kilkenny, into curves and slopes, hills and dales, piles of rock, and extensive spreads of level though high ground; hills and dales are thickly or wildly planted; and mountain streams, made rough and interesting by the stony impediments in their course, seek their way through the bending and shivered banks and fantastic woods; sometimes leaping over an unusually steep barrier. The waterfalls send their chafings among the woods and hollows, which on all sides, and at a distance, reply; and these voices of nature, together with the nearly similar noise of the rustling trees, or the crackling of their knotted arms in the blast, are the only, or the overmastering sounds that disturb the solitude.

"Extrinsic interest has lately attached to this fine scenery on account of its having been the last residence on earth of a lady not-unknown in the literary world. In fact, the present proprietor is a Mr. Tighe; and here the gentle author of 'Psyche,' that gentleman's aunt by marriage, breathed the last notes of her femininely sweet song, and the last breath of a life she was almost too good and pure to have longer breathed, in a bad and gross world. Here she sang, in sighings of the heart, her last melancholy farewell to the 'Odours of Spring;' and, alas, the flowers she addressed had not wasted their perfume till they were transplanted to her grave. A beautiful girl, long the humble *protegée* of the minstrel, culled them with her young hands, and in recollection of notes that the silent tongue had once murmured, placed them on her bed of clay, and thus in the tears of beauty and of youthful sorrow, they were there nurtured. The grave is one of many in the church-yard of the village that skirts the domain. The river runs smoothly by. The ruins of an ancient abbey that have been partially converted into a church, reverently throw their mantle of tender shadow over it: simple primroses and daisies now blossom round. It is a place for the grave of a poetess.

"But when Tresham visited this district, it had, for him, the single yet abundant interest of its own beauty. Even as he approached it, the introductory scenery grew fair and enchanting. The country outside of Kilkenny was uniform; but at last, from the highest point of a rough, mountain-road, his eye was at once flung over a semicircular extent of hill, dell, and mountain, broken into every desirable shape of the picturesque, and thrown and tossed about, as if in the awful sportiveness of the creating hand. Hill bestrode hill, the guardian giants of the race appearing pale and mysterious in the distance; while through the midst, in the depths of a spacious valley, the lady Nore curved on her graceful course.

"It was the first approach of an unusually fine evening in September, and the red sun, setting over an extreme vista at Tresham's back, lackered all the opposite scene with gold : producing, at the same time, those stretching shadows that make evening the painter's best hour for the study of his *chiaroscuro*. At every turn of this road the scene only changed into another mode of beauty. From a nearer point appeared the lowly village of Inistiogue; a few white cottages, glinting, like white stones, at the bases and in the mighty embrace of hills, richly planted. Its light and not inelegant bridge spanned the crystal river, groups and groups of trees massing behind it; and, over all, the high grounds of Woodstock rising in continued and variegated foliage. Tears of pleasure filled Tresham's eyes. He felt it was happiness to live in so fair a world; alas! he enjoyed the scene as if he had been doomed to enjoy it."

Amidst these quiet haunts Banim loved to linger. The first round of life's great ladder of fame was, he fancied, passed; the jostling crowd who, panting and eager, thronged its foot, were no longer to be feared; and day dreams, such as only the young poet knows, made bright and joyous the hopeful musings of that autumn after he had seen "one of his sky-rockets go off." It was not that he felt unwilling still to labour and fast, and watch and wait. Fame to him was like that image of Love in "Gondibert"—and made all and everything bright and sunny—

"As if the thing beloved were all a Saint,
And every place she entered were a shrine."

The sad times of walking about the streets for lack of lodging—of "whistling for want of a dinner," were past—but the strong will, the earnest love of literature, were true and daring as ever. Plays, Essays, Novels, and Poems were designed, and talked over with Michael, who was the confidant now as ever.

It is a well known fact, that the genius which constitutes the Dramatist is nearly akin to that which forms the Novelist ; and in discussing the plans of his future life with his brother, Banim resolved to make his next venture as a writer of Irish fiction. At this period (1821) Miss Edgeworth was in the full possession of the public taste as the best and only Irish novelist. That reputation which she had obtained through the "Tales of Fashionable Life," and through the "Moral Tales," was out-topped by the success of the "Essay on Irish Bulls," and of "Castle Rackrent." These, however, were but the elegant drawing-room portraitures of Irish life and character, which might be represented in conjunction with the performances of that famous bear, in "She Stoops to Conquer," who only "danced to the genteelest tunes." They wanted vigour and individuality, and were entirely deficient in that dramatic power, without which any—most of all an Irish—novel must be weak. Admirably as Miss Edgeworth's genius might qualify her for the composition of her inimitable fictions inculcating moral precepts ; excellently as she might construct that most difficult of literary labours—a story for children, or for young people,—she wanted many, very many, attributes peculiar to that phase of genius which can obtain, and keep secure, the title of *the* Irish novelist. Banim knew well that his countrywoman possessed ability of a very high and polished order; he felt that in entering upon the world of literature as a writer of Irish fiction, he should be prepared to take his place beside, if not above, one who enjoyed all that strength which is derived, in literary matters, from a preoccupation in the public mind. He was fully impressed with all the might and force of these facts, but Sir Walter was his ideal of a National Novelist; from this ideal nothing can be more dissimilar than that discoverable in the style and tone of the works of Miss Edgeworth. Banim had known the people of whom he desired to write from childhood; he wished, like Galt, to draw his scenes and plots from the characters and events furnished by the every day world around him. As we shall, hereafter in this portion of his biography learn, he thought that from the body of his acquaintances the "studies" for many novels might be made. The scenery of his native county, and various portions of his native city, were to form his still life—they but required careful description to become the external nature of his fictions. The human nature he would find in the humour, in the pathos, in the tender hearts, or in the wild fierce passions of the Irish peasant.

In the year 1821, the Roman Catholics were just beginning to make their chains " clank o'er their rags;" the battle against Tithes was being fought; O'Connell had not, as Sydney Smith said, "lapsed"; the reign of Captain Rock was flourishing, and all the wild nature of the people was aroused. Banim's feelings were in unison with those which actuated the great mass of his countrymen; and thinking thus, Banim resolved to attempt that which many others have tried to accomplish—to raise the national character in the estimation of other lands, by a portrayal of the people as they really were; but at the same time to vindicate them from the charges of violence and bloodthirstiness, by showing, in the course of the fiction, the various causes which he supposed concurred to draw forth and foster these evil qualities. He fancied that of the lawlessness of the peasant he could discover the actuating principle in that bitter thought of Shylock, which teaches that those oppressed will in their turn oppress; and he longed to be their champion. The Irishman had been the blunderer of the stage for years—his stupidity being only equalled by his vulgarity and coarseness :—not alone on the stage was he misrepresented, the novelists had likewise held him up to ridicule, he was their butt or their adventurer—a species of commingled "Gil Blas" and "Vanillo Gonzales," speaking a barbarous English with a most abominable brogue—and in the whole range of the drama or of fiction, the only moderately fair portraiture, before the appearance of the "Tales by the O'Hara Family," of an Irishman, was to be found in the Sir Callaghan O'Brallaghan of Macklin's "Love à la Mode," and in the Sir Lucius O'Trigger of "The Rivals." Whether Banim knew these mistakes of former writers, or whether he was incited in his project by the success of the Waverley Novels, is now a question of little moment. Doubtless he knew that half the merit of Sir Walter's wonderful fictions consisted in their nationality, their naturalness, and their truthfulness. Fielding and Smollett and Macklin had caricatured the Scottish character in precisely the same manner as that adopted towards our own countrymen : yet despite the ridicule of the older wits, Scottish character will be truly understood; and from Oldbuck and Dumbiedikes—from Baillie Nicol Jarvie, " rest and bless him," and Caleb Balderston—from Rob Roy and Jeanie Deans—from all so dissimilar, and yet so Scottish in their individuality, the world has learned to know Scotland in her people. And to accomplish such a work as this for Ireland, was the great aim of Banim's efforts—the object which from this period, and at all after times, was ever honestly before him. We are here writing of the reasons which induced him to become an Irish novelist, and are now but recording the plan and scope of the projected works,—hereafter we shall, in the proper place, discuss the various topics connected with the tone and style of composition marking these excellent fictions.

Much as Banim longed to become the novelist of Ireland, yet knowing the great difficulties to be encountered and surmounted, he hesitated and feared and doubted. Whilst roaming through the demesne of Woodstock, whilst revelling mentally amongst the various scenes of sylvan loveliness of the landscapes around Inistiogue, he spoke of all his hopes and fears to his brother Michael. Michael was all courage and trustful aspiration. From the period at which he had ceased to be a pupil of Mr. Buchanan's " English Academy," he had been engaged in business as an assistant to his father. He had been, as we have already seen, the constant correspondent and adviser of John: he knew little of books, but much of the men who formed the world in which he lived. These were precisely the men who were to make up the characters of John's projected novels. Michael urged his brother to proceed : he knew nothing of the literary jealousies, the carping, the injustice which must be encountered in working one's way to the public eye. He believed in John's genius; he had gloried in his progress; he had been his confidant in his unhappy first love; he had been his nurse in the long and terrible sickness succeeding the death of Anne D———; and now he was his best and truest friend, for he kept him firmly fixed to one plan of many, promising success. They talked of plots and scenes; they repeated old stories, and criticised their adaptability for the novel or romance; and thus Michael became confirmed in his estimate of his brother's genius, and John learned the great advantage to be derived from the judgment, and kind but honest criticism of Michael. And he learned more :—in discussing their plans, and in relating the country tales that seemed most suited for John's purpose, Michael related one particular story so well, so clearly, so graphically and with so genuine a pathos, that John determined upon venturing all his hopes of success in an Irish Novel— a novel to be written in separate tales—one, at least, of which should be written by Michael—and thus, amid the green fields of Inistiogue, were the "Tales by the O'Hara Family" planned, and a joint system of writing commenced, which rivalled in popularity the "Canterbury Tales" of the sisters Lee. Michael was unwilling to join his brother in this plan; he doubted his ability; a book and printers were awful things in his eyes—but John insisted—implored : he would correct; he would be in London, Michael would serve him by shortening his work—the "filling stuff" of the volumes would be supplied by Michael's story if it served no other purpose; the story was a good one,—he might depend on John's judgment for the truth of the opinion; and at length it was agreed that each should commence composing forthwith, Michael to write the story he had told to John, John to prepare the other tales necessary to complete the ordinary three volumes—and each was to submit his work to the judgment and correction of the other.

This joint plan having been arranged, another joint plan was to be undertaken, in which John was to appear as chief actor. In his wanderings around the neighbourhood of Inistiogue he had selected, as his chief resting place, the house of John Ruth of Cappagh, a very old and steady friend of his father. John Ruth was what is, or used to be, called a "gentleman farmer"; one of those who with good land and low rents made up the somewhat spendthrift race of Irish "strong farmers." His house was well built and warmly thatched; it had its fool, its lame cook, its herd of hangers-on, its guests, whose days were idleness and whose nights were too frequently drunken revels. He was amongst the last of his class, and as many of our readers in this age of staid, sober Incumbered-Estates-purchased farms may not be aware of the causes which conduced to make Irish "gentlemen farmers" incumbered landholders, we here insert, from "The Nowlans," Banim's sketch of Aby Nowlan, the original being a cousin and neighbour of John Ruth:—

"Daniel Nowlan had an important bachelor brother, who was godfather to his second son, had given certain characteristic symptoms of a liking for the boy, and would most probably take him home one of those days, keep him in his house, 'and make a man of him.' Some few close critics now and then hinted, indeed, that no such hasty conclusions ought to be drawn from the symptoms alluded to, or from the general character of Mr. Aby Nowlan; or, supposing John to have been transported to his house, it did not follow, they said, that he would be much the better for the change; for 'Masther Aby's house was a wasteful house, and money went out of it, a power of money,' no one knew how or where; and, in fact, the hints on this subject were so many, that we feel it our duty to bring more fully before the reader the character and condition of Mr. Aby Nowlan.

"He was the first Roman Catholic 'gentleman farmer' of the district, inheriting, almost undividedly, the profit rents of many farms taken from time to time by his father, at very low terms and on very long leases, tilled and cultivated with skill and industry, and at last brought to such perfection, as on his deathbed to leave the premature old man the willing of almost a real estate of about one thousand a year. And, by the will he made, old Nowlan seemed perfectly to understand the importance of his acquisitions: for, in imitation of the proprietors of real estates around him, he would have, in his eldest son, a representative also; while three other sons, Daniel among the number, were left but scantily portioned; Murrough, the second, being apprenticed to a saddler in Limerick, and, when out of his time, turned off to shift for himself upon three hundred pounds and a blessing; Davy, the third, similarly disposed of 'in the grocery line;' and Daniel, the youngest, favoured, at the same rent under which the old man himself held it, with a lease of part of the ground on which we now see him living and thriving, and which, indeed, was the beginning of his prosperity.

"In fact, a gentleman, 'a real gentleman,' old Nowlan would leave behind him in the person of 'Masther Aby;' and it was not by independence alone, but by education and accomplishments too, he sought to confer this character. For himself, who had the making of the estate with his own two hands, late and early, through fair weather and foul, 'the larnin' would have been no use to him, and might have proved an injury; but the son who was to get all, ready made to *his* hand, and live the life of any gentleman upon it, why, it well became him to put something besides his mark to a lease or a receipt, and to be able to read any book that might come in the way, and to keep his accounts in 'pin-writin,' rather than on 'a tally,' and to have a word in his cheek before the best in the land; nay, to understand the soggarth's Latin itself, and not 'to have it thrun away upon him, like a cow or a horse.'

"But old Nowlan's endeavours, in this second view, were not as successful as his previous industry; he found it easier to make a thousand a year for his son, than to make that son a scholar or a gentleman. In vain did he send him to the best schools in Limerick; 'Masther Aby' either learned nothing in them, or did not stay in them long enough to learn anything. Sometimes he was turned home, like an incurable out of an hospital; sometimes he came home of his own accord, and, without speaking a word, or showing the least change in a face, always, from youth to old age, unchangeable, sat down to dinner in his father's parlour; and, more than once, when the old fellow thought that by dint of a good horsewhip he had succeeded in prevailing upon him to return to his 'schoolin,' that is, when after a sound flogging he had shut the door in his face, 'the young masther' has been discovered, months after, quietly passing his days under the roof of some distant tenant; eating, drinking, and sleeping; whenever it was possible, riding a horse; and scarcely ever opening his heavy-lipped mouth to a creature around him.

"In wrath and stern resolve, old Nowlan fell upon a plan, suggested by an action he had seen performed by the blockhead himself. At about twelve years of age, Aby was well skilled in dogs of all degree, and there was a certain pointer of his kennel which took an objection to breakfast on 'stirabout,' just at the very time when, in consequence of the animal's real or supposed state of body, stirabout was deemed, by good judges, its best diet. So soon as, after repeated efforts, Aby saw that the dog would not share the breakfast of its brother-and-sister dogs, he was observed silently to unchain it, lead it out into the middle of the yard, secure it to a large stone, place before it a platter of the objectionable food, stand by until a reasonable time was afforded for dog or man to form a decided opinion, and then flog it with a steady hand, again adjust the platter, again stand inactive, again flog, flog, and so continue, until some kinderhearted person beguiled him from his employment, or until his father, at last recognising the matter, came out with another horsewhip in his hand, not for the dog, but for the dog's master.

"And on this hint, old Nowlan acted in resolute prosecution of his plan to make his eldest son a scholar. Mounting a good horse, he rode, not to the ablest, but to the severest pedagogue in Limerick, and proposed an unusual pension for Aby's board and education, on the following provisos : that, first, Aby should get neither breakfast nor dinner until he had previously breakfasted 'dacently' on his morning and afternoon tasks, or else upon three distinct whippings, morning and evening ; second, that, to prevent elopement during the day, he should be chained by the neck and leg to a block of wood sufficiently large and heavy to hinder him from running, or even walking fast ; and, thirdly, that to guard against the like accident at night, all his clothes except his shirt should be taken from him as he lay down in bed, and not restored until the chain and log were in waiting for re-adjustment at the hour of getting up : 'an if the bouchal won't ate his stirabout now,' said old Nowlan, when the bargain was ended, and Aby regularly installed in his log and fetters, 'why, he may just folly his own likins.' And, notwithstanding the boasted wisdom of the arrangement, and the unremitting watchfulness and attentions of the pedagogue, 'the bouchal' did contrive to 'folly his own likins :' for, upon a winter's morning about eight o'clock, and about a fortnight after his father had left him in the school, a vision of 'the young masther,' habited solely in a draggle-tailed shirt, appeared walking up to the house, just as the old farmer was on his way to a fair at Nenagh ; so they met in the little avenue, and Aby's first salute from his affectionate parent was a lash across his shoulders, at which, wincing somewhat, he turned down the avenue again, and showed symptoms of a retreat to a tenant's house ; but the father spurring his horse, intercepted, and by words and continued lashes, exhorted him into the Limerick road, kept him in it for miles, always foiling his efforts to double to the right or left ; until as Limerick came in view, Aby, roused to a dogged despair, rushed through a gap down a descent to the Shannon, gained the river's edge before his father could baffle his sudden movement, plunged headlong in, and, as he had ever been too lazy to learn to swim, would most certainly have been drowned, but that a fisherman's cot paddled to his assistance, picked him up, and returned him to the arms of his now afflicted and remorseful parent.

"This was his last trial. From this day out, Aby never saw the loathsome interior of a school ; though to the hour of his death, his dreams often surrounded him with its villanous circumstantiality. Old Nowlan, in addition to his caution of his former pertinacity, consoled his heart with various reflections; such as, when he was cross—'hard to make a silk purse out iv a sow's ear; hard to dhraw blood from a turnip; man proposes, God disposes:' or, when he recollected that Aby could indeed write a tolerably fair hand, and read a book without much coughing and hemming; and, fair time being allowed, and no hurry, work out a sum upon a slate to the effect of 'what would six sacks of wheat come to at — the sack?' and find out London and Dublin upon any map he was used to, with other considerable things;—why, when the old man took this to mind, he would comfort himself with—'half a loaf is betther nor no bread;—take an inch if you can't get an ell;—too much of one thing is good for nothing;' &c. &c.

"The stupid harmlessness of Aby's character had further influence on the natural feelings of the parent: 'Avoch, poor boy, there wasn't a bit of bad in him; an' the heart was in the right place, anyhow;—an' he was no sich omadhaun, neither; smooth water runs deep: he could see as far into a mill-stone as another: he knew more nor a cow did of a bad shillin'; lave him to himself; jist let well enough alone; you'll never see him atin' pavin'-stones for phayties:' and in time, this negative admiration amounted to real love; even of the dolt's clumsy person, set features, and staring eyes, the father became fond; nor was Aby's taciturnity any check on their fire-side communions, for, just as one can talk for hours to a dog, in imaginary reply to its set gaze, or the wagging of its tail, old Nowlan easily managed long conferences with his eldest son.

"In a word, 'Masther Aby' was a mere animal of a very inoffensive and perhaps amiable class: not a fool—that gives no idea of him: an animal is the word,—an animal with an animal's wants, and with no mental stimulus to strive for anything beyond their gratification.

"Aby Nowlan however, had, in common with his father, an ambition to be thought a gentleman; but he manifested it in a tamer and more slavish way than his father would have done. To wear, like 'Square Adams' (meaning Squire Adams) of 'Mount-Nelson,' (or some such ridiculous name conferred on a bit of barren ground once called Killavochery, or Ballybrochlehin, or Coollavoorlich, and still surrounded by similar ones)—to wear like him, who was the county magistrate, beforementioned, a very blue shining coat with very bright buttons, a canary-coloured waistcoat, top-boots, and fawn-coloured smallclothes; to ride like him, a good hunter to every hunt, and like him, and especially to him and his nine sons, and score friends, to give great meat dinners, and 'lashins' of claret, port and sherry, and all in the timid hope of being recognised as the boon companion, and no more, of a man of less actual wealth, and of no more actual rank than himself; this was the weak, mean and superfluous way in which stupid Aby Nowlan tried to become a gentleman. And, to his heart's content, the 'quality' allowed him to make the experiment; day after day, night after night, 'Square' Adams, and his ranting and roaring, cursing and swearing, sons and cousins, friends and followers (himself as great a roarer and blasphemer as any amongst them), would honour 'the bachelor's house' with their noise, voracity, guzzling and drunkenness! While 'Mrs. Nowlan' had a numerous circle to tea above stairs, the 'masther' gloated, with staring eyes, and with scarce a word in his cheek, on all this glory in the parlour; so that his candle, thus lighted at both ends, blazed away famously.

"But whether or no these loose courses of Mr. Aby Nowlan were attended with the results hinted at by his neighbours, remained more than doubtful, for no symptom of declining grandeur yet appeared: the house might still be found full of company; and as much wine and whiskey-punch were drunk in it as the oldest tenant could remember."

John Ruth* had been unlike his cousin, the original of this sketch; he had not been a drunkard, but he had been somewhat unfortunate in his farming speculations, and he was not the man to raise himself into competence when he had once fallen from his position. But in the incident of Banim's life which we are about to relate, this circumstance weighed lightly with him.

* This is not the only instance in which Banim has introduced his wife's family name: for example, in "The Fetches," he gives the name Ruth to his heroine "Anne."

John Ruth had three daughters—all pretty, and well educated for their position in life. Banim, as their father's guest, was frequently their companion: he was not the fiery-souled adorer of the days when he wooed Anne D——; the hard and iron realities of his life in Dublin had taught him, that love which begins without calculating upon mutton chops, lodgings and coal, is likely to expire in the daily struggle for the procuring of these necessaries—yet he was ardent enough to love the youngest daughter of his host—even though she were dowerless. He had known Ellen Ruth little more than a fortnight when he told her that he loved her. He did not ask her then to marry him; he left Kilkenny for Dublin. He published a pamphlet on the proposed testimonial commemorative of the visit of George the Fourth to Ireland, and after arranging his affairs in Dublin, preparatory to removing to London, he returned, in the month of February, 1822, to Kilkenny. He then found that his love of Ellen Ruth was returned by an affection as warm, and fond, and true as his own; and after a courtship of less than five months, John Banim in his twenty-fourth year, and Ellen Ruth in her nineteenth, were married on the 27th of February, 1822. A pure heart, a sweet kindly face, and great love and trust in her husband, were all the fortune she brought him; and as we recall now the patient care, the tender, never-flagging zeal with which, in after years, she bore her part as wife, and nurse, in many a weary month when her husband slept but for minutes, to awaken to hours of agony, we can apply to her the beautiful lines in Gerald Massey's "Poor Man's Wife"—

> "Her heart it was lowly as maiden's might be,
>   But hath climb'd to heroic height,
> And burn'd like a shield in defence of me,
>   On the sorest field of fight!
> And startling as fire, it hath often flasht up
>   In her eyes, the good heart and rare!
> As she drank down her half of our bitterest cup,
>   And taught me how to bear."

On the 13th of March, 1822, less than one month after their marriage, Banim and his young wife set out for London, really to seek their fortune. To the student of literary history, how many memories the words "seeking his fortune," and "settled in London," bring back upon the mind. Johnson rises first—the great, heaving figure is before us—he has failed as "a dominy,"—his weary years of sorrowful youth, and disappointed early manhood are past, and now he seeks but bread by the labour of his brain. David Garrick, with his skipping step, and bright black eye, can work his way, and his little vanities but help him onward; but the deep, loving soul, with thoughts and hopes for all, is gloomy and distressed; he lives somehow, "genteely," at an eightpenny "ordinary," "with good company, sir;" and he hangs about Cave's at St. John's Gate. He hopes on, he calls upon Wilcox the bookseller, with a letter of introduction, and requests employment as a literary man; Wilcox looks at him, measures his burly frame, scans his heavy face, and tells him he had better "buy a porter's knot." But he still perseveres; he has a poem with him, an imitation of Juvenal, and Dodsley liking it publishes it for him, and when his "London" appeared, Samuel Johnson was "settled in London." Goldsmith comes next to London—poor Goldsmith! his has been a wild, wandering life; but man and woman, age and youth, had ever loved him as he loved them. He is at first an usher in a school—what he thought of that employment he has told us in his "Life of a Philosophical Vagabond;" he leaves the school and sets up as a physician at Bankside, and he "has plenty of patients, but no fees." He too hangs about the publishers; a little pock-marked man, very shabby indeed, for this was before the days of William Filby the tailor, and the "peach-coloured suit;" but he works on, as he ever did, hopefully, giving pence in charity when he himself lived on pennies. And when the world thought Sterne a great novelist, thought Beattie a great poet, thought Kelly a great comic writer, Heaven knows poor Goldsmith might have despaired, even if Newbery had not retained the "Vicar of Wakefield" for two years, even if Coleman had not thought so meanly of his play, as to refuse to paint a new scene for a thing which he was sure must be damned. These woes he suffered before he was "settled in London," and yet Oliver Goldsmith died 2,000*l.* in debt—truly we may exclaim with Johnson, "Was ever poet so trusted before?" Then Tom Moore goes to London; bright-souled Tom, with his light purse, his glowing fancy, and his loving heart; he had no dark days save when he wanted a new coat; he forgot this care too in a supper with "Incledon and Irish Johnson," and thought of it only when he was asked to dine by "the Honourable Mrs. Gardiner, an English woman, but she has an Irish heart;" he is happy because the Prince accepts the dedication of "Anacreon:" and thus Tom Moore is "settled in London." Gerald Griffin goes to London; a boy, fresh from the blooming fields of his native place, founding his hopes of success upon his tragedies

"Aguire," and " Gisippus ;" only in his twentieth year, and with no friend in all the great city save one—John Banim. What a struggle was his! " Cheated abominably" by Magazines to which he had contributed; translating a " volume and a-half of one of Prevot's works for two guineas ;" disgusted with his employments, " there was so much shuffling and shabby work," but yet he was ever hopeful, and Gerald Griffin was only " settled in London" when his " Collegians" appeared ; and as his other novels were written at all times, and in all places, so this was written " against the printer," and as it was required.

These are the memories which arise as we record the going forth of John Banim to seek his fortune in London, and to obtain a home for his wife in that unknown place. And truly his home was her home—they had no home save his, save that home which he should procure, and support by his own exertions; and with a hurried leave-taking they quitted the old folks at Cappagha and Kilkenny. It was a speedy farewell, but one in which good wishes came from the souls of the home-stayers. There was only the " God bless you," of the father and mother; the " God speed ye," of the neighbour; the " God be with ye," of Michael and the sisters—and, last but not least, the firm grasp of the hand, and the honest smile of the servant, as she half laughing, half weeping, said, " More power to you, Misther John." And so, passing from the scene of his joys and sorrows, John Banim went forth to London; and as he and his wife moved away towards that vast city of all earthly evil and good, they proved the beautifulest thing in all the world—woman, in her blooming youth, clinging to man in the strength and energy of genius—two whose hearts beat but as one; whose life was faith, and hope, and love—faith in the bliss of to-day—hope in the work of the dreamy future—love in all times and in all fortunes. And as they entered the city, so they entered the reality of life, and began to learn that solemn truth of Goethe, " Ernst ist das Leben."

He arrived with his wife in the metropolis on the 23d of March, 1822. He had no friend in all that world, he had very little money, but he possessed all the courage that ever dwells in the strong, deep heart of genius—and he required all, its fullest, sustainment. Most literary men have commenced the struggle of London life with no claims upon their exertion save their own needs; and in the from-hand-to-mouth existence of a young adventurer, who must be prepared to wade and buffet in the tide of men around him, ere he can hope to swim smoothly along the deep, broad stream of popularity, this circumstance of being sole is of great importance; it eases the load of anxiety and care; and be such a young man's course right or wrong, he knows that in his failure he alone can suffer; if he succeed, his reward must be in the hereafter of a future fame, and in the love of a wife wooed and won in days not perhaps happier, but more secure in that realized fame—a good name with, as Goldsmith said, the author's " real patrons—the booksellers."

Banim, however, thought not of these things. Forth from home he went, with his young wife, and his first residence in London was at No. 7, Amelia Place, Brompton—the house in which John Philpot Curran had lived the last months of his life—the house in which he died, on the 14th of October, 1817, and which John Banim entered, as a resident, on the 29th of March, 1822. It was the last of a row of nine houses, and around it were green and pleasant fields, and a nursery garden, which now forms the ground of Pelham Crescent. Banim was elated at gaining possession of these lodgings. His first pilgrimage in London (every literary man who is worth the name, has some long-selected spot in London, to which he makes a pilgrimage on his first visit) had been to the scene of Curran's death; a lodging-bill was in the window—" I," as he afterwards said, " bolted in, I took the rooms at once, that I might dream of Ireland, with the glory and halo of Curran's memory around me." Here, amidst the semi-rurality of a London suburb, he fixed his residence, and he thus, in his first letter to the dear friends in Kilkenny, describes his lodgings, and relates the feelings and emotions with which his heart is filled :—

"LONDON, 7, AMELIA PLACE, FULHAM ROAD.
"*March* 30*th*, 1822.

" MY DEAR FATHER AND MOTHER,—We got into London on Monday evening. Tuesday, Wednesday, and Thursday we spent lodging-hunting. We settled here on yesterday. We are pleasantly situated as regards accommodation; and when I retire to the back drawing-room, which I have fixed upon for my study, I am as quiet as if I were in a wood. Exclusive of the conveniences I enjoy, there is a charm attached to my abode, that recommended it to me above all others; I breathe the very air of inspiration, I sit in the same chair, I lounge on the same sofa, and think, read, and write in the very study where John Philpot Curran sat, lounged, and thought.

"Four years of the latter part of this great man's life were spent in the rooms I now occupy. His thoughts, even yet, perhaps, float about my little study; and when I lock the door, and sit down, I almost imagine I can get them into a corner and make them my own."

The day following that on which he entered these lodgings, he commenced preparations for a vigorous performance of his duties as an author. He details to Michael, in the following letter, the course which he had adopted, "to keep," as he said, "the fire in and the spit turning."

One can fancy the brave, true-hearted "country boy," sitting at the breakfast table, with a good appetite, in which "Ellen keeps him in countenance," earnestly searching the advertisements of *The Times* for some employment that might suit him; and wondering, like Tom Pinch, that so many people wanted what others offered to supply, yet apparently the parties never met. We can fancy him, after a fortnight of these hopes, and fears, and expectations had elapsed, writing thus so heartily and honestly, as he ever wrote, to Michael :—

"LONDON, *April 4th*, 1822.

"MY DEAR MICHAEL,—Do not be so uneasy about me; I am in the receipt of a weekly stipend, that is, paid weekly, but it is a settled annuity, which keeps the pot boiling very well.

"As soon as I was fixed I took up a newspaper,

looked over the advertisements, saw a new periodical advertised, wrote immediately to the proprietors, furnishing some specimens of my capability ; was treated with immediate attention, and soon engaged, and I am right well pleased with the concern altogether.

"And now you must praise me, and say that I have not succeeded badly at the outset, considering that I am only an Irish country boy.

"I work hard, to be sure, to meet my engagement ; it is what I expected, and what I like. I am not indebted to a single introductory letter : this to me is delightful—to work one's own way, without incurring obligation, sweetens labour.

"I was at work the second day after I got into a fixed abode. I will take amusement, when I can do so consistently with my industry : plenty of time for that : in the meanwhile, I repeat it, is it not delightful to feel myself getting on in a strange world, by my own efforts alone ?

"The expense of travelling has been very great, and the cost of living here out of all proportion with Kilkenny. Then why, you will say, saddle yourself with a responsibility to create the expense ? My dear Michael, this is my answer—I have purchased by my outlay, rational happiness, settled habits, and a continual stimulus to future exertion. With the money I have expended I am as happy as any fellow can be, in my humble sphere. I am in excellent health and spirits. My appetite may be said to be too voracious for my income ; and further, Ellen keeps me in countenance in this respect. I go to bed early, rise early, drink nothing but water or tea ; work with a liking for it, all the day long, and I have my cheerful fireside, with a companion thereat whose smile cheers me after my toil."

This letter was written in the month of April; and early in the July following a weekly paper, entitled *The Literary Register*, was started, and Banim was engaged upon its staff, and was also occasionally employed as its editor. This was his first step as a literary man in London, and he believed it to be a fortunate one, for it proved to him that "a country boy" might succeed, had he but ability and industry; and in reply to some anxious questions of Michael's, regarding his position and prospects, he wrote thus:—

"LONDON, *July 27th*, 1822.

"MY DEAR MICHAEL,—Your affectionate queries shall be answered. I am well off, better than I deserve to be, with a rational prospect of doing gradually better. I am a more industrious fellow than I was ever before. It is my delight; it agrees with me. My health is good; my domestic happiness equal to my anticipation. My time is my own; that is, I can apportion it as I please, consistently with my duties; and I patiently and resolutely await the coming of events."

Amidst all his own cares and wants, he was at this early period as anxious to serve a young man, a young Irishman in particular, who needed assistance, as in after days, when in the full possession of his fame, and of his influence, he aided Gerald Griffin with that heart-whole kindness which caused Gerald to write from London to his brother, "what should I have done if I had not met Banim? mark me! that is a man—almost the only one I have met here." Indeed, he was never weary of assisting needy brother-authors by advice, and by kind words spoken in their favour to those who could really advance them; and money too he would give, but he had it rarely to spare: he was not, however, inclined to encourage the folly of those who consider that London is a city where wealth can be made, in any profession or walk of life, without energy and patience. The following letter to Michael gives an amusing account of his treatment of a young Irishman who had requested his counsel and direction, on certain matters connected with a proposed visit to London in search of employment, as an apothecary's assistant. The plain good sense of the letter is very deserving of the attention of young gentlemen of large aspirations, but small experience, who fancy that an Irishman in London is a very wonderful and clever fellow, and must excel the natives of England or Scotland. Banim wrote thus:—

"LONDON, *August 8th*, 1822.

" MY DEAR MICHAEL,—Your inclosure from Mr. Mac Gawly is curious: let me quote for you; he requests me to inquire into the state of the medical profession in London; and says, 'would you have the goodness to acquaint me if there are facilities to Irishmen, to obtain appointments at the houses of apothecaries?'

" What the deuce! (Lord forgive me) nonsensical work is this he gives me to do? By what means am I to make out that vaguely generalised study—the state of the medical profession in London? What does he, or what can he, mean by facilities to Irishmen, to become druggists' assistants? Have they not the same facilities possessed by Scotchmen, Welshmen, any men? I think I would not be serving Mr. Mac Gawly, did I induce him to venture over here. Depend on it, he would find it hard, even had he every facility, to pound his way through the bustling and shouldering of this place of rivalry."

Banim's prospects were now becoming brighter; he had been engaged on other periodicals, through the ability which had distinguished his contributions to *The Literary Register*: so far he had been fortunate; but his wife became ill, her life was in imminent danger, and in the month of November, 1822, she was delivered of a still-born child. These combined sorrows were the clouds of his married life; but yet he bore up against them hopefully, manfully—above all, Christianly. If to-day were dark, to-morrow might be sunny; and his life was as that shown in the stanza of Shakspere,—

> "O, how this spring of love resembleth
> The uncertain glory of an April day,
> Which now shows all the beauty of the sun,
> And by and by a cloud takes all away!"

His present griefs and future hopes were thus told by him to Michael; and, short as the letter is, there shines a noble, beautiful heart through every sentiment which it contains:—

"LONDON, *November* 22d, 1822.

"MY DEAR MICHAEL,—Ellen has just escaped with her life; her confinement was premature, and our lovely little infant came into the world still-born. My expenses have been great, between nurse, doctor, and apothecary. But God has done all for me; notwithstanding that I have encountered real difficulties, I may say I enjoy absolute comfort. I can put my hand in my pocket for every shilling circumstances require, and my purse is never positively empty.

"Conceive how grateful I ought to be to heaven for my real independence, hardly earned, but the sweeter for that very reason.

"My salary has been increased, and I earn something by contributing to other periodicals."

Mrs. Banim regained her health very slowly. Constant labour of the brain was required from the young husband, that money might be procured to meet the increased expenses of his wife's illness. We know nothing more interesting, in the whole wide range of literary biography, than the account given by Banim, in the following letter to Michael, of his position. It is not painful, or disagreeable in its details of an honest, poor man's needs; for the sorrows of the time are relieved by the hope, and trust, and content by which he is sustained; and he required all his cheerfulness: he wrote in a house where his wife lay ill— where his servant lay sick; he was at his desk about fourteen hours each day; he had "doctors, and their bills *galore;*"* and now it was that he found the usefulness of the stern discipline of the time when he walked about the streets for want of a bed, and whistled for his dinner, being not the first by many and many a score, who has involuntarily and unconsciously learned, in the school of early poverty, those lessons of self-denial and self-discipline, without which success

* *i. e.* in plenty.

seems to be problematical, if not impossible, in any and every walk of life. There is a charming, lovable, honest simplicity in the confession—that, much as he liked a glass of punch, he never has it now; and one can suppose that as he wrote he recalled the happy evenings when with his father, and Michael, and Mr. Buchanan, he sat by "the little octagon table" in the old man's "sanctum sanctorum," when the pleasant jokes went round with the bottle; and things were somewhat changed, for—"By the life of Pharaoh, sir, if I do not ply and tease the brain, as wool-combers tease wool, the fire should go out, and the spit could not turn." The letter to which we have referred is the following, and was written about a month after Mrs. Banim's premature confinement:—

"LONDON, *December* 22d, 1822.

"MY DEAR MICHAEL,—I sit down to reply to two letters of yours for which I am in your debt.

"Ellen continues to go on tolerably, though not as rapidly as my opinion of her constitution led me to hope.

"You say you will favour me with your cordial criticisms. My dear brother, you could not more materially serve me. I give you my word, I throw off all matters for the *Register*, as I do this letter, and without half my present stimulus or purpose. I must write—must stuff the gaping maw of that weekly glutton, with anything to fill it. Pages—pages! that is the cry. Well, too well I feel convinced that part, often the whole of every packet, I shoot off at the office, is bad, meagre stuff. But here is my difficulty. I have not time to hunt for these parts, in order to fix them and avoid their repetition. By the life of Pharaoh, sir, if I do not ply and tease the brain, as wool-combers tease wool, the fire should go out, and the spit could not turn.

"By-the-bye, I am held pretty tight at present. My poor Ellen is ill, and my very good servant, as if for the purpose of adding to my difficulties, has got some confounded stoppage in her throat, and is in bed too, not able to swallow. Matters have been thus for a week back, and we have doctors and their bills galore. To meet the unavoidable increase of outlay, I am obliged to knuckle down to my work, and to live close —close, myself. You may remember, I used to like a cheerful glass. Not one libation now, even to the temperate fireside Bacchus. I am in great spirits for all that; I am always so, thank God for it."

These labours here recorded: this "teasing the brain," this "knuckling down to his work," this "living close, close," at length produced its inevitable results, and the poor, brave heart, whilst stout as ever, was overcome by the necessities of the weaker frame— the sword was outwearing the sheath.

In the hour of his utmost extremity, at the time when Banim most required health and energy, a terrible sickness settled upon him, the malady of his life began, and to him the awful moral of Cowper's lines was taught by a fierce discipline of agony—

"Read, ye that run, the awful truth,
 With which I charge my page;
A worm is in the bud of youth,
 And at the root of age."

Early in the year 1823, the racking pains which had afflicted him during the twelve months succeeding the death of Anne D——, returned with all their violence.

The tortures which he endured, in head and limbs, were increased by the thought that a delicate wife was now dependent upon him for support, and, as a

"Sorrow's crown of sorrow,"

his physician ordered an entire cessation of all literary employments. This was a woful sentence. It meant that he must consign himself to beggary, or become, with his wife, a burden upon his father, to whom it had been his earnest hope that he might, at no distant period, be an assistance. All was dark and gloomy around him now, and at the very time too when success seemed to be within his grasp. The despondency of his first sickness returned : no hope—no rest —pain by day—pain by night—pain even in dreams —and waking hours but offering objects to rend the heart ; for, as time passed on, he fancied that his position with the publishers and the readers became weaker and more uncertain.

He wrote at length to his father, informing him of his condition, and stating that he feared he should be forced to claim the shelter of his roof for himself and for his wife. To whom could he fly from pain and want, but to those for whom every pulse of his heart had ever beat warmly in the dawn of fame and manhood, as in the days of hopeful, dreaming, loving youth?

He was, however, spared the sorrow of this return to Kilkenny. With rest, and skilful medical attendance, he was, after the lapse of some months, restored to health ; and with the first indication of its return, he thus, with a buoyant spirit, writes to his father :—

"We are wrong to anticipate twenty cloudy days, because one is overcast. Praises be to Heaven, I am better and likely to mend. My Sangrado frightened himself and frightened me, and I terrified you all at home too much. I must not, however, write so constantly; I must devote four hours per diem to exercise, for some time."

Whilst writing thus hopefully of his health, his means of support were much diminished. He was unable to spend sufficient time at his desk to keep up his connexion with the periodical press as in the days before his illness, and therefore he was forced to endure many wants, many privations. But, as usual, he hoped; and as his connexion with the weekly press decreased, he became a more regular and better paid contributor to the monthlies. This circumstance was advantageous to him in one very important particular; his work was no longer task work, filling stuff, struck off for the printer, and against time; and he had therefore leisure to produce papers of a more finished and more carefully written character. With recovered health he changed his residence from 7, Amelia Place, to 13, Brompton Grove, where he had for neighbours, in Grove House, first William Wilberforce, and secondly, William Jerdan.*

His leisure, shortly after taking possession of these lodgings, was rendered still greater by the termination of *The Literary Register*, which closed its publication with the 44th number, in May, 1823.

With leisure came back the old love of dramatic poetry; and amidst his other occupations, he found

* No. 13, Brompton Grove, was lately occupied by a stonemason. Gerald Griffin succeeded Banim in these lodgings, which are separated from Grove House only by Hermitage Lane—which takes its name from the Hermitage—the house occupied by Madame Catalani, during her residence in England. It was, after she left it, converted into a private lunatic asylum.

time to compose a tragedy, which he entitled "The Prodigal." The plot was well conceived, the situations most effective, and the language glowing, yet vigorous. The chief character, "The Prodigal," resolves to murder his father; he is led on by passion; the perpetration of the crime is checked by remorse, and in the moment of committal the foul design is abandoned. "The Prodigal" was accepted at Drury Lane Theatre, and parts were cast for Kean and Young.

Banim had just succeeded in getting his tragedy accepted, when there arrived to him from the county Limerick, bearing a letter of introduction, a healthy-looking, handsome youth, who had come to London to seek his fortune and to secure his fame by the sale or representation of two tragedies, which he carried with him from his native place; it was poor Gerald Griffin, all genius and hope: but knowing as little of London or the booksellers as did Parson Adams when he commenced that famous journey to the city to negotiate the sale of his two volumes of sermons. Griffin had found much difficulty in discovering Banim's residence; and whilst seeking it, he heard from an acquaintance that Banim had a tragedy in rehearsal at Drury Lane, entitled "The Prodigal;" and thus, even before the future friends had spoken, one of Gerald's hopes was crushed; *he* had a tragedy in his trunk, and which he had called "The Prodigal Son." At length the two poets met; and Griffin, in a letter to his brother William, thus describes their interview:—

"LONDON, *December 29th*, 1823.

"MY DEAR WILLIAM,—I mentioned to you a few days since, that I had seen Banim. I dined with him on

Thursday; there were Mrs. Banim, and an Irish gentleman, and we had a pleasant evening enough. He had read 'Aguire' twice. He went over it scene by scene with me, and pointed out all the passages he disliked. He then gave me his candid opinion, which was, that after making those alterations, the play ought to be accepted, and to succeed. He gave it very high praise indeed, especially the third and fourth acts, which he said could not be better. Parts of the others he found fault with. The piece would not suffer by the loss of those passages, as he thought the acts too long. He recommended me to persevere in writing for the stage ; and if I did so, to forswear roses, dewdrops and sunbeams for ever. The fate of the unfortunate Vespers of Palermo told me this before. Poetry is not listened to on the stage here. I could not, on the whole, have expected Banim to act a more friendly or generous part than he has done. On the second day I called on him (Saturday), he made me stop to dinner. I put the direct question to him, whether, from what he had seen, it was his real opinion that I should be successful as a dramatist. His reply was, that he thought I had every claim ; and since I had dealt so candidly with him, he advised me to write on, and that he would do everything for any piece I wished to bring forward, that he would do if it was his own. With respect to the present piece, he advised me to leave it in * * *'s hands until he sends it to me, and not call or write to him. If he knows anything of him, he says he will keep and play it. I am very sorry I did not see Banim first. In that case I should long since have known its fate, as he could have procured me an answer from the committee in ten days. With regard to his present views, he has placed me on my honour not to breathe a word of them; therefore, on that subject I can say nothing; but I may talk of the 'Prodigal Son,' as I had before heard of it. You recollect I mentioned the coincidence in name with a play of mine. I asked him about it. He showed me sketches of it in his note-book. The story is the same, and the scene is laid in the same place, so that all my fine visions are knocked on the head there. He also lent me part of another manuscript tragedy of his, which will come out at Covent Garden, in which I found the counterpart of my character of Canabe. Is not this vexatious? But enough of theatricals, as Lucy calls them. It would be a great advantage to me if I could keep my lodgings for some time, as with such a friend as Banim, acquainted in the first literary circles in London, and willing to give me every assistance in his power, there can be little doubt of eventual success. He is in high estimation at the theatres, and says he will procure me an answer immediately to any piece I wish to present. He has lent me a new French tragedy, which was sent him by Talma, a very fine piece, as far as I have read." *

Banim's regard for Griffin's interest did not cease here. The letters of the latter are everywhere filled with acknowledgments of Banim's kindness towards him. He advised him in his literary ventures. Gerald writes to his brother William, in February 1824, " Banim is very kind to me. On my calling on him, he urged me to alter 'Aguire' in those passages he pointed out, and told me that he still persevered in

* See "Life of Gerald Griffin," by his Brother.

his opinions of it: that there were scenes in it, which for stage effect, and every requisite, could not be better." Again, he writes: " I had a visit from Banim the other day. What with the delays and disappointments I have met since I came here, it is only his encouragement, and his friendship, that keep hope alive." " Banim's friendship I find every day growing more ardent, more cordial if possible."

Thus this true-souled Irishman acted. He did not fear a rival. He suggests improvements in Griffin's plays ; " Banim made me an offer the other day, which will be of more immediate advantage than the tragedy, inasmuch as I need not abide the result. He desired me to write a piece for the English Opera House. When I have it finished, he will introduce me to Mr. Arnold of Golden Square, the proprietor, who is his friend, and get me immediate money for it without waiting its performance. Banim offers me many introductions. He is acquainted with Tom Moore, Campbell, Ugo Foscolo, and others of celebrity. *What would I have done if I had not found Banim? I should never be tired of talking about and thinking of Banim. Mark me! he is a man—the only one I have met since I have left Ireland, almost.*"

Whilst thus active in kindness and good offices to his young friend, Banim was pushing his own way in the world. He had become the chief adviser of Thomas Arnold, the proprietor of the English Opera House, and contributed many operatic pieces to the establishment. These were but the things of an hour and are now forgotten ; but to the close of his connexion with Mr. Arnold he found him liberal, honourable, and a steady friend.

He had commenced, in 1823, the composition of his intended novel, and had written to Michael, urging him to hasten the completion of his story, which was, as had been agreed upon, to form a portion of the volumes. Michael had little time to devote to literary pursuits. From morning till night he was engaged behind his father's counter, and in literary composition he had had, since leaving school, no practice beyond drawing up a business account, or writing a letter to John. But John had praised his talent as a storyteller; had asked him to write a tale for the forthcoming work; and as John, a judge of those things—a literary man himself—had approved his efforts thus, he determined to make the required attempt.

But how was the attempt to be made? He could not start from a customer to write down the thought of the moment; but when did genius ever fail in expedient? Michael Banim had naturally a good memory; his story was one founded on facts; and accordingly whilst he was behind the counter, with busy hands discharging all the multifarious duties of a shopman in a country town, his fancy was busily at work, weaving the scenes of his narrative, and when he retired to his room at night, he committed the already formed scenes to paper, and the early morning generally found him clothing his thoughts in words, and thus the powerful story, entitled "Crohoore of the Bill Hook," was composed and written.

The first portion of the manuscript was transmitted to John for perusal late in the year 1823. By return of post, a letter of praise and thanks was written to Michael, and entreaties for more were pressingly urged. The progress of the composition was necessarily slow, but scrap by scrap it was forwarded; and, as had been agreed upon, John's portion of the works,—" The Fetches" and " John Doe,"—was sent to Michael, each brother acting as critic to the other, and thus the *nom de plume*, "Tales by the O'Hara Family," was in every point a reality—John taking the name Abel O'Hara, Michael assuming that of Barnes O'Hara.

The brothers commenced their joint tales in 1823, and during the succeeding twelve months, John's letters are chiefly devoted to criticism upon his own and his brother's contributions to the series. Amongst these letters, the following is the most important. It extends to fourteen pages of very closely written letter paper, and in our mind contains the whole principle of the novelist's art. It is valuable not alone to the young novelist, as teaching him how to write, but it is equally useful to the critic and to the reader, as it teaches them how to judge and how to appreciate. It was carefully considered; and although commenced on the 2d of May, 1824, was not concluded until the 4th of June following. It should be borne in mind that the letter is not a didactic essay, but a friendly communication addressed to Michael, and is meant to convey true principles rather than to exhibit a finished style. The letter is remarkable also as being the production of a man only in his twenty-sixth year, yet showing a knowledge of the sources of all the secrets of construction which have rendered the novels of Scott and Galt so famous, because so life-like.

This letter, too, is important, as it gives the writer's impressions of his literary brethren. He had fallen into the common error of supposing, or assuming, that literary men are exactly what their peculiar styles of composition might lead one to suppose them : just as many visitors of the theatre assume the tragedian to be a grave, austere man ; and fancy the comedian is all fun and jokes, when in the quietude of private life.

The passage in the letter which refers to Washington Irving is extremely interesting, as it shows that the opinion formed by Banim of his goodness of heart, in 1824, was fully supported by the testimony recorded by Moore in 1821. Banim writes :—" I have had opportunities of coming into close contact with Geoffrey Crayon; he is natural as his sketches—*a man who would play with a child on a carpet.*"

How exquisitely this passage, in italics, supports an entry in Moore's "Diary," relating to Irving. Moore and "Bessy" have resolved, in the year 1821, whilst residing near Paris, to give a children's ball in honour of "little Tom's" birth-day. The children, in dancing, have shaken the floor in some parts of the room, and what follows is thus described by Moore :—

"Our dance to the pianoforte was very gay, and not the less so, for the floor giving way in sundry places ; a circle of chalk was drawn round one hole, Dr. Younge was placed sentry over another, and whenever there was a new crash, the general laugh at the heavy foot that produced it caused more merriment than the solidest floor in Paris could have given birth to. Sandwiches, negus, and champagne crowned the night, and we did not separate until four in the morning. *Irving's humour began to break out as the floor broke in, and he was much more himself than ever I have seen him.*" *

* See " Memoirs, Journal and Correspondence of Thomas Moore." Edited by the Right Hon. Lord John Russell. Vol. III. p. 213.

The letter is as follows :—

"LONDON, *May 2d*, 1824.

"MY DEAR MICHAEL,—I have read attentively, and with the greatest pleasure, the portion of the tale you sent me by J. H——. So far as it goes, I pronounce that you have been successful. Here and there, I have marked such particular criticisms as struck me, and them you may note by referring to the margin. I send you the MSS. of my tale, and I request your severest criticisms; scratch, cut, and condemn at your pleasure. This is the first copy. Looking over it, I perceive many parts that are bad; send it back when you can, with every suggestion you are capable of making. Read it for the whole family in solemn conclave. Let father, mother, Joanna and yourself sit in judgment on it, and send me all your opinions sincerely given.

"I have met some eminent literary characters lately, and many, of whom I had formed high notions, fall far short of my expectations.

"I will say no more about these; and at your peril keep my gossip to yourself. Hap! hap! it is dangerous to meddle with edged tools; a chip from an angry *homme de lettres*, would cut deep.

"I have had opportunities of coming into close contact with Geoffrey Crayon; he is as natural as his sketches—a man who would play with a child on the carpet, and one of the few *littérateurs* I have known whose face and character are in sincere keeping with his talents.

"I have found, that to write fine and enthusiastic passages in a book—to deify virtue and honour, and melt with pathos—it is not always necessary to have a heart. Genius is frequently the artificer; mimicking rich feelings and warmth of soul, while the writer may be cold and vicious. Put it out of your head, that genius and worth always go hand in hand; the reverse it has been my lot to know, alas! too often.

"To turn again to your tale. Two of the personages do not stand out sufficiently from the canvas. Aim at distinctness and at individuality of character. Open Shakespeare, and read a play of his, then turn to the list of *dramatis personæ*, and see and feel what he has done in this way.

"Of a dozen characters, each is himself alone. Look about you; bring to mind the persons you have known, call them up before you; select and copy them. Never give a person an action to do, who is not a legible individual. Make that a rule, and I think it ought to be a primary rule with novel writers.

"Suppose one was to get a sheet of paper; draw up thereon a list of persons, and after their names, write down what kind of human beings they shall be, leaving no two alike, and not one generalised or undrawn. After Shakespeare, Scott is the great master-hand of character, and hence, one of his sources of great power. To show you clearly what I mean; not a creature we ever met in our father's penetralia, resembled the other. There might be somewhat of a conventional, outward similarity, arising from their pursuits, habits, and amusements being similar; but each was, notwithstanding, distinct.

"I think that in writing a tale, every character in it should be drawn from nature. It is impossible all should be absolute originals. Human nature being the same, in all ages and in all climes, it cannot be hoped now-a-days that a writer can be the discoverer of a new character. It can be no more than the same dough, somewhat differently shaped. Habits of country, habits of station, habits of any kind, will diversify; but human nature is the same now that it ever was. I say one can scarcely draw an original character; but I say, draw like nature; no matter what kind of nature you draw from, provided that the likeness be not that of a disgusting object. After all, there is nothing common-place in nature.

"Since I am on this, I may as well tell you how, as I think, character ought to be marked. Apart from propriety of language and thought, fit words and fit ideas for each person, (and by the way lift up both your hands, and wonder how Shakespeare makes his people walk before you *without any other means,*) character can be indited by portraits of the face and person, with allusion to the expression and conformation of both; by painting dress, by describing gait, motion, gesticulation, and by the tone of the voice sometimes. I here purposely omit the downright easy way of telling us at once, that a man is a good, or a wicked fellow. If you sharpen your eye and ear on these points—I see you are pretty sharp already—you can, either from your recollections, or present and future study, in society, and among men and women, every hour in the day, gain truth, and conviction, and pleasure.

"If either of us could only delineate the peculiarities we daily witness in those we meet, success would be the result. All will appreciate a likeness; and the artist who can convince every beholder, that he has transferred to his canvas, each peculiar mark of the individual he paints, will be praised, and he deserves it.

"For example, only draw well for me in a novel, little round-paunched, puffing Rogerson M——, who used to lament so pathetically over the hardships of a soldier's life, when as a member of his yeomanry corps he was ordered to mount guard. Give me the clinging of his wife and daughters, round their unwieldy, asthmatic warrior, as he issued forth, to sit all night before a good fire in the tholsel of Kilkenny, and drink his punch to give him valour. No enemy within forty miles of him, and he, doughty hero, physically unable to raise his ponderous musquet to his shoulder, were twenty rebel pikes coming full tilt against his wizend.

"Many of his brothers in arms occur to my mind just now. Johnny M——, the linen draper, who bore no good will to the house of Hanover, 'being Protestants,' but who, to escape the very improbable fate of being hanged as a papist on the permanent gallows at the gaol door, put on the King's livery and groaned and sweated beneath the King's firelock—Johnny M——, whose 'quick march' was a gouty trot, and who would not, in obedience to orders, or by persuasion, put a bullet into his gun, lest, in his own words, 'it might hurt somebody.'

"Paint for me to the life, our old parish priest, Father O'Donnell, hat, wig, jock coat, worsted stockings, shoe-buckles, as he appeared and spoke, when he patted our heads, and approved of our proficiency in catechism.

"Give me Tom Guinn, hat, gaiters, watch, pipe, and his horn tinder-box; his peculiar jokes, his frequent big words, and his gurgling laugh at his own conceits. For a reckless bully, boy and man, remember Michael

B———: I might, but I will not here, increase the list.

"Get fourteen or fifteen of any of the persons you ever knew; put them into scenes favourable to their peculiarities, their individualities can be exemplified, without straining after the point; in proper situations, set them talking for themselves; by their own word of mouth, they will denote their own characters, better than any description from your pen: thus will you dramatise your tale, and faithful drama is the life and soul of novel-writing. Plot is an inferior consideration to drama, though still it is a main consideration.

"Do not say that I am dictatorial, or that I consider you to be a subject for a drilling; but let us unaffectedly compare notes as often as we can, and both will be benefited.

"This long letter of mine is a disjointed affair, taken up from time to time as I find opportunity; all the remarks are thrown in a hurried, and, of course, disarranged way together, but you will, for my sake, endeavour to reduce them to method.

"A few words more, as to the mode of studying the art of novel-writing. Read any first-rate production of the kind, with a note-book. When an author forces you to feel with him, or whenever he produces a more than ordinary degree of pleasure, or when he startles you—stop and try to find out how he has done it; see if it be by dialogue, or by picture, or by description, or by action. Fully comprehend his method—his means for the effect, and note it down. Write down all such impressions. Enumerate these, and see how many go to make the combined interest of one book. Observe, by contrasting characters, how he keeps up the balance of the familiar and the marvellous, humorous, serious, and romantic.

"This would not be imitation, it would be study; what, I will venture to say, great men have done with their predecessors—what painters do in the study of their art."

Whilst thus directing his brother, he was anxiously engaged in various literary employments, and all his leisure was given up to the construction and composition of his portion of the tales. His wife's health was still very weak, and was a cause of constant anxiety. He had, as his own ailments decreased, commenced anew that overtaxing mental labour which had before affected him so disastrously,—and again the pains of head and limbs returned, and once more he was forced to lay aside his pen: on this occasion however, the attack, although fully as violent as either of the former, was not of so long continuance, and when again at his desk he was gay and hopeful as ever,—and he wrote to his father thus:—"I am snug: calculating like a spider in his corner." An unlucky simile by the way, in every respect—save the curious perseverance of the insect.

This illness had, like the other attacks, rendered him, as he said, "tight;" but he no longer thought of seeking a refuge at home, as his reputation was now fully established with the publishers of serials; and in Arnold he had a judicious, yet kind friend. His chief care still arose from the ill health of his wife—and hoping that this might pass away, and that with time he might, by his own genius, gain a competency sufficient for the support of all whom he loved, he wrote the following letter to Michael; it is creditable not alone to the writer, but to all whose names are mentioned in it:—

"LONDON, *June 2nd*, 1824.

"MY DEAR MICHAEL,—My poor Ellen is improving. My anxiety is principally on her account, and she repays me by affection. I always thought, that if knapsacked with a responsibility, I would not be deaf or negligent to or of my duties, and I trust I have proved that this opinion of myself was not self-flattery.

"That my dear Ellen, and my dear Joanna, should live together in love and unity, is my great wish and my hope too. To see them working, or reading, or making their womanly fuss near me, and under my roof, and mutually tolerating and helping each other, and never talking loud; and my mother, my dear, dear mother, sitting in her arm-chair looking at them, with her old-times placid smile; and my father and you doing whatever you liked. Tush! Perhaps this is foolish and Utopian of me. Yet we *must* live together: that is the blessed truth. Such a set of people were not born to dwell asunder. And, perhaps, the old times would come back again after all. What is the reason, I ask, that after a little while we should not club our means, and dwell, as Mr. Owen preaches, in one big house, every mother's son and daughter of us; and have good feeling, good taste and economy presiding over us? More unlikely things have happened. After the world is seen, it does not bear to be gaped at every day; and the only true aim of a rational creature ought to be, humble independence on any scale, and the interchange of those little and tireless amiabilities, that in a loving, and virtuous, and temperate circle, make life indeed worth living for—to me. And without these, life is a compulsion; a necessity to breathe without enjoyment—to sweat without a reward."

These longings for home life were but day dreams: the visions of that cloud-land future of which we all, at times, catch glimpses, but into whose happy valley we seldom enter.

Although these intended kindnesses to his family were but things of the future, there were kindnesses of the present to be performed, and of these Griffin was still the object. They were fast friends, and Banim consulted him frequently upon the merits and demerits of the tales, as the brothers proceeded in the work; and yet a coldness, for a time, checked the growth of their friendship, and might have destroyed it for ever, but that each was good and true in heart. It was not a quarrel, rather a misunderstanding commencing through some *apparent* slight done to Banim, and increased by Griffin's morbid delicacy, and horror of patronage. Of the causes of this misunderstanding we gather the facts from the following extracts from various letters appearing in Griffin's Life by his brother:—

"The looking for lodgings, for an engagement, and several other matters took up my time so entirely, that I was compelled to break an appointment I had made with Banim that I would call on him for a particular purpose—to have my criticism, as he did me the honour to say, on a work which he is sending to the press, and which, so far as I have read, is really a delightful performance. The consequence was, when I did call, it had been sent off, and though his manner was as friendly as ever, I could see that what he considered the neglect had somewhat cooled him. I could not explain then, and I perceived that he thought the apology I did make, a very lame one indeed. However, I did explain after nearly three weeks' absence, and received two or three days since a letter full of kindness and friendship; in short, everything that I could wish. I should almost like to transcribe part of it here; it would so fully show you what manner of man he is." In another letter of a later date he says: "You ask me of my dramatic prospects. I have done nothing—I *could* do nothing in them while I was prevented from calling on Banim— my kind, my true friend—which I have not done these two months. The restraint in this instance is absolute torture to me, when I consider what a cold return I must appear to make to his most friendly and pressing invitations. Since I wrote last I have heard or seen nothing of him." "I cannot tell you here the many, many instances in which Banim has shown his friendship since I wrote last; let it suffice to say, that he is the sincerest, heartiest, most disinterested being that breathes. His fire-side is the only one where I enjoy anything like social life, or home. I go out occasionally in an evening, and talk or read for some hours; or have a bed and leave next day."

So far we can understand the kindness of Banim, and Griffin's hearty appreciation of it; but when the latter had been, as he states, two months absent from Brompton Grove, Banim thought that some serious obstacle must have interposed to cause so long an estrangement. He accordingly sought Griffin's residence, and with much difficulty discovered it—" a small room in some obscure court near St. Paul's." Griffin was out; Banim called again next day, and with no better success; and upon questioning the landlady as to the apparent circumstances of her lodger, he was shocked at finding that Griffin was badly dressed, still more poorly fed, in low spirits, and rarely going abroad by day, fearing to encounter his acquaintances in his pitiable condition. It was low enough, and Gerald afterwards, in a letter to his father and mother, described its horrors:—

"It was then that I set about writing for those weekly publications; all of which, except the Literary Gazette, cheated me abominably. Then, finding this to be the case, I wrote for the great magazines. My articles were generally inserted; but on calling for payment—seeing that I was a poor, inexperienced devil, there was so much shuffling and shabby work that it disgusted me, and I gave up the idea of making money that way. I now lost heart for everything; got into the cheapest lodgings I could make out, and there worked on, rather to divert my mind from the horrible gloom that I felt growing on me in spite of myself, than with the hope of being remunerated. This, and the recollection of the expense I had put William to, and the fears—that every moment became conviction—that I should never be enabled to fulfil his hopes or my own expectations, all came pressing together upon my mind and made me miserable. A thousand and a thousand times I wished that I could lie down quietly and die at once, and be forgotten for ever. But that, however, was not to be had for the asking. I don't think I left anything undone that could have changed the course of affairs, or brought me a little portion of the good luck that was going on about me; but good luck was too busy elsewhere. I can hardly describe to you the state of mind I was in at this time. It was not an indolent despondency, for I was working hard, and I am now—and it is only now—receiving money for the labour of those dreadful hours. I used not to see a face that I knew, and after sitting writing all day, when I walked in the streets in the evening, it actually seemed to me as if I was of a different species altogether from the people about me."*

These painful circumstances were sufficient to sour the mind of any man; and doubtless Griffin looked on all the world around him with disgust, whilst Banim, rising in fame, saw—as indeed he ever saw save when racked by pain—only the bright side of life. He returned to Brompton Grove, from the poor lodging of his friend; he wrote to him kindly and openly, yet delicately, offering pecuniary aid freely, as he had already offered and given the assistance of his counsel and of his influence, and Gerald, the kindest, fondest, most patient soul, among all the suffering, enduring thousands of the great struggling city in which he lived, was so warped from his own proper self, as to reply coldly and abruptly, and with a harsh refusal, to an offer which sprang, as he then thought, from pragmatic and impertinent officiousness. The coolness was, however, but for the day: Griffin hardly knew why he deemed himself offended. As his biographer writes:—"It seems to have been a mystery even to himself, if we may judge by the following introductory sonnet to 'Suil Dhuv,' one of the 'Tales of the Munster Festivals,' in which he evidently alludes to it. There is something affecting in the little pleading allusion he makes to his struggles

* Life of Gerald Griffin. By his Brother.

and ill success, and in the humble confessing spirit in which the sonnet is written. It would appear, too, from the first of those passages which I have marked by italics, that there was nothing in Mr. Banim's manner of conferring the favour, that in Gerald's opinion could at all justify the mode of its rejection:—

I.

I hold not out my hand in grateful love,
    Because ye were my friend, where friends were few,
Nor in the pride of conscious truth, to prove
    The heart ye wronged and doubted yet was true—
It is that while the close and blinding veil,
    That youth and blissful ignorance had cast
    Around mine inward sight, is clearing fast
Before its strengthening vision—while the scale
Falls from mine eye-balls, and the gloomy stream
    Of human motive, whitening in my view,
Shows clear as dew showers in the grey morn beam,
While hearts and acts, whose impulse seemed divine,
    Put on the grossness of an earthlier hue,
I still can gaze and deeply still can honour thine.

II.

Judge not your friend by what he seemed, when Fate
    Had crossed him in his chosen—cherished aim,
When spirit-broken—baffled—*moved to hate*
    The very kindness that but made his shame
More self-induced, he rudely turned aside
    In bitter, hopeless agony from all,
    Alike, of those who mocked or mourned his fall,
And fenced his injured heart in lonely pride.
Wayward and sullen as suspicion's soul,
    To his own mind he lived a mystery—
But now the heavens have changed, the vapours roll
Far from his heart; and in his solitude,
    While the fell night-mares of his spirit flee,
He wakes to weave for thee a tale of joy renewed."

Whilst these events were occurring, Banim had disappointments, and sources of uneasiness, quite as depressing as those which surrounded Griffin. His tragedy, "The Prodigal," had been accepted at Drury Lane Theatre early in the year 1823; the parts had been cast, and it was supposed that the great Edmund Kean was satisfied with his character in the piece. Such, however, was not the fact: Kean had grown fastidious in his parts, and thus it became a matter of impossibility to produce the piece at Drury Lane; and Banim, being unwilling to risk its success with less able performers, withdrew it from the hands of the manager, and it was never afterwards offered for representation. He thus states the causes of its non-production, in a letter to his father and mother; and it is worthy of notice, that even with the depressing fact before him— that his play was unacted, not through want of merit, but because the chief performer wrangled about his part, —the letter is in the following uncomplaining style:—

"LONDON, *June* 16, 1824.

"MY DEAR FATHER AND MOTHER,—Since I had the pleasure to write you some account of my theatrical progress, other revolutions have come round.

"Mr. Kean, after accepting his part in my tragedy of the 'The Prodigal,' and attending with the other performers to two readings, has declared that he will appear in no new play that does not give him one superior character. Such is the statement made to me; whether it be true, or but partially true, I cannot positively determine.

"After some difficulty I have succeeded in withdrawing the play from the hands of Mr. Elliston of Drury Lane, and expect to have it brought out at Covent Garden, the two principal characters to be played by Charles

Kemble and Mr. Young. In better hands they could not be.

"I could give you a specimen of green-room jealousies and contentions, that might be amusing, and I may do so at some other time."

A letter was brought to Michael by the same post which bore the last, and in it Banim thus relates the ill success of Sheridan Knowles's play, "Caius Gracchus," and recounts the difficulty which he himself experienced in obtaining the manuscript of "The Prodigal" from Elliston.

"LONDON, *June* 16*th*, 1824.

"MY DEAR MICHAEL,—'Caius Gracchus' did not deserve its fate. The author, as I learn, submitted to have his production cooked in the green-room, and after the cookery it was 'dished'—to use a cant word, signifying that it had been made unpalatable.

"I called on the manager for my MS. 'Oh! yes, yes, certainly,' he said, 'to-morrow; don't for the life of me know where to lay hand on it. But to-morrow.' On the morrow, accompanied by a friend, I met Mr. E——n; he expressed a willingness to give up the play, 'but really, and indeed, did not look it out since.' 'Then don't trouble yourself,' I said, 'I have another copy, somewhere. I think I can find that'—'Oh! for the world, would not give you such a job—I'll send it to-morrow.' I walked off, and made another perfect copy, which I have now ready for Covent Garden."

The play was not produced at Covent Garden; and though it was considered by those who read it as the most admirable of all Banim's dramatic pieces, though he appears to have prized it highly himself, preserving it with especial care, even to within a few months of his death; yet, after a most careful and anxious search amongst his papers, no trace of it can now be discovered.

He still worked closely at the Irish stories; and continually incited Michael to hasten with his portion. He criticised, advised, and encouraged the latter, and as a specimen of the style in which these letters were written, we insert the following:—

"LONDON, *July* 10*th*, 1824.

"MY DEAR MIKE,—I think I recognise your tithe-proctor, Peery Clancey; the portrait is so accurate I could not mistake the gentleman. Your next door neighbour, Mickle Ryan, is your original, and you have not outstepped nature, or misrepresented facts, in the slightest degree.

"You have given some of my people a good castigation; you have frightened me in fact, and almost made me hopeless of them. Don't spare one of them however—better *you* should deal with them than critics of less bowels or humanity.

"You must adopt my amendment. The woman, singing the keenthecawn, must be the mother of Terence, not his wife; kill his wife—I decree her death; by slaying her, you give a very rational increased incentive to the wretched widower's thirst for vengeance.

"You tell me you intend to cut off the proctor's ears: slice them close to his head by all means; do not leave a shred; no honest man will say that he does not deserve the cropping."

His wife's ill health, and a slight attack of his own pains, were again pressing upon his slender resources;

and being unwilling to delay his task—the completion of the tales—by entering into any new engagements with publishers, he earnestly and anxiously endeavoured to discover some means by which his purse might be replenished speedily, without much labour or delay. His last sovereign had dwindled to half; his credit he did not wish to test, and with ideas quickened, by what John Taylor quaintly calls, "Wit's whetstone, Want," he resolved to correct, and offer to the publishers, a series of miscellaneous essays which he had from time to time composed, and which now swelled to the proportions of an octavo volume. He arranged the manuscript for inspection in a few hours, and early the following morning set out in search of a purchaser. He valued the papers lightly, and his hope of finding a publisher willing to buy them was almost forlorn. Mrs. Banim spent that lonely day in anxious expectation of his return. At length, late in the evening, he entered their little drawing-room. He looked weary and despondent, and seating himself by his wife's side he gazed mournfully in her sad face: he drew her towards him, kissed her tenderly, but spoke not a word. She feared to question; but after he had sat in silence for a minute, he sprang from his seat, crying, " Ellen, my darling, hold out your dress for a present," and in a moment he threw into her lap a shower of bright clinking guineas—and kissing her once more, whilst his eyes laughed out in all the joy of his heart's triumph, he cried, "There, Ellen, there are thirty guineas, the price of the essays."

The essays thus opportunely disposed of were published in 1824, in one volume, by Simpkin and Marshall, and bore no author's name; they were entitled

BIOGRAPHY OF JOHN BANIM. 141

"Revelations of the Dead-Alive," and extended to 376 pages. In the first chapter, the rather odd title of the book is thus explained. The writer states himself to possess the power of sleeping at will for lengthened periods, and during these periods to possess the faculty of, as it were, going out of himself; a species of self-acting clairvoyance. He has been enabled by a peculiar American root, to extend the periods of sleep to a length much beyond that which, unaided by its power, he could accomplish. After a slumber of one hundred and ninety-eight days and a quarter, he is enabled to relate, and does record in the succeeding chapters of the book, the events of one hundred and ninety-eight years and a quarter; or, as he writes. " I was dead one hundred and ninety-eight days and a quarter, and for every day I saw a year of time, so that when I came to life again, I had observed what was, and is to be, in the lapse of one hundred and ninety-eight years and a quarter, a year for each day;" and in the relation of these experiences consist the " Revelations of the Dead-Alive."

The " Revelations " are, for the chief part, very clever hits at the follies, fashions, and manners of the year 1823. Amongst the fashions of that period was a most absurd reliance on the system of Phrenology— then rendered a very imposing question by Gall— which Banim thus satirizes:—

"They spoke of a gentleman who had invented a new and approved science of moral physiognomy, deduced from Messrs. Spurzheim and Gall; and deduced I may in every sense say, for, leaving them in possession of the head, it seized on the feet; thus, perhaps, pushing the matter to extremities. Mr. Klapptrapp made the cover of leather usually worn by these members, equivalent to the integument of the cranium in Mr. Gall's system, and hence his science derived its name of Ocreology. Prior, I believe, has ingeniously set to work in his smart poem of Alma Mater, to discover the residence of thought in the human machine; and, if I mistake not, traced it indifferently to the limbs. Such at least was the floating recollection in my mind, that, at the first mention of Mr. Klapptrapp's theory, made me think something might come of it.

"Mr. K.'s attention was first seized by observing that after a man has worn a boot or shoe for a considerable time, his feet give it a particular set, and also particular markings, that raise and fix the leather at certain points of the insteps and toes, into greater or smaller convexities: these in the end become confirmed on the outward surface, so that when the shoe or boot is even thrown away or cast aside for ever, they keep their places and shapes. The varieties of bumps thus insured to boots and shoes were, he next observed, as endless as the varieties of human talent and general character; and here and at once was a coincidence too remarkable not to be curiously analysed.

"So Mr. Klapptrapp became industrious, and in the very infancy of his inquiries, ascertained the strong-marked difference between the bumps conformed on the boot of a very vulgar and brutal man, and on that of a very refined and amiable man. No one, he well remarked, can have been without noticing the horrid conformations acquired by the boots of a huge waggoner or Smithfield badge-man, who from constant use of same has fully impressed them with the knuckles and twistings of his broad, bullock-like, splay-foot. Only hang up by their side a pair of genteel old boots, such as may have been worn to the welt, by a scholar or philanthropist, and can you not instantly vouch the exact kind of intellect and heart that once put in motion the different limbs to which both were once appended?

"This was the foundation of Mr. Klapptrapp's system. He followed it up with a zeal, a perspicuity and minuteness I cannot pretend to detail: first, contrasting general differences, and then—his eye and intellect becoming quicker by practice—at last establishing the nicest subdivisions and distinctions, so that bring him a pair of cast-off shoes or boots he had never before seen, and he told you, within a bump, of the wearer's talent and morality.

"When Mr. Angle introduced me into his study, we carried

with us a pair of shoes that had been left behind by a man recently hanged for a shocking murder; and the moment Mr. K. laid his eyes on them, he proclaimed their sanguinary conformation. In this he was fully warranted by the appearance of the organ of destruction which, as I recollect, is formed by an unusual swell of the outward knuckle of the great toe, leaving a correspondent knob on the outside of the shoe or boot; and which, in this instance, peculiarly verified its nature by having burst through the leather on or about the night when the homicide committed his bloody act.

"We found the philosopher surrounded by rows over rows of old boots and shoes of every possible class; and I listened with much interest and deference to his lecture of some hours, upon the virtues or vices, genius or stupidity, of those by whom they had once been worn. There was the last pair of Waterloos that John Thurtell had doffed, authenticated by certificates under the hand of each collector of curiosities who had possessed them, from Lavender or Ruthven down to Dr. Klapptrapp; and the benevolent and cautious, and heroic cut-throat and brain-pounder came in for his future as well as present vindication. By felicitous chances other shoes and boots of other remarkable characters of this day, had been snatched from oblivion: but while all proclaimed the admitted and general excellence of the individuals they professed to illustrate, they also suggested curious differences, in minute points indeed, between the real and self-asserted characters of some of those persons. Lord Byron's boot, for instance, wanted the organ of amativeness; hinting that notwithstanding all a man may rhyme about the passion, he need not, as a consequence, ever feel it; or that, *vice versâ*, as Shakspeare says, one may be

———'over *boots* in love,
Altho' he never swam the Hellespont.'

Neither did Mr. Hazlitt's shoe exhibit much of this organ. I was surprised to see a pair of Sir Walter's evince almost as much constructiveness as ideality, and not so much secretiveness as I had expected. Wordsworth, after all, left behind him a pair of shoes indicative of little veneration, while time, tune, order, causality, and locality were jumbled together in them. Mr. Southey's had a strong bump of self-esteem, now equivalent to self-conceit; Ugo Foscolo's had no combativeness; Coleridge's no form; Hogg's no wit; the author of Lacon no inhabitiveness; and Bowles's very little weight and momenta.

"It will be here remarked, that Mr. Klapptrapp had unceremoniously transferred to his leathern knobs all the organic names invented by his predecessors; which, however common to both the names might be, I own I regarded as a plagiarism unworthy of his genius."

Banim did not, however, spare the literary profession. That was the age of reviewing, in the sense in which Macaulay understood it, ten pages to himself to ten lines of his author; or reviewing was committed in another manner, but by inferior minds—one connecting page of the review to ten pages of the author; and thus, when poetry was before the critic, he became —to the injury of author and publisher—nothing more than a paste and scissors purloiner, and might truly say with Falstaff, "I have abused the King's Press most damnably."

Of these two classes of reviewers, and of the newspaper critics, the "Dead-Alive" thus expressed his opinions:—

"'How many periodicals have you?' said I.

"'By act of parliament, three. *There* was another curse of the age we have so often alluded to, and one other slow but sure rot in its literature. Every periodical, great and small, had its own friends and its own coterie, or its own political opinions, and right or wrong, mawkish or extravagant, as its contributors might have been, they were partially deified, and their literary opposites run down in the same breath: and thus a most dangerous jumble of tastes frittered away the public mind, until puzzle begat languor, and languor indifference, and both an utter neglect of every new book and author.'

"'It seems to me,' I continued, 'that in another view, periodicals must have produced the decay you speak of. A small volume of poetry costs five shillings, and it will contain the bad as well as the good of an author; and you purchase his errors and slips, which you don't exactly want, along with his brilliant bits and savoury passages. Behold on the other hand a grand army of reviews, of all shapes and prices, from five shillings down to fourpence, in many of which was to be had the cream of from five to five-and-twenty authors together, carefully skimmed for your sipping palate, and ready for use at your tea or coffee in the morning. Moreover, you bought ready-made opinion for your money, a few shillings or pence, as it might be, and so were saved the trouble of forming your own. And what man or Miss in his or her senses might be expected to pay a great deal for so little, when with a little, he or she could have the great deal?'

"'No one did so,' said Mr. Drudge: 'the "reading public" rested satisfied with periodicals alone, and the author was left on the publisher's shelf. Of course no author would continue to write for the profit of other persons only; so the pen was at last totally abandoned, and the sole comfort resulting to authors was to see their monstrous tyrant, the periodical press, sharing with themselves a common ruin and oblivion.'

"'The periodical press?' I exclaimed; 'truly, sir, it was a species of steam-loom, or thrashing or winnowing machine, that with its short methods and unnatural despatch, threw thousands of honest people out of bread.'

"'I wonder,' said Mrs. Drudge, 'they never rose out against it, as about the same time the indignant trades, weavers, and spinners, and carders rose out against the mechanical encroachments—monopoly indeed—of Manchester, Glasgow, and other manufacturing places. Surely, if the great body of authors were united (but that was, in itself, rather a difficulty), one night would have been sufficient for the demolition of all the periodical presses in London and Auld Reekie.'

"'Or I should have chosen a more legal proceeding,' said Mr. Drudge. 'It is my fixed opinion that a good action—Authors v. Reviewers—might have been made out, to go for damages to a special jury in King's Bench. I think an author might have crippled them in a thumping verdict, not on account of their defamatory praise or censure, but on account of their piratical quotations. Where was their right to republish, without end, the best part of a man's book? Was it not as black piracy as if the promulgators of the sixpenny Cain did so, without any dull or prattling remark at the head, the tail, or between the passages?'

L

"'Here is a curious little book that, among other curious things, gives us some notion of the views entertained by applicants for employment to a periodical editor, of their self-measured fitness for the office,' resumed Mrs. Drudge; 'shall I read from it a letter found among the papers of a gentleman, who, it would seem, once swayed a miscellaneous periodical of the time?'

'*To the Editor of the Universal and Multifarious Magazine.*

SIR,—Being at present disengaged, I have no objection to tender my services for the advantage of your respectable journal. I do not much care into what department you may put me, as I think I shall be found fit enough for any. Indeed, if agreeable to you, I should rather like to do, now and then, a little on every topic. I write essays off-hand on all subjects. I am particularly liable to be struck with the minutest errors of a literary work, and particularly slow at comprehending what an author means by a beauty: hence you can estimate my capacity for your review sheet. By the help of a lexicon, and a friend of mine, a young Cantab, I scruple not to say I should be quite competent to detect the bad orthography of a Greek quotation; and should an error happen, you know we could lay it either on the author or the printer, as might suit our convenience. I make poetry myself, on one leg, so you cannot doubt my capacity to be a flogger and mangler of all new poems, particularly the successful ones. By the way of poetry, I have a large blue book of original sonnets, odes, &c. lying by me, with which I shall be happy to harmonize your last sheet, on reasonable terms; but I wish it to be understood, that they must go in at double the rate of my prose contributions.

Send me to the King's Theatre, if you like: I am no great adept myself, nor indeed can I boast a good ear, and in honest truth have never heard an Italian song; but a musical dictionary is within my reach; a dear friend of mine frequents the opera: so I could manage a brisk technical paragraph for you. Of the drama I ought to know something; I have trod the boards myself, before now, and since then have written a play which would have astonished the town if the silly managers had produced it. So don't spare me at Drury Lane or Covent Garden.

But I request one department entirely to myself—the fine arts: for although I know little of the matter, my brother is an artist of long standing; his pictures have been twice turned out of Somerset House, and he promises to furnish me with critiques on the works of the council, and particularly of the hanging committee. As to the rest, I know no subject more easily handled by a writer completely ignorant of it. Only compile a list of painters' names, and the cant of the painting room; boldly arraign Sir Joshua's lectures; compare pictures and styles that may be as antagonistic as north and south; slip in such terms as glazing, and scumbling, and toning, and keeping; conclude by saying your kettle is singing to make whiskey punch, and the thing is done. HORACE HANDY.'"

We have given these extracts as specimens of a work little, if at all, read in these days, and as affording an example of Banim's ability in an excellent style of light composition, very dissimilar to that for which he is best known.

To resume—once more the dreaded malady returned, and days of pain were succeeded by nights of sleepless watching. Still he bore up manfully against all odds, and amidst his sorrows, the dear friends of the old house in Kilkenny were as close to his heart and as warm in his memory as ever. He wrote thus to Michael,—

"LONDON, *November* 15*th*, 1824.

"DEAR MICHAEL,—Tell me how this weather treats my poor mother. As to me, leaving me otherwise in good health, it brings a score handsaws, chisels, and corkscrews, to work all at once, on every inch of my thighs, legs, shins, feet, and toes. I roar out from the pain, and I cannot restrain myself; the other night I was awake from lying down to rising, all the while in torture."

This attack was not of long continuance, and with the new year, 1825, came the satisfaction of having completed the "Tales by the O'Hara Family," for the purchase of which he was, in January, in treaty with Colburn.

CHAPTER IV.

"TALES BY THE O'HARA FAMILY" PUT TO PRESS—"THE BOYNE WATER" COMMENCED—A PUBLISHER'S RUSE—"TALES BY THE O'HARA FAMILY" PUBLISHED — THEIR SUCCESS — SHARE OF MICHAEL AND JOHN BANIM IN THE SERIES—LETTERS—SICKNESS OF MRS. BANIM—SLIGHT RETURN OF HIS OWN ILLNESS —LETTERS—PROGRESS OF "THE BOYNE WATER"—VISIT OF JOHN BANIM TO DERRY—TOUR OF MICHAEL BANIM THROUGH THE COUNTY LIMERICK — EACH BROTHER COLLECTING MATERIALS FOR "THE BOYNE WATER"—LETTERS—ENGAGEMENTS WITH ARNOLD OF THE ENGLISH OPERA HOUSE—LETTERS FROM GERALD GRIFFIN — FRIENDSHIP BETWEEN HIM AND BANIM — VISIT OF JOHN BANIM TO KILKENNY—MICHAEL'S ACCOUNT OF IT—LETTERS—PUBLICATION OF "THE BOYNE WATER"—LETTERS—SECOND MISUNDERSTANDING WITH GERALD GRIFFIN— "THE NOWLANS" COMMENCED—LETTERS—RELIGIOUS FEELINGS —HOME THOUGHTS—LETTERS.

WE have related the various phases, sometimes sunny and frequently clouded, marking the life of John Banim, and we have now reached that epoch of his life-history in which, when in his twenty-sixth year, he had completed "The Tales by the O'Hara Family," and had succeeded in obtaining a publisher. Now had come the time for which, through all the sorrows of the weary past, he had toiled and hoped. True, it was not his first triumph, he had known that joy which elevates the dramatist when his thoughts are filling the hearts of an enraptured audience; he had heard great actors in his "Damon and Pythias," and, as some noble passage in the play had charmed the listeners, he had seen the surging, swaying crowds applauding to the echo. But this was a triumph too uncertain, and too much dependent upon the mass, and, in the probable success of "The O'Hara Tales," he fancied that he saw the brightest dream-land of his brightest reverie—fame, competence secured, a happy home for Ellen, for his mother, for all; the full fruition of that charming aspiration which he expressed to Michael when he wrote: "That my dear Ellen, and my dear Joanna, should live together in love and unity, is my great wish and my hope too. To see them working, or reading, or making their womanly fuss near me, and under my roof, and mutually tolerating and helping each other, and never talking loud. And my mother, my dear, dear mother, sitting in her arm-chair looking at them, with her old-times placid smile; and my father and you doing whatever you liked. Tush! Perhaps this is foolish and Utopian of me. Yet we *must* live together: that is the blessed truth. Such a set of people were not born to dwell asunder. And, perhaps, the old times would come back again after all. What is the reason, I ask, that, after a little while, we should not club our means, and dwell, as Mr. Owen preaches, in one big house, every mother's son and daughter of us; and have good feeling, good taste, and economy presiding over us? More unlikely things have happened. After the world is seen, it does not bear to be gaped at every day; and the only true aim of a rational creature ought to be, humble independence on any scale, and the interchange of those little and tireless amiabilities, that in a loving, and virtuous, and temperate circle, make life indeed worth living for—to me. And without these life is a compulsion: a necessity to breathe without enjoyment—to sweat without a reward."

These were his hopes and heartiest wishes—success in literature could alone for him secure their attainment, and once attained, life would be fair as

"A light upon the shining sea."

But, even whilst correcting the proof sheets of the first series of "The Tales," he was preparing materials for a novel, and he wrote thus to his brother:—

"LONDON, *January* 17*th*, 1825.

"MY DEAR MICHAEL,—I am reading hard for a three-volume tale, and, if our present venture succeed, I may hope for a fair price."

He was not, however, at all forgetful of his success as a dramatist, and he still negotiated for the production of "The Prodigal" at Covent Garden Theatre, having, as we have already related, failed in inducing Elliston to accept it for Drury Lane. But in this attempt he was, as the reader has been informed, unsuccessful, owing to disagreements with Edmund Kean.

Disappointments connected with this tragedy were not his only causes of uneasiness. Mrs. Banim's health had not improved, and she was directed by her physician to pass a short period in France. In the following letter Banim describes his position, his cares, his hopes, and his expectations. The old kindly home love is bright as ever—whether in joy or sorrow; struggling or prosperous—home, his wife and his mother, are always at his heart. And yet how strange it seems that his love should cling so firmly to those scenes where he had known many sorrows, many pains, and, save in childhood, no joys. Can it be that this thought of the lamented Arthur Henry Hallam is true, and that "Pain is the deepest thing that we have in our nature, and union through pain has always seemed more real and more holy than any other." Thus, at all events, John Banim wrote to his father :—

"LONDON, *January* 28*th*, 1825.

"MY DEAR FATHER,—I have to inform you, that I have kept back at Covent Garden to watch the fate of a play by ——. This play I judged would not succeed, and my judgment has proved good. It was repeated only twice. I may expect to come on, when Young returns to his engagement, in about six weeks. The stage apart for a moment, pleasant little matters are occurring elsewhere. Our publishers, being highly pleased with the matter now in progress, *engage* liberal terms, should our venture have luck. Yesterday I received a proof of their good opinion, in the shape of a handsome snuff-box, with which I intend to present you when we meet. So far, my dear father, with other seasonable assistance from my good friend Mr. Arnold, who receives my small theatrical pieces freely, I am very comfortable, considering that I have had to win my way in a scramble, where no human being was interested to lend me a hand. I think I have not altogether done badly. I have been hère three years, and I do not owe a shilling. I am now esteemed in the market. Alas! literature is a marketable commodity, as well as any other ware, and sells according to its quality. But, if able, my regular business will soon send me to Ireland, and afford me the happiness of embracing my family.

"One regret I must feel during my visit; I shall not be accompanied by her who has for three years been the sharer of my struggles—the only friend in my exile. Ellen has been ordered to seek a milder clime for awhile, and I must convey her to France for a period. She is not very or dangerously ill : I send a medical certificate to her father to convince him of this; but still her removal has been pronounced necessary, and I owe her too much to counteract the injunctions of her physician.

"Michael gave me charming assurances in his last letter of my dear mother's good health. Were she ever so ill, I know the expectation of seeing ME (you see I am growing riotous in my own good opinion) will speedily make her well."

He accompanied his wife to France, and having secured apartments for her, he returned to London, and to its labours. In the following letter, written a few days after he had reached London, he informs Michael of the progress of "The Tales" through the press, and hints at his returning illness :—

"LONDON, *May 9th*, 1825.

"MY DEAR MICHAEL,—I remained scarce a day in France after I saw Ellen housed : yet short as was my absence from London, matters got into a pretty pickle with the printers before I came back.

"The labour of getting 'Crohoore' through the ordeal has been hideous : almost every sheet of him came back to me three or four times. It is tremendous work to compel English types to shape themselves into Irish words. Happily he is now equipped for his *début*, as well as I can shape him. 'The Fetches' is disposed of also, and I am through the first hundred pages of the last volume. I have been leading a solitary life since my wife left me: but no help for that. To keep me alive I have plenty of work on hand, and there are fair prospects in view.

"My health has been only tolerable; as Shakespeare hath it,

'—— The moon, the governess of floods,
Pale in her anger, washes all the air,
That rheumatic diseases do abound.'

"I greatly fear and dread mother has also had her visitation, if the weather has been such in Ireland as we have had here."

Upon the eve of the publication of "The Tales," the next letter was addressed by John Banim to his brother, and in it he details a little publishing *ruse*; one of a class of which many instances have been afforded in London, during the anxiety of the public to possess books containing information on the countries surrounding Sebastopol:—

"LONDON, *April 6th*, 1825.

"MY DEAR MICHAEL,—Our tales have not been announced in the usual manner, and I will tell you why.

"A certain literary gentleman, an Irishman too, of undoubted talent, being aware of the nature of our volumes, started with a spirited publisher, and got out notices, and it became rather an amusing race between us. He would come occasionally, in the most friendly manner, to hope I was going on well. Pen against pen it was, as fast as they could gallop. Mounted on my grey goose quill I have beaten him, as to time at all events. It was necessary to keep him in the dark by leaving our books unannounced. What may be the further result of our race is yet to be seen. There is quackery in all trades, from the boudoir to the pill-box.

"I purpose to be in Derry, two hundred miles north of you, in a few weeks, and in some time after I will run down to Kilkenny to shake hands with you all, and hear my poor mother call me her own '*graw bawn*' once again."

The visit to Derry, mentioned in this letter, was undertaken for the purpose of gaining an accurate knowledge, from personal observation, of the scenery and character of the country around the Boyne; and this knowledge was turned by Banim to excellent account, as may be perceived in those admirable descriptions introduced in that novel upon which he was then engaged, "The Boyne Water."

The "Tales by the O'Hara Family" appeared on the 7th of April, 1825, and their success was, from the first day, unquestionable. Gerald Griffin wrote to his brother, and described Banim's triumph thus: "Have you seen Banim's O'Hara Tales?—if not, read them, and say what you think of them. I think them most vigorous and original things; overflowing with the very spirit of poetry, passion and painting, if you think otherwise, don't say so. My friend W—— sends me word that they are *well written*. All our critics here say that they are *admirably* written; that nothing since Scott's first novels has equalled them. I differ entirely with W—— in his idea of the fidelity of their delineations. He says they argue unacquaintance with the country; I think they are astonishing in nothing so much as in the power of creating an intense interest without stepping out of real life, and in the very easy and natural drama that is carried through them, as well as in the excellent tact which he shows, in seizing on all the points of national character which are capable of effect; mind, I don't speak of 'The Fetches' now. That is a romance. But is it not a splendid one? Nobody knew anything of Banim, till he published his 'O'Hara Tales,' which are becoming more and more popular every day. I have seen pictures taken from them already by first-rate artists, and engravings in the windows."

Literary fame, however, was not the only point to be considered; the pecuniary reward of merit was a very important consideration. The fame, indeed, belonged entirely, so far as the public knew, to John; but Michael, living at home quietly in Kilkenny, had formed very prosaic ideas, and thought, very naturally, that if the public admired "The O'Hara Tales," the public ought to prove its appreciation by purchasing them; and he wrote to John, requesting information upon the interesting topic comprised in the short question, "How do the books sell?" John's reply we shall just now insert, but we would here draw the reader's attention to the facts already related, in which we have detailed the plans of joint contribution agreed upon in the composition of the "Tales by the O'Hara Family."

The first tale of the series, entitled "Crohoore of the

Billhook," was written by Michael Banim, who wrote also the opening chapter, descriptive of a "Pattern," in "John Doe," the third tale of this first series: the remainder of this tale, and the entire of "The Fetches," the second tale, were written by John Banim; but, as was agreed upon, each brother submitted his contributions to the earnest criticism of the other.

And when one comes now to examine these fictions, to mark their vigour and dramatic power, to note those qualities indicated by Griffin, who wrote of them, "they are astonishing in nothing so much as in the power of creating an intense interest without stepping out of real life, and in the very easy and natural drama that is carried through them, as well as in the excellent tact which he shows in seizing on all the points of national character," we must agree with Gerald in his estimate of the merit of the series. These qualities attributed by Griffin to "The Tales" appear more clearly in the fictions subsequently written, but the ability of the brothers is not the less plainly shown. And it is, indeed, strange that two young men, the one a shopman to his father, planning his scenes by day whilst attending to his business duties, and stealing his leisure from the night; the other, a hard-worked literary man—one who, as he said himself, should "tease the brain, as wool-combers tease wool, to keep the fire in and the pot boiling," could have been able to produce those novels which, though entering upon a pre-occupied branch of literature, obtained and secured attention from the earliest publication. In John Banim's case, too, it should be remembered, that he was forced to write when he *could* write; that is, he wrote at such times as he could snatch from his ordinary engagements: sometimes when racked in body by his own pains, sometimes when racked in mind through sympathy for the ill-health of his wife. But the strong bold will, the earnest hope of success, bear the mental hero above every sorrow—the victor of every woe—and thus is proved the wisdom of Wordsworth's thought—

> "A cheerful life is what the Muses love,
> A soaring spirit is their prime delight."

In the following letter those qualities of mind are proved, and his industry and mental courage are most admirably displayed:—

"LONDON, *May 1st*, 1825.

"MY DEAR MICHAEL,—You ask me a very vital question, How do the books sell? Very well.

"The publishers are quite contented: big with hopes, and withal benevolent. On mature reflection, I venture to solve another important query; I deem you should neglect neither your business nor three new volumes. Plan out three tales, and work at them from time to time at your leisure, and I think I can obtain for you a remunerative price.

"I will be ready with a tale in three volumes by Christmas, and I propose you should be prepared for the next trial. For my tale I will visit every necessary spot in the north and south. Derry, Lough Neagh— thence to the Boyne, and then to Limerick. I have christened the tale before its birth. It is to be called 'The Boyne Water.' I have sent you all the criticisms; in no case have we got a drubbing. We have yet to undergo the scrutiny of the monthly and quarterly periodicals. This I can tell you to inspirit ou—the good Belles Lettres critic of the Quarterly has read our volumes, and has deigned to praise them in high quarters.

" Man alive, hold up your head and have courage."

A few days after the date of this letter, John Banim sailed for Ireland, and reaching Dublin safely, he at once set out for Belfast. His occupations in the North were thus described, in a letter to Michael:—

"COLERAINE, *May* 28*th*, 1825.

" MY DEAR MICHAEL,—Lest you should be uneasy at my staying longer than I proposed, I write to say I am well, and have only been delayed by the uninterrupted interest of my route from Belfast. I walked a great part of the way along the coast to this town; having forwarded all my baggage, trusting to Him who feeds the sparrow and the raven, for a meal and a bed. My adventures have been considerable in the way of living alone. I sometimes slept in a sheebeen house, sometimes in a farmer's house, and sometimes in a good inn; and only I thought myself too ill-dressed a fellow, I might have shared the hospitality of a certain lady of high rank.

" But what scenery have I beheld—grand, exquisite: the Causeway, from which I have just returned, the best part of it. You may look out for me towards the end of the next week. One thing is certain—I will meet a hearty welcome at the old house where I first saw the light."

Back to "the old house," and to his mother, came "her own *graw bawn*," with love as warm and heart as true as in the past-by days of childhood, when he stole from his playmates to watch over her safety, fearing that "Farrell the Robber" might carry her away. And here, the student of literary biography will, doubtless, observe how beautifully this man's nature shines, unchilled by adversity and pain, unspoiled—so unspoiled—by success, and by the golden hopes of the brighter future.

One can fancy this deep-hearted man returned to "the old house" where he "first saw light," and where he had known such joys and sorrows, such real cares and such cloud-land visions, as, happily, few men experience in their darker phases: Joanna and Michael rush forth to greet him, and the more sober, but not less intense joy of the father and mother need no word-painting. It must have been the realization of a dream-vision, one of those glimpses of paradise, fading as the morning arises, and leaving but a regretful memory of joys never to return again.

Thinking thus, we addressed Michael Banim, and added,—"tell us how you all received John when he came to you from his northern tour;" and Michael answered us, "You may be sure the absentee received a hearty welcome in the old house. On a Sunday evening he came amongst us, the evening of all others we could best enjoy ourselves There was the family board, with something more choice even than the usual Sunday fare, to mark the event. The well-known faces were all around it once more. No one absent. There was the new comer, in the identical chair, and on the same spot, he used to occupy. There was the dinner prolonged unreasonably, by questions and answers, interruptive of mastication. When the table was at length cleared, there was the jerking of chairs into as close contact as possible. And there was the cheerful glass, in which to hob nob with the restored struggler. Truth to tell, I fear that three of the circle, the old man and his two sons, dipped somewhat deeper than discretion or respect for the Sabbath evening warranted.

"This meeting of kindred after separation, bore likeness to a gushing fountain, one of whose channels had been interrupted; the others insufficient to carry off the waters; the temporary obstacle removed, the whole affluence came forth babbling and sparkling in the sunshine. There was no cloud that we could see, on that Sunday evening, over us. There was frequent laughter, ringing out, and without rhyme or reason. There was a tautology of endearing epithets. There was the voluble enjoyment that marked a jubilee."

Banim did not continue long in "the old house;" and early in July he was back once more in London at his desk, engaged in that ceaseless round of work; truly

> "Twilight saw him at his folios,
> Morning saw his fingers run,
>   Labouring ever,
>   Weary never
> Of the task he had begun."

His visit to Kilkenny had not been entirely one of pleasure. He had planned, with Michael, the outlines of future novels, plays and poems. He had now no doubts or fears, and the great prizes of genius, that is, such prizes as England gives, golden wreaths, were all, he fancied, within his grasp, to be secured by industry. Within three years he had *made* for himself a reputation by honourable, but unflinching work; and he looked upon it but as the stepping place, the mound which should be raised before his hopes could blossom in complete fruition.

"Time, the subtile-thief of youth,"

had never yet affrighted him; the past was but a dead past; all life, and the bliss of prosperity were in the future—and that life and bliss were to be wrought out of the life and labour of the present.

A few days after his return to London, he wrote thus to Michael:—

"LONDON, *July* 16, 1825.

"MY DEAR MICHAEL,—I am stripped to the shirt sleeves, the weather is so hot, not scampering abroad, but in my oven-like study, plying the skreeking pen might and main, for it is a terrible atmosphere here: the glass up to fever heat, and, except the rabid, who appear now and then, not a canine frequenter of the streets visible. The race of dogs seemeth extinct."

Whilst "plying the skreeking pen, might and main," he learned from Mrs. Banim that she was now sufficiently restored to health to bear the atmosphere of England; and accordingly on the 24th of August he set out for France, and returned with her to his new home in Mount Street; and Gerald Griffin succeeded him in the occupation of the old lodgings in Brompton Grove.

All his unoccupied time was now devoted to the completion of "The Boyne Water." Griffin visited him frequently, and was fully acquainted with all the details of the work. He wrote to his brother, William, "Banim has been all over the north of Ireland, and has brought here the world and all of materials for his new novel. He has spent an immense deal of labour and study in acquiring a perfect knowledge of all the historical records of the period; and procured a great deal of original information, and other matters, during his ramble." In weaving these materials, so gathered, into his novel, Banim seemed to forget even the friends in "the old house," and Michael wrote anxiously to Mrs. Banim, requesting that she would correspond with him, as John seemed lost to all honesty in paying epistolary debts. Mrs. Banim's reply was as follows, and it reminds one of Dora Copperfield's experiences of the "pursuits of literature."

"LONDON, *September* 30*th*, 1825.

"DEAR MICHAEL,—John is so much occupied at present, that I scarcely ever see his face from nine o'clock in the morning to six in the evening—when, after rapping for some time at the ceiling, for he works over head, I go up to his door, put on the most hungry face I can, and complain of my starving state: then only can I get him to come down: when he issues forth, he is the true picture of stupidity. He has himself denied to all visitors, since our arrival from France, and the whole, long, long day, he is shut up, with his plaguy 'Boyne Water.'"

Nearly a month after the date of this letter, Michael received the following from John, and in it we perceive the first indication of doubt as to the *politics* of "The Boyne Water:"—

"LONDON, *October* 25*th*, 1825.

"MY DEAR MICHAEL,—You have made me shake and shiver, by bringing before my eyes the ticklish ground on which I stand, with respect to the present novel: and you have almost driven me to despair, by telling me to look for increased reputation—or——. I almost give up the hope of realizing the wishes you have formed, of what I ought to produce. No writer can pronounce on his own realization of his conceptions. Unfortunately we often value a production according to the pains and care we bestow on it—hence we are indifferent judges of ourselves—I have good materials, if I can but use them to advantange. Your notes on Limerick and the contiguous country, have gone beyond my expectation—I return you my thanks for all you have done. Apart from the matter I wanted, your memoranda are rich, and suggestive to me of a continuance of such things by both of us conjointly, to be followed, some time or other, by the publication of 'Walks through Ireland, by the O'Hara Family.'"

At length, as the novel advanced towards completion, he seems to have become still more nervous on the subject of its probable success. Michael had warned him that in adopting the political tone so strongly colouring the tale, he was endangering its popularity with a large section of readers: and truly it was most dangerous ground. Gerald Griffin, however, did not participate in, or encourage these fears—but then he never feared anything; his soul was like a lark, always soaring. He wrote to his brother, William, thus:—"I dined with Banim last week, and found him far gone in a new novel, now just finished, 'The Boyne Water,' (*good name!*) which is far superior, in my humble judgment, to the 'O'Hara Family:'" that he spoke to Banim as he wrote to his brother, there can be little doubt, and John seems to have regained his self-reliance, and to have taken to himself the counsel he had offered to Michael, when he wrote — " Man alive! hold up your head and have courage."

The following letter, written a few days after that last inserted is most interesting: the anxiety that Michael should correct freely; the humble confidence in his brother's judgment; the holy spirit of belief, which—however much, in one point, a worshipper of another creed might dissent from it—yet none can refuse to admire in the man, all render this letter worthy of the true-hearted writer:—

"LONDON, *November 6th*, 1825.

"MY DEAR MICHAEL,—With this you will receive the first volume of 'The Boyne Water.' I expect to go to press in a month from this day, so read it immediately, and return it as promptly as you can.

"Be very candid in your remarks, because I ought to be made to know myself: and don't you, at least, through a false delicacy, let me lead myself astray—every man's vanity blinds himself, to himself, of himself.

"This morning (Sunday), accompanying Ellen to Communion, I was delighted with the fair and beautiful sight of a crowd of other communicants, of every rank and age, clustering to the Sanctuary. Some old Chelsea pensioners were there. The lame, the blind, and the tottering: and there were boys and girls of very tender age, mixed with these infirm old men. Leaning down to minister the bread of comfort and of life, to those stumblers on the grave's brink, and those young adventurers on a world of temptation, was a most reverend looking priest — with long white hairs, who to my knowledge is one of the most zealous, virtuous, simple-minded men alive. My dear Michael, as I looked on, the recollection of our first communion together side by side, and of the devotion and holy awe that filled my heart at the time; and the remembrance of our aged and benevolent parish priest bending down to us with the sacrament in his fingers, came refreshingly to me, like the draught from a pure spring; and a long train of innocent days and blissful times, passed before me — with my thoughts recurrent to boyhood."

"The Boyne Water" was commenced in July, 1825, and at Christmas of that year the three volumes were in the hands of the printer; and early in the year 1826 it was before the critics, who gave it a very severe and rough reception; their criticisms, however, were directed against its politics rather than its literary merit, or its structure of plot and scene.

It was published as a fiction "By the O'Hara Family," but, writes Michael Banim to us,—" With the exception of examining the locality of the Siege of Limerick (the siege of the violated treaty as it is called), and the tracing of Sarsfield's route from the beleaguered city, to the spot where he surprised and destroyed the reinforcement of cannon on its way from Kilkenny, I had no direct concern in this tale. It passed through my hands during its progress, and I pruned, and added, and corrected *ad libitum*."

Roughly, however, as the critics used this book, the reading public were its very warm admirers; but, better than all, to one who wanted money, Colburn offered a very large sum for the next tale by "The O'Hara Family;" and John, closing with the proposal, commenced writing his novel, "The Nowlans."

The northern tour of John Banim was but part of that extended one required to be undertaken and completed, before the entire scenery of the localities introduced into "The Boyne Water" could be described from actual observation. Time, however, did not permit him to traverse this route himself, and Michael was enlisted as the note-taker of the southern districts. From the notes so taken the descriptions of Limerick, and the surrounding country, in "The Boyne Water," were written.

Michael's tour, however, was remarkable, as an adventure occurring in its progress, suggested to John the powerfully written, but painful novel, "The Nowlans." Michael Banim has, with his usual kindness, written for us the following account of this incident to which we have referred, and it will be observed that John, with consummate ability, wrought out the idea suggested by Michael:—

"While pursuing the track of Sarsfield on his route to intercept the reinforcements destined to strengthen the besiegers of Limerick, I journeyed on foot, through the Slieve Bloom Mountains, tracing my way principally by the traditionary information given by the people. I kept an itinerary as I went along, referable, not only to the purpose of my journey, but descriptive also of the peculiar and impressive scenery around me; and of the existing characteristics of a little known, but, as they appear to me, a very fine people.

"My adventures during this excursion were not without interest; and, after it had been ascertained satisfactorily that I was not a gauger, coming to spy after potteen sellers and potteen stills, I found courtesy and kindness, and disinterested assistance, all through the mountain range.

"It was my fate to seek shelter for the night at the house of a farmer named Daniel Kennedy. His warm and comfortable dwelling was in a mountain hollow, known as Fail Dhuiv, or the Black Glen. The peculiarities of this out of the way homestead, the appearance of the dwellers therein, and the details of the unostentatiously hospitable reception given to me, were faithfully reported in my note-book. Extracted thence, almost word for word, my veritable account forms the introduction to the tale of 'The Nowlans.' There was a sick son on the night of my visit occupying the stranger's bedroom, about whom the good woman of the house and her daughters appeared to be most anxious. I could not, for this reason, be accommodated in the apartment usually reserved for guests, and my bed was made up on the kitchen table. The home-made sheets and blankets, white as snow, and redolent of the sweet mountain breeze in which they had been bleached, were most inviting to a weary pedestrian, as I was; and I slept luxuriously that night on the kitchen table, under the roof of Daniel Kennedy of Fail Dhuiv.

"The circumstance of the sick son, who, I could learn, had been away, and who, in his illness, had come home to seek the ministry of his affectionate kindred, gave the idea, and no more than the idea, of John Nowlan—the hero of the new tale." *

---

* The broad humour of the following passage from Michael's introductory letter to "The Nowlans," we have always considered quite worthy of Smollett or Fielding. "Abel O'Hara"

Whilst John was engaged upon "The Nowlans," Michael paid him a long-promised visit in London, in

has been drenched by a heavy shower in the mountains, and returning to Nowlan's house finds that—

"All the family stood at the threshold to receive me; exclamations of condolence came from every tongue; and, almost by main force, the old woman, her daughters, and the robust maid-servant, forced me off to a bedchamber, where I was commanded to doff every tack upon me, and cover myself up in a neat little bed, until every tack should be well dried. In vain I remonstrated: Mrs. Nowlan and her handmaid whisked off my coat and vest, even while I spoke; the latter, squatting herself on her haunches, then attacked my shoes and stockings; Peggy appropriated my cravat; and I began to entertain some real alarm as to the eventual result of their proceedings, when away they went in a body, each laden with a spoil, and all renewing their commands that I should instantly peel off my Russia-ducks and my inner garment, drop them at the bed-side, and then retiring between the sheets, call out to have them removed.

"I did even as I was bid; and when properly disposed to give the appointed signal, Cauth Flannigan, the maid of all-work, speedily attended to it, re-entering with something on her arm, from which her eye occasionally wandered to my half-seen face, in a struggle, as I thought, and I believe I was not wrong in my reading, between most provoking merriment, and a decent composure of countenance; 'The misthess sent this *shirt*, Sir—only it isn't a shirt, entirely, but one belongin' to the misthess, becase it's the washin' week, an' the sickness in the place, an' all, an' the misthess couldn't make off a betther at a pinch'—— and, laying it on the edge of the bed, Cauth strove to hide her giggle and her blushes by stooping to take up the last of my drenched garments. When she had again retired with them, I examined the nicely-folded article she had left with me, and, truly, it was *not* 'a shirt entirely'—but—what shall I call it, Barnes?—a female shirt, haply; the personal property, as Cauth would have it, of Mrs. Nowlan; yet, from the earnestness with which that zealous Abigail strove to impress the fact upon me, as also from the hasty erasure of an initial, near its upper edge, I had my own doubts, while I put it on, concerning the identity of its owner."

the summer of 1826; and then it appeared that John had, in his letters, detailed only the good and cheering facts connected with his life, and had but too well concealed the slow, but certain progress of his malady. Though only in his twenty-eighth, he seemed, at least in his fortieth year; his hair was grizzled; his face was wrinkled; his limbs were so weak that Michael feared, lest he should fall in the streets as they walked together; and then, during Michael's visit, he was witness of one of his brother's paroxysms of pain, and though he had seen—had even been as his nurse during—his first illness, after the death of Anne D——, yet this attack, though but of a few hours' continuance, frightened him by its violence, although when it passed away John was gay and hopeful as ever.

Whilst thus working and suffering, he once more, through his anxiety to serve Gerald Griffin, became estranged from him. It would appear that Banim had induced him to write an operatic piece for the English Opera House, which Arnold accepted through Banim's recommendation, agreeing to give 50*l*. for it, and Gerald wrote to his brother, "Much as I had known of Banim's kindness, I hardly looked for this great promptitude." This piece was entitled "The Noyades;" but though Griffin received every encouragement to write on from Arnold, yet fearing lest it might be supposed that Banim was in any way his patron, for he had, as his brother states, "an almost morbid horror of patronage," he sent two other pieces under the *nom de plume*, "G. Joseph," to the Manager. He had quite sufficient influence with the latter to secure a favourable reception for his pieces; as, by his essays on the Italian and English Operas, published in

"The Town," and in which he had endeavoured to excite a taste for purely English music, and characteristic English recitative, he had gained very considerable reputation. The facts of this misunderstanding, within the scope of this portion of Banim's Memoir, are thus related by Gerald Griffin's biographer :—

"Gerald, though fully sensible of Mr. Banim's kindness, and friendly solicitude about him, could not by any effort wholly divest himself of the instinctive reluctance he felt, to place himself under deep obligations to one upon whose good nature he had no other claim than his own difficulties; and his friend, conscious of this feeling, was perhaps too observant of the least expression which betrayed it. The consequence was—as soon as an opportunity of rendering Gerald a service occurred—some unhappy misconception on both sides. After the former misunderstanding, Mr. Banim, far from losing interest in Gerald's welfare, sought anxiously to render him services in the only manner he saw they would be accepted, by procuring him a market for his labours. Aware of his dramatic talent, he was continually urging him to write for the theatres, and especially for the English Opera House, where, from his own intimacy with Mr. Arnold, he was sure any recommendation of his would meet with attention. He at last obtained a piece from Gerald, to be presented at the English Opera House, out of which, some time after, arose the following correspondence :—

'*Thursday, August 18th*, 1826.

'MY DEAR SIR,—Yesterday, I handed your piece to Mr. Arnold. He read it instantly, and agreed with me in thinking it one of a high order. Here and there, however, I suspect you will have to cut and alter—and perhaps your songs must be re-written, and appear with less poetry, and more *set*-ableness about them. I conclude that your little drama will be produced this season, and some day soon, I'm to have the pleasure of introducing you to Mr. Arnold, who thinks very highly of your dramatic power, I assure you, and whom you will find possessed of all the technical acquirements calculated to mature it.

' My dear Sir, faithfully yours,
' JOHN BANIM.'

'*Thursday Evening, August* 18*th*, 1826.

'My dear Sir,—I shall be obliged to go into the city tomorrow, so that I must take this opportunity of mentioning, that I have just seen Mr. Arnold. I gave him the piece with the alterations, of which you spoke to me, and he said he would read it again, and supposed he should have the pleasure of seeing you in a day or two. Talking of money matters—for he spoke of the mode of payment, though he said nothing decisive—I'm such a stupid awkward fool, that I could scarcely understand the business properly, but I thought there appeared to be some feeling on his part, of unwillingness to incur risk, or some such thing. If this was at all the case, I certainly should not take any remuneration, previous to its being produced. My feeling on this subject is a great deal that of indifference, but if the piece were found profitable to the theatre, I should by no means be content that it should be otherwise to me—and that is all I feel about it. I should be perfectly satisfied to let the piece be played, and let Mr. Arnold calculate its worth by its success. I trouble you with this, my dear Sir, in the hope that you may make use of it, as far as you think proper, in case Mr. Arnold should speak to you on the matter as he said he would. A far greater object than any payment in specie to me would be the being enabled to take my trial soon. How can I apologise to you for all this?

'I am, my dear Sir, yours sincerely,
'Gerald Griffin.'

" It is evident that the feeling of 'indifference' which Gerald expresses in this letter, related entirely to the *mode* of payment, as to whether it should be absolute and unconditional, or dependent upon the success of the piece. Mr. Banim, however, seems unfortunately to have formed some misconception of the expression, as appears by the following letter:—

'*Tuesday Morning, August* 23*d*, 1826.

'My dear Sir,—Yesterday, after calling another day without seeing him, Mr. Arnold spoke to me finally about your piece. He is well disposed towards it, and, if you permit, will act it. I could see none of the indecisiveness you mentioned in your last, nor did he say a word that could make me believe he thought he ran any risk in the matter. Perhaps you mistook him in your interview. He now desires me to inform you that you may get paid in proportion to its success on the established terms of his theatre, or sell your drama at once for fifty pounds, including the publishing copyright. Should you prefer the former mode of remuneration it will be necessary for you to ascertain by calling on him, what are the usual terms of paying authorship in his theatre *by nights*. I know nothing of it. I invariably prefer a certainty beforehand; indeed he got a piece of mine for less than he offers for yours, and I believe I have not been a loser. Mr. Howard Payne did not, I am informed, receive more from Covent Garden, either for his Clare, or Charles II.

'Miss Kelly has been ill, and perhaps but for that, your piece would now be in progress. Mr. Arnold still thinks he will produce it this season. You inform me that your feeling on that subject is one of a great deal of indifference. This I must regret, particularly as I have been the cause of giving you trouble in a matter which does not interest you. I assure you at the time I first wrote for the English Opera House, and waited month after month even for an answer, I would not have been indifferent to whatever chance might have got my piece read and answered two hours after it had been handed in, and the transaction finally brought to a close in a few days.

'I am, my dear Sir, truly yours,

'JOHN BANIM.

'However you may decide, Mr. Arnold hopes to close with yourself.'

'*Tuesday Evening, August* 23d, 1826.

'MY DEAR SIR,—I have just received your letter, which I hasten to answer. I am exceedingly obliged to you for all the trouble you have taken with the play, and am most gratified with the conclusion. I feel the entire extent of the obligation which you have conferred upon me; I always felt it, and I thought I said so in my first letter, but a mistake you have fallen into with respect to my last, renders it necessary for me to explain.

'The indifference of which I spoke (as probably you will find by referring to the letter) related entirely to Mr. Arnold's mode of payment, or indeed payment at all in the first instance, as, from the conversation I had with you on the subject, and the subsequent interview with Mr. Arnold, I concluded that nothing worth being very anxious about was to be done in the way of money, at a summer theatre. It was far from an object of indifference to me, however, that a play of mine should be produced. When you thought I meant to say this, you gave me credit for a greater piece of coxcombry than I was conscious of. It has been the object of my life for many years; I could not profess to be indifferent about it, still less could I be indifferent to the nature or extent of the obligation when conferred. Let me beg of you to take this general assurance in preference to any construction which possibly may be put on casual words or sentences.

'I am, my dear Sir, very truly yours,
'GERALD GRIFFIN.

"To this letter, which certainly seems sufficiently explanatory, Mr. Banim unfortunately returned no answer, believing, as he afterwards mentions, that both parties were content, and all cause of misunderstanding removed. Gerald, however, very naturally expected some acknowledgment of the fact, and not receiving it, ceased to urge any renewal of an intimacy, the interruption of which he felt did not rest with him. It would seem extraordinary that Mr. Banim, after having always evinced such a kind interest in Gerald's affairs, and received so ample an explanation of the slight misconception which occurred, did not evince some sign of returning confidence; but I believe the fact to be, that before an opportunity occurred for declaring it, a new and more annoying cause of jealousy arose. At the time that Mr. Banim's works were in the very highest estimation, and when indeed the assistance of no new author could have added to their reputation, he offered Gerald a place in the O'Hara Family and urged him to contribute a tale. To a person wholly unknown, and whose most successful work could not have procured for him a third of the price from the booksellers which could be obtained for it as one of the O'Hara Tales, this was a very generous proposal. It was, however, declined by Gerald on the plea that he was unequal to the task. Hollandtide appeared some months subsequent to this, and almost immediately after the conclusion of the correspondence respecting the drama accepted by Mr. Arnold. It was hardly surprising that under such circumstances Mr. Banim should feel he was treated disingenuously, especially as he was convinced Gerald had Hollandtide written at the time he declared his inability to write a tale for the O'Hara collection. This, however, was really not the case. Most of the tales in Hollandtide were written in an inconceivably short space of time (not more than two or three months,) before their publication, and entirely at my constant urging, and I can testify from the difficulty I had in inducing him to make the effort at all, how very diffident and doubtful he was of success. I do not mean that he exactly underrated his own powers, but I believe he did not think that his engagements with the periodicals, which he could not give up, would allow him sufficient time and consideration to attain the success he was ambitious of, in a regular work of fiction. In any event, indeed, I do not believe he would have joined an author of established fame in his labours, however advantageous it might be in a pecuniary point of view. If there was any one object dearer to him than another in his literary career, it was the ambition of attaining rank and fame by his own unaided efforts, or at least without placing himself under obligations to those on whom he felt he had no claim; but independent of this, and highly as he must have appreciated the kindness of Mr. Banim's proposal, he might not unnaturally conclude that the public would consider his own early efforts as indebted for success, more to the assistance of his eminent friend, than to any original or independent merit they possessed. He had besides, on all occasions, an almost morbid horror of patronage, arising partly from a natural independence of mind, but yet more from the depressing disappointments of his early literary life. When first he came to London, he sought by a few introductions and the friendly exertions of literary acquaintances, to bring his productions favourably before the public, but without the slightest success. His powers seemed to be undervalued precisely in proportion as he made interest to procure them consideration, until at length disgusted by repeated failure, he resolved in future to trust wholly to his own unfriended exertions, and if they should not sustain him, to abandon the struggle. It was soon after forming this resolution that success first dawned upon his efforts, and that he was anxiously sought for as an anonymous contributor by the editors of periodicals, who, when he was previously introduced to them, would give him nothing to do. In proportion as his success increased, the remembrance of the many mortifying disappointments he had formerly experienced seemed to sink more deeply into his mind, and he gradually acquired a degree of sensitiveness with respect to patronage, that made him recoil from even the ordinary and necessary means of obtaining attention for his pieces. This may have influenced him much less with respect to Mr. Banim than others." *

Matters rested thus, and we shall hereafter, at the proper time, resume the history of this disagreement, and the happy, honest, ingenuous reconciliation of these two excellent men.

Michael returned to Kilkenny in August, 1826; and when he left London, "The Nowlans" was entirely finished, and he had acted as the critic upon it; but in six weeks after he had reached his home, "Peter of the Castle" was forwarded to him for his corrections. This story is founded upon the character of one well known in the neighbourhood of Kilkenny some few years before the period of which we write. "The Nowlans" and "Peter of the Castle" form the second series of "The Tales By The O'Hara Family," which was published in November, 1826. The series was thus dedicated:—"To Ireland's True Son and First Poet, Thomas Moore, Esq. With the Highest National Pride in his Genius as an Irishman, These Tales are Inscribed." It would appear that Moore, although blundering in his recollection of the words of the dedication, was pleased with it; and when in the year 1830 he visited Kilkenny, whilst staying with the late Mr. Bryan of Jenkinstown, he made the following entry in his "Diary," under date September 8th:—"Walked with Tom into Kilkenny, to show it to him. Called at Mr. Banim's (the father of the author of the 'Tales of the O'Hara Family,' who keeps a little powder and shot shop in Kilkenny), and not finding him at home, left a

* Life of Gerald Griffin, Esq. By his Brother.

memorandum * to say that I had called out of respect to his son. Took care to impress upon Tom how great the merit of a young man must be who, with not one hundredth part of the advantages of education that he (Tom) had in his power, could yet so distinguish himself as to cause this kind of tribute of respect to be paid to his father. I have not, it is true, read more than one of Banim's stories myself, but that one was good, and I take the rest upon credit. Besides, he dedicated his second series to me, calling me 'Ireland's free son and true poet,' which was handsome of him."†

It would, perhaps, be almost impossible to suggest any plot more powerfully conceived, and more vigorously elaborated, than that of "The Nowlans." It is, in truth, the analysis of passion : love in every phase —its pathos and its rage ; and when we close the book, saddened by the fate of poor Letty Nowlan, and her misguided lover, we feel how truly the epigraph which Banim selected from Gray describes the lot of the hero and heroine :—

> "These shall the fury passions tear—
> The vultures of the mind."

The whole vigour of Banim's genius was engaged in the construction of this novel ; and it was, in its first edition, disfigured by some passages which his more sober judgment led him afterwards to omit. If, however, we take this novel, solely as a specimen of what

* The memorandum was as follows, and old Mr. Banim valued it most highly, and always carried it about with him in his pocket book :—" Mr. Thomas Moore called to pay his respects to the father of the author of 'The O'Hara Family.'"

† "Memoirs, Journal, and Correspondence of Thomas Moore." Edited by the Right Hon. Lord John Russell. Vol. VI. p. 136.

Banim's genius could enable him to achieve, and if we compare *all* its parts, considering them as a whole, it must be classed amongst the most powerful fictions of the time, and if not the first, certainly of the first rank. Doubtless if it be not taken as a whole, the melodramatic character appears too boldly, but this is an objection which might, with equal force, be urged against "The Bride of Lammermoor," and "Eugene Aram." Possibly it was through regarding particular characters only, that Miss Mitford was induced to write—"John Banim was the founder of that school of Irish novelists, which, always excepting its blameless purity, so much resembles the modern romantic French school, that if it were possible to suspect Messieurs Victor Hugo, Eugène Sue, and Alexandre Dumas, of reading the English, which they never approach without such ludicrous blunders, one might fancy that many-volumed tribe to have stolen their peculiar inspiration from the 'O'Hara Family.'"*

The success of the "The Nowlans" was most satisfactory; but as reputation and competence were reached, disease and pain advanced with more violent and confirmed tenacity. Still he wrote on; none knew how nobly and bravely he worked; for, though it was easy to measure his hours of toil, who could measure that toil done in wringing, agonizing, burning pain? "He looked forty," says Michael, "though not eight-and-twenty:" his hair was grizzled; his face wrinkled, and he tottered as he walked, if the distance were many

---

* "Recollections of a Literary Life; or, Books, Places, and People." By Mary Russell Mitford. Vol. i. chap. 2. "Hardress Cregan," in "The Collegians," appears to us much more French than either "Tresham" in "The Fetches," or "John Nowlan."

doors off. During four months he never communicated with his family in Kilkenny, because he would not tell them of his illness; and at length, when Christmas, with its joys and sorrows, had come round once more, and when he believed that his health was somewhat improved, he wrote thus to Michael, in the old hopeful tone, bowing before the will of the Almighty in that same spirit in which Galileo said of his lost sight, "it has pleased God that it should be so, and it must please me also." In this letter nothing is omitted or forgotten, and home is home still, and every memory of other days is around his heart, as warmly cherished as if he had known neither the elevation of success nor the depression of withering sickness and disappointment :—

"LONDON, *Christmas Day*, 1826.

"MY DEAR MICHAEL,—I have just got your letter of the 21st. How could you suppose I should forget the hob nob at six this evening? we will chink our glasses to you with hearty good will and fond remembrance.

"When you were with me you insisted on my promise that I should be very candid with you in future regarding the state of my health. It was an injudicious engagement for me to make, or for you to exact. Why should I afflict those who love me?

"I have been very ill, but, under good treatment, am now much better. The pains came on with violence, accompanied by numbness and chilliness in the limbs, and general exhaustion. So I set to work for the best advice. You were right in saying that the pains are not at all rheumatic or gouty. My most excellent, as well as eminent, medical friend, after a long examination of me, touching my pursuits and mode of life for some years, and a careful consideration of the symptoms, decides that the brain pan, or my substitute for such, has been overworked; and that nervous debility, locally producing my ailment, has been the result. His treatment is preventive as well as stimulating. I am interdicted from much study of any kind; desired to take my ease; to live well, at the same time that I swallow tonics, and submit my poor body to the shower bath. My dear Michael, this is a hard sentence against me. If I am not to study, what am I to do? But let me not murmur. Let me not forget the goodness of God to one so unbefriended as I was, nor anticipate the withdrawal of His guardianship. With His help I shall mend, and the prospect will brighten again.

"By the way, I shall never forget the first morning I took a shower bath. A shock I had reckoned on, but for the tremendous one I felt, my mind had made no provision. I had scarcely touched the string, and brought down the first shower, when I manfully plunged straight forward, bursting open the door of the bath, and allowing the water to inundate the room. To heighten the scene, Ellen and a favourite cat were slumbering in bed in the next apartment, and when they heard the mixed commotion, they repeatedly manifested, each in her own way, their extreme astonishment and alarm thereat.

"To return; I said I am much better, and but for the diabolical London weather that surrounds me,— enough to relax the system of the big metal Achilles in Hyde Park,—I should be better still.

"It is some time since I have written to you: I did not care to annoy you when I was very ill, and I dare not, after my engagement, misrepresent facts. As far as acute torture, sleepless nights, and total prostration of frame could go, my worst enemies need not have wished me to suffer more.

"The second series go on right well; but the publishers say they are too strongly written, too harrowing, and, in parts, too warm and impure. The latter portion of this judgment, I regret to say, is merited. I have made a mistake, and must not again fall into the same error.

"Now a word or two as to yourself. I like the sketch you have sent me extremely well. You tell me you have read extensively, and that you have good materials for a story, if you thought yourself able to turn them to account. I tell you that you are able. One of your greatest drawbacks is your mean opinion of yourself. If we do not feel that we have power, we will not attempt to exercise it. I saw and said from the beginning, from my view of your first scrap of Crohoore, that you had the requisite qualifications; and now, when my opinion has been strengthened by that of the public, I urge you to think better of yourself—go on with your intended tale—I will handle it as before—have confidence in yourself, and, with God's help, the result will please you.

"Now—here goes for an effort: I will walk to the next post-office as well as I can, to drop in this letter, then home to a rib of beef, and then 'the people over the water'—hip, hip, hurra!

"This with best heart's love from Ellen and from

"J. B."

"The last paragraph of this letter," writes Michael, "may require explanation.

"At home in Kilkenny, as the clock struck six on each Christmas evening, all glasses were filled to the brim: when the last vibration ceased, my father raised his bumper, and gave the toast—

'HEALTH AND LONG LIFE TO POOR JOHN AND ELLEN FAR AWAY.'

By agreement, as the clock struck the same hour in London (we overlooked the difference of time) there was the answering toast of—

'HEALTH AND HAPPINESS TO ALL AT HOME.'

Even when our mother was no longer able to leave her bed, her glass of wine was brought to her, and she joined in the pledge from the inner room."

CHAPTER V.

ANXIETY FOR FAME AS A DRAMATIC POET—COMPOSITION OF HIS TRAGEDY "SYLLA"—HISTORY OF THE TRAGEDY—COMPARISON OF IT WITH THE "SYLLA" OF DERRICK AND JOUY—EXTRACTS FROM IT—LETTERS—PROPOSED VISIT TO THE SOUTH OF ENGLAND—RESTORED HEALTH—FRIENDSHIP OF JOHN STERLING—VISIT TO CAMBRIDGE—RESTORED HEALTH OF MRS. BANIM—URGING MICHAEL BANIM TO CONTINUE JOINT AUTHORSHIP—LETTERS—BUOYANT SPIRITS AND NEW PROJECTS—REMOVAL TO EASTBOURNE—OPINION OF MICHAEL'S TALE, "THE CROPPY"—ACCOUNT OF ITS COMPOSITION—A DAUGHTER BORN TO JOHN BANIM — CORRESPONDENCE WITH GERALD GRIFFIN — REMOVAL TO SEVEN OAKS—ADMIRABLE LETTER TO MICHAEL UPON THE COMPOSITION OF A NOVEL AND THE SELECTION OF CHARACTERS—INCIDENTS SUGGESTED AND OLD STORIES RECALLED—THE BEAUTIES AND ART OF GREAT NOVELISTS DISPLAYED—LETTER FROM MICHAEL SHOWING RESULT OF THIS ADVICE IN THE PRODUCTION OF "THE GHOST HUNTER"— ILLNESS — LETTER TO MICHAEL — LITERARY OCCUPATIONS DESCRIBED — BEAUTIFUL ACCOUNT OF HIS HOME LIFE—HIS CONDITION, THE BODY RACKED, BUT THE MIND GLOWING — DELIGHT AT RENEWED FRIENDSHIP OF GERALD GRIFFIN—THEIR LETTERS TO EACH OTHER—REMOVAL TO BLACKHEATH — ILLNESS AND PROSTRATION OF STRENGTH—REMOVAL TO THE FRENCH COAST ADVISED BY PHYSICIANS—ANOTHER SERIES OF "TALES BY THE O'HARA FAMILY" HURRIEDLY WRITTEN BY JOHN BANIM, AND PUBLISHED UNDER THE TITLE OF "THE DENOUNCED"—REMOVAL TO FRANCE.

IT will have been remarked by the attentive student of Banim's mind, as exhibited in his letters, that the old love of poetry and of dramatic composition, recurs frequently in evident forms. It was, indeed, never entirely lost, and he seems to have cherished hopes of brilliant and steady success in that most difficult of all literary labours, the production of a really poetical, original drama.

He was ever, in his leisure hours—and these, truly, were few—engaged in poetic composition; he had no pleasures, save those springing from literature. In this, he did not resemble Scott, or Byron, or Pope, or Moore; and he, more than any literary man of our time, could declare, with the great Chancellor of France, D'Aguesseau, "le changement d'étude est toujours un delassement pour moi." The hero of his drama was always selected from those historic names, whose deeds, and crimes or virtues, have afforded the fullest scope for the display of the genius of the dramatist and the art of the actor. It is also worthy of remark, that in all his dramas, as in all his novels, Banim ever chooses the portrayal of the wildest and fiercest passions, or the most harrowing and striking situations.

Ancient history seems to have been the storehouse whence he selected his plots; "Damon and Pythias" was one of these subjects thus drawn, and of its treatment the reader has been already enabled to judge; but, in the latter months of 1826, Banim commenced the composition of his tragedy entitled "Sylla," and it was completed in the last week of January, 1827. He appears to have supposed that his play was the first attempt to paint the character of Sylla in the English language; and, doubtless, his was the first attempt worthy the theme. A drama in three acts, and entitled "Sylla," was, however, written by Derrick, and printed, though never performed, in 1753; it grossly misconceives the character of the Dictator, and makes him, in addition, sing three songs.

By a strange coincidence Derrick founded this drama on, and in part translated it from, a French play of the early part of the seventeenth century, and Banim formed his tragedy upon, and in part translated it from, the "Sylla" of M. Jouy: and thus it comes to pass that the only dramatic authors who have taken Sylla for their subject have had one common fountain of inspiration—a French original. Of his own design, and of his opinions of Sylla's character as conceived by M. Jouy, Banim thus wrote:—

"The present is, so far as the writer is aware, the first attempt in the English language to illustrate, by dramatic action, the character of Sylla, and to account plausibly for the motives for his last astounding act of power—namely, his laying down the dictatorship. That the man, and the events of his public life, particularly the one specified, are strikingly dramatic, will not be denied; and the previous want of an English tragedy, built with such materials, is almost as striking. Perhaps it may have been caused by the apparent difficulty of the task. It is quite true that history supplies very little to make such a task easy. Sylla's heart and mind have been less unveiled to us by old writers, than have those of any other celebrated personage of antiquity. His own reasons for some of his actions—actions, sometimes noble, sometimes atrocious, always startling,—remain at best but as matters of guess-work to us. The outline of his character is blurred to our eyes. We do not understand him. Cæsar, Antony, Brutus, Catiline, and a score other citizens of old Rome, occur to our thoughts like intimate, well-known acquaintances, while of Sylla our notions are vague and unformed. As to what must have been truly his state of mind, when he laid down the palm and purple, and dismissed his lictors in the Forum amid a crowd of people, from scarce one of whom he had not good reason to dread a stern and dangerous remonstrance regarding his reign as dictator—upon his reasons for this prodigious and sublime act of hardihood, history is silent. And hence indeed would seem to arise such a difficulty as had just been conjectured. If you make a man the hero of a play, you must necessarily make him speak in his own person;

and just as necessarily, sooner or later, in the progress of your five acts, you must make him account, out of his own lips, *for what he does*. But how is this to be easily effected with an historical character, of whose *incentives to what he does*, ancient historians seem to decline all explanation?

"In another country, however, a tragedy of 'Sylla' has been produced, and its author, M. Jouy, of the French Academy, has, in his own apprehension, found no obstacle in the way. Upon the authority of Montesquieu, that gentleman refers to what can be nothing, or little less than patriotism, not only Sylla's abdication, but even his usurpation of the dictatorship, thus— (I quote from M. Jouy's preface to his tragedy):—

"'Sous la plume de l'auteur de *la Grandeur et Decadence des Romains,* Sylla devient le réformateur de Rome; et veut les ramener à l'amour de la liberté, par les horreurs de la tyrannie, et quand il a suffisament abusé du pouvoir dans l'intérêt de la république, qu'il ne separe pas de ses vengeances personnelles, satisfait de la leçon sanglante qu'il a donné à ses compatriotes, il brise lui-même la palme du dictateur qu'il a usurpé.'

"And therefore—

"'Ce n'est point Sylla si imparfaitement esquissé par Plutarque, c'est ce Sylla si admirablement indiqué par Montesquieu, que je veuille à reproduire sur la scène.'

"But there is no reason, notwithstanding M. Jouy's preference, why Montesquieu, who lived about seventeen hundred years after Sylla, should be authority for his patriotism, when Plutarch, who lived only about two hundred and twenty years after him, says nothing on the subject, nor Appian, who was a contemporary of Plutarch; nor Valerius Maximus, who lived very nearly a century still closer to Sylla. And since Montesquieu could not have derived his reading of Sylla's motives from these authorities, where did he get it?

"There is a point still more perilous to M. Jouy, and a curious and rather astonishing one it is. What M. Jouy says for Montesquieu, that writer does not say for himself. Nay, he says the very contrary, as follows—'La fantaisie qui lui fait quitter la dictature *semble* rendre la vie à la république, mais dans la fureur de ses succès il avait fait des choses qui mirent la Rome dans l'impossibilité de conserver sa liberté.'—And Montesquieu supplies a frightful list of the things which Sylla did, tending to destroy the liberties of Rome. It will further be noticed, from this last quotation, that instead of ascribing to patriotism Sylla's abdication of the dictatorship, Montesquieu, very conveniently for the exercise of his own penetration, absolutely calls his motive or impulse upon that occasion, 'whim,' and nothing else. But the fact is, M. Jouy, in presenting to a Paris audience a tragedy of 'Sylla,' tried, in order to ensure success for his drama, to paint in its hero the character of Napoleon; and, as history stood in the way of such a project, he had very little hesitation in getting rid of it. He hit his mark however, with indeed considerable assistance from Talma, who gave an imitation of the companion of his youth, even to the adjustment of his own stage wig; and the worthy Parisians flocked night after night to enjoy, under the name of the old Roman dictator, the political sentiments, allusions, and even personal peculiarities, of the great chief, then uppermost in their thoughts—I was going to say affections. M. Jouy could have written his tragedy in a fitter view than this.

"Having said so much in admission of the difficulties of the present attempt, I hope I shall not incur the charge of temerity for having engaged in it at all. With very little assistance certainly, I have had to sit down, and, after careful study, venture a new solution of the enigma of Sylla's dark character, and, above all, of the last grand act of his public existence. If I have failed, let me be judged only as severely as the reader's recollections of history will warrant. Nor shall I attempt to conciliate in a preface, his good-natured dispositions towards my dramatic scenes, by a detailed account of why and wherefore I constructed them as they are, for if they do not tell their own story, so far at least, they tell nothing. It is useless trying to argue a man into a conviction of the plausible."

Banim did not, however, by the foregoing observations, intend to depreciate the merit of M. Jouy's tragedy : Banim's drama was one of action rather than of narration ; three years being substituted for the three hours of M. Jouy, and nearly the whole of the non-historical characters of the French tragedy being abandoned. The two first acts of the tragedy, as written by Banim, have no counterparts in that of Jouy :

but the audience scene in the third act is taken from his play, whilst its first sixteen, and six concluding, lines are translated from it: all the intermediate passages are original in Banim's tragedy. The scene between Julius and Sylla in the fourth act is parallel to that between Claudius and Sylla in the French play. The historical situation in the fifth act was open to both, but the incident of Julius attempting to stab Sylla is probably suggested by the scene in the French play, in which the imaginary heroine, Valeria, endeavours to accomplish the same deed; the chief identity, however, between the two plays is the adoption by Banim of Jouy's Catiline.

This tragedy, although completed in the year 1827, was not offered for representation until the spring of 1837, and was performed at the Theatre Royal, Hawkins' Street, Dublin, in the month of June, of the last-named year. Of its cast, and reception, we shall write at the proper time.

Whilst labouring in the old track, with hopes bright and buoyant, amid pains and wants, he lived but in the terrible battle against those ever-recurring illnesses of which he so often writes, yet so seldom complains. And now, to his own woes was added that weak and uncertain health which preyed upon his Ellen. "Repose," said the physician, "is necessary for both." But where was repose for the deep heart that knew no joy save that which sprang from honest, noble, mental work—what repose was there for one whose support was wrung from energetic thought, from—as he wrote— "teasing the brain as wool-combers tease wool, to keep the fire in and the pot boiling." When they told him of repose, of rest, of change of air and scene, and when he marked his own worn and haggard face, which Michael describes as "making him look fully forty though little more than twenty," how bitterly he must have applied to himself the lines of the "Prisoner of Chillon,"—

> "My limbs are bow'd, though not with toil,
> But rusted by a vile repose,"—

for, be it remembered, whilst he could write, whilst *unthreatened* by his physician, he had few regrets; but how sadly must he have felt whilst writing the following letter to Michael:—

"LONDON, *February* 3d, 1827.

"MY DEAR MICHAEL,—For the last week I have been projecting a visit to the southern coast with Ellen, for both our sakes, and under advice. In fact, we both require good air, and everything else calculated to give a new stock of health. Since my last I have suffered much in a relapse, and, though again relieved from absolute pain, remain exhausted and feeble."

This projected visit was not made, for with some few days of revived health came new projects, and now, as in latter years, Banim ever longed to escape the thought that his strength was broken.

In these times of which we write, John Sterling was rising into that reputation so short-lived yet so brilliant, and of which Thomas Carlyle and the late Archdeacon Hare have given us such interesting memorials: young, witty, earnest, and good-natured, Banim and Sterling were formed to love each other; and it is worthy of notice, that amongst all the portraits made of Sterling by his artist-friends, a little sketch by Banim is considered the most spirited and truthful. The regard of each for each was warm and open, and in the following letter to Michael we gather some knowledge of the sympathies by which they were mutually bound. One can fancy John Sterling joining in a debate at the famous Union on "the Catholic Question," and laughing more loudly than Peter Plymley at the arguments of the anti-emancipationists:—

"LONDON, *March 1st*, 1827.

"MY DEAR MICHAEL,—Soon after my last to you I got so well that, instead of running down to Hastings as I had intended, I accompanied, on a visit to Cambridge, a young friend of mine, Mr. John Sterling, a talented member of the University. I was present at a debate on the Catholic Question at their Union. I give this piece of intelligence, apprehensive that you may be terrified at my silence. My excursion has agreed with me; I am now well, and so is Ellen.

"The attention shown me at the Alma Mater of England, and the great interest they take in Ireland, were very gratifying, and joined to the pure air and generous excitement, have made me a new man in point of spirit and nerve.

"Write instanter to
"ABEL O'HARA."

Poor Abel O'Hara! Just six weeks after the writing of this buoyant-toned letter, bitter, bitter sorrows are upon his noble heart. The terrible tortures of his limbs have returned; painful remedies have been prescribed and endured, but with little effect. His wife is sick; his furniture has been taken in execution for debts incurred during his former and present illness;

his pen is idle; his mother is ill; and yet he can, amidst all his many cares, show gleamings of the ever-living love of literature, can urge Michael to renewed exertion, and—most beautiful trait of all—he rejoices that in the new edition of "The Nowlans," the too highly coloured scenes of ardent passion are altered and amended. The letter is as follows:—

"LONDON, *April* 13*th*, 1827.

"MY DEAR MICHAEL,—After all my resolutions, I have not been able to leave London hitherto, and I know you will be sorry to hear the cause. Continued attacks of my old complaint in the limbs, producing almost the command of my medical advisers not to go to the country till I had fully tried the effects of galvanic operations: these are now ended with, I hope, some good result, and our seats taken to Hastings for to-morrow morning.

"I believe I before told you, that I have not been allowed to exert myself since the commencement of this attack. Now I have to inform you (God be praised) that to the present day I have remained almost idle; so that everything connected with our future prospects depends on you—that is, if you have not a new series of tales, ready to be transcribed by me against the 1st of July, we must be out of the market.

"After the loss of my furniture in Sloane Street, my idleness ever since, and the joint expenses of Ellen's medical men and mine, and apothecaries, which is immense, to say nothing of living meantime, my banker's account must be materially influenced. In fact, if I had a bit of despondency in me, this heavy visitation of sickness, with its consequences, would make me hang my head.

But be assured, I still keep a stout heart, and a hope, not without reason, in the future.

"In the second edition of the second series of our tales, just out, I have corrected some of the more glaring improprieties of the first. Again, as to your contemplated three volumes, you have been turning the matter long enough in your mind to be able to go to work, and you must not conclude that everything which displeases you as bad, or *vice versâ*, is so. No man EVER fully completed his own original thought.

"Need I say how grieved I was to hear of my mother's attack. This weather will make her better; at all events if I did not sympathise with her in spirit, I did in body; that is not much comfort to either of us."

To an appeal so touching, so pathetic as this, Michael Banim could not be insensible. "From time to time," he writes to us, "during the year 1826, and in the first months of 1827, I directed all my leisure hours to the composition of a three-volume novel, and the result of my labours was the Third Series of 'Tales by the O'Hara Family'— the novel known as 'The Croppy.' This, like my former tale, passed through my brother's hands previous to publication." It was almost completed when the last melancholy letter reached Michael; the manuscript was forthwith dispatched to London, and from Eastbourne, whither after the date of his last letter he had removed, John addressed the following letter to his brother:—

"45, SEA HOUSES, EASTBOURNE, *June 20th*, 1827.

"MY DEAR MICHAEL,—When last I wrote, I told you I proposed being in town the 1st of June, and asked you to send your manuscripts to Colburn. Accordingly on the 1st of June I was in town, and I got the manuscripts the 2d; such, it is worthy of remark, are the blessings of punctuality, such the agreeable effect of two people being able to rely on each other in their arrangements.

"Days, after my return to Eastbourne, were exclusively devoted to a careful perusal, or rather to careful perusals of your tale. Your anticipations of failure, though they did not convince, put me on my guard against deciding too partially, and precisely, as I felt, I now candidly assure you, that I think you need not apprehend failure in this your trial."

The opinion here expressed of "The Croppy" was fully supported by the opinion of the public—it was, and most justly, considered fully equal in merit to any of the fictions written by "The O'Hara Family."

Rendered somewhat easy in mind by the assurance that the reputation of "The O'Hara Family" was secured for the present, Banim's satisfaction was increased at the same period by the birth of a daughter. He thus announced the event to his mother:—

"EASTBOURNE, SUSSEX, *July* 22*d*, 1827.

"MY DEAREST MOTHER,—I have to inform you that on Friday night last you became grandmother to a big daughter—who gives such proof of lungs, as to disturb the whole village. Amongst the multitude of women now congregated about me I go for very little indeed, in fact I seem of no importance whatever in their eyes."

Banim had been long anxious that Michael should visit him, and now he urged the matter specially, and claimed the visit as one due to him in honour of his child, and as a welcome to her. Referring to this period, Michael writes to us thus:—

"In fulfilment of a year-old promise, I joined the father and mother of the 'big daughter,' in the August of 1827, at the sea-side village of Eastbourne, in Sussex. —When I visited him in 1825, I had observed a sad change in his appearance: he now looked as if twenty years had elapsed since we met. He stooped: his face (all except the eye) was that of an elderly man, and even with the aid of a stick, he could not walk one hundred yards at a stretch. Notwithstanding, I found him still hearty and joyous, and hoping against all probability for recovery. Of course I did not act so unfeelingly as to undeceive him by giving my own conviction. He removed from Eastbourne to Seven Oaks, in Kent, when the winter approached and the sea breeze began too frequently to roar and lash the waters; his health seemed to improve with the change of weather.

"I remained as his guest from August to November, and during this time I put the last volume of 'The Croppy' out of my hands, reading for him every evening the result of the day's work, and adopting his suggestions as I went on.

"I read in MS. at the same time, the rough copy of a tale, which he had put together between whiles and in the lapses between his attacks of pain. This was done without the knowledge of the doctors. He could not submit to the sentence of positive idleness: the tale I allude to was published the year following, under the title of 'The Anglo-Irish.' It was of a different character from the 'O'Hara Tales,' and was not announced as proceeding from the same authors.

"I cannot say how the 'Anglo-Irish' was received—I believe indifferently. The full power of the writer's mind was not brought to bear on it; unhappily, there was a physical inability to strain the brain to its tension at the time it was written."

The reader will remember that a coldness, arising from misconception, had estranged Gerald Griffin and Banim, in the year 1826, and that all correspondence between them had ceased. However, in October, 1827, the following letters were written, and which are here quoted from Gerald Griffin's Life by his brother.

"24, NORTHUMBERLAND STREET, REGENT'S PARK.
"*October* 19*th*, 1827.

"MY DEAR SIR,—I have been endeavouring to find you in vain, since my return to London. I enquired at Mount Street, at Mr. Colburn's, and from Mr. Arnold, but I could only learn that you were then at Hastings. In case I should not be able to see you before I leave London, I wish to communicate in writing what could be done with more satisfaction in person.

"Had I had the pleasure of seeing you before I left England this letter might be unnecessary, and I am very sorry now that I did not. I wish to explain to you more fully the cause of the long silence which we both seemed to expect should be first broken by the other, and the fault of which I am ready to acknowledge, rested with myself. The fact was, I felt hurt by your letter, in which you charged me with wanting a sense of the advantage I had derived from your kindness, (which charge, recollecting the temper of my previous letter, I fear you were not without grounds for,) and acting on that feeling, I wrote again, what I at the time thought ought to be a satisfactory answer. I expected a few words to say whether it had been so or not, but they never came, and thence that absence which you say astonished you. It was an error, I acknowledge, but yet not wholly without excuse. I never entered your house without reluctance, even when you were most warm and kind; excuse me if I could not do so when you seemed to wear an altered face. That, and that alone, was the cause of my absence.

"For the rest I have only to say, I owe you much, and I thank you. If it has seemed otherwise to you, believe my present assurance. It must have seemed otherwise, or you would not have left my letter unanswered. Be a good Christian —forget and forgive.

"I hope to leave a parcel directed for you at Mr. Colburn's, of which I request your acceptance, begging at the same time that you will keep my secret, as it is not my concern alone. I take also this opportunity of assuring you of the sincere delight with which I heard of an event in your family, which must have been a source of much happiness to you.

"I have another favour to beg of you, which I am sure you will not hesitate to grant me. It is, that you will expunge from the play which you presented for me, the passage in the scene between the Irishman and the hero, comprising the few sentences just before 'she talks philosophy.' You may laugh at my introducing this matter, but I am unwilling to trouble Mr. Arnold myself, and the passage may be objectionable. Once more wishing you all the health, happiness, and peace which you can desire or deserve, I am, with sincere esteem and gratitude. "Yours,

"GERALD GRIFFIN.

"My words have so often failed to convey what I intended, that I am not without apprehension, lest by any possibility I should again be misconceived. I wish, therefore, to say once more distinctly—and to entreat you to understand and believe it —that the only feeling at present on my mind, is that of sincere regret for what has passed, and anxiety that you should be satisfied of it. Either in vanity or in folly, or in whatever you please I thought I filled *too humble a part* in the whole transaction, and this made me fretted with myself, and forward to anticipate a slight, where I am certain on proper reflection none was intended. It was not what you deserved, but it was my mistake; your not answering my letter confirmed me in this bad feeling, which, as I have learned to correct, I hope you will no more remember. G. G."

To this letter Mr. Banim at last sent the following reply, which led to the subjoined correspondence, ending in a perfect renewal of their former intimacy and good understanding.

"BATH HOTEL, PICCADILLY, *November*, 1827.

"MY DEAR SIR,—You mistake in thinking that I have ever had the most remote notion of a misunderstanding with you. The last letter we interchanged on the subject of your drama, a year and a half ago, seemed to me quite satisfactory. When you were leaving town about six months after, your note suggesting that some peculiarity, (or a word to that effect, or perhaps stronger,) of your own mind must have caused your previous doubts, I recognised as a most ample, though unnecessary explanation. I became assured you were content, as I was, with our renewed good understanding, and sincerely in this feeling, I desired, in a letter I wrote to Limerick, to your cousin last April, to be kindly remembered to you. I do not know how I shall make further answer to your letter of the 19th October, received by me only two days since; one sentence alone—viz., 'I never entered your house without reluctance, even when you were most warm and kind,'—sounds somewhat strangely to my ear, because, during our years of close intimacy, when your visits were always welcome to me, I had never supposed such to be the case. I have written to Mr. Arnold to the effect you wished.

"The parcel you do me the favour to procure me, has not appeared at Mr. Colburn's.

"I am, my dear Sir,
"Yours very truly,
"JOHN BANIM."

No date.

"MY DEAR SIR,—When I received your last letter (late on November 6th,) I hurried off to the Bath Hotel, in the hope of being able to see you, but was much disappointed at finding you had left it that morning. I am pleased to learn my mistake, but I was led into it by your letter of last January, and, allow me to say, your long silence after my former note on leaving London. Your remembrance I never received.

"You will oblige me by accepting these volumes, which

though faulty enough, may yet answer the purpose for which I send them. I leave London to-morrow morning, and regret much that all my efforts should have failed in endeavouring to see you, the more especially as I do not purpose returning for some considerable time.

"The feeling which renders one reluctant in trespassing on the kindness of a good friend, I can scarcely think so new or strange as you seem to imagine. I should be very sorry it was so; but I ought to remember a conversation on this subject which showed me that your opinions on this matter were different from those of "My dear Sir,

"Yours sincerely,

"GERALD GRIFFIN."

"For 'reluctance' read ' diffidence,' and perhaps we may agree."

"SEVEN OAKS, KENT, *April 17th*, 1828.

"MY DEAR SIR,—Not till the other day, when I ran up to town, did I receive, at Mr. Colburn's, the 'Tales of the Munster Festivals,' with the accompanying note. How long they had previously lain there I cannot tell, nor has a reference to your note enabled me to decide, as it is without date; but I feel very uneasy under the apprehension that you may have sent them about the time of publication, because if you reckoned on their speedy transmission to me, your not hearing from me in the meantime, must have seemed to place me before your eyes in a light very different indeed from that in which I sincerely wish, as I ever have done, to be regarded by you.

"My best thanks for the volumes. I have read them with the highest gratification, and warmly congratulate you on the talents they display, as well as the success they have met with. That you thus at last triumph in a great degree, as I hope, over the neglects and annoyances of your first residence in London, is to me a matter of some triumph also, to say nothing of the pleasure it affords me, because in common with all who were known to you, I claim the foresight of having long destined you to no common fortune in the battle for literary fame. Accept my very best wishes for your continued and augmented success.

"I am very sorry you did not see me at the Bath Hotel last autumn, or that I did not soon after get something like the note that accompanied your tales. The simple explanation of one simple word given in the postscript of that note, would have saved me ever since the exceedingly painful feeling of thinking you unkind; but I now heartily rejoice at being undeceived, and the hand that you hold out I take, aye, and shake, exploded as is the custom, not only with an unalloyed feeling of, believe me, warm esteem and friendship, but with a lightened bosom, and a mind more at rest, than the idea of our estrangement would allow me to experience.

"I hope you will drop me a line very soon. I shall be very uneasy till I know you have got this. Accept my most grateful thanks for the handsome terms in which my tales are mentioned in certain printed pages. Mrs. Banim joins me in kindest remembrances and good wishes, while I remain,
"My dear Sir,
"Yours, truly and affectionately,
"JOHN BANIM." *

As we shall presently find, this revived friendship was a source of deep satisfaction, and the following letter increased this pleasure: how much it increased it, the reader can judge who has marked the deep devotional spirit so frequently apparent in Banim's letters. Upon his first acquaintance with Griffin he had found him embittered by sorrow and neglect, and almost hopeless; he had begun to doubt those divine truths of which he had seldom thought, and, longing to escape from life and sorrow, tried to fancy himself,

"A vapour eddying in the whirl of chance,
And soon to vanish everlastingly."

He was never a sceptic in the full meaning of the term, but he exemplified a grave truth of Charles Lamb's—"Few men think, until forty, that they are mortal;" and this was the secret of Gerald's errors,

* See "Life of Gerald Griffin, Esq., by his Brother," p. 231.

from which the following letter, for which we are again indebted to Gerald Griffin's Life, declares his release :—

"PALLAS KENRY, IRELAND, *April* 22*d*, 1828.

"MY DEAR SIR,—I had the happiness to receive late last night your most acceptable and friendly letter, for which I return you my warmest thanks. It was a pleasure indeed, which I had almost despaired of enjoying, but it was not on that account the less delightful. It made amends, and ample amends to me, for a great deal of bitter reflection—such as I shall be careful never to give occasion for while I live—and it afforded me likewise the satisfaction of feeling that I had not overrated the generosity of your character. Whatever faults had been committed, whatever misconceptions had arisen, I was confident that when I had endeavoured to explain the one, and freely acknowledge the other, you would not continue to withhold from me that friendship which was one of the most valued consolations of my life, and the loss of which I could never have considered in any other light than as a deep misfortune.

"The books I sent to Mr. Colburn's when I was leaving England, a few days after their publication; knowing, however, that you were not then residing in London, I could not be sure that you had received them before I got your letter. I do not know whether I mentioned to you in the note that accompanied the volumes, that I had, immediately on receiving your letter (about ten at night), run down to Piccadilly in the hope of seeing you, but to my great disappointment, I found that you had that day left the hotel. I regretted the circumstance extremely, as I was assured that a personal interview would have done more to accomplish a clear understanding between us, than any written explanation.

"And now, my dear friend, that we do fully understand one another; now that you do so kindly and unreservedly admit me into your friendship—a happiness of which I am prouder than I can easily express—will you permit me to offer one suggestion that may prevent a recurrence of those unhappy mistakes by which I have suffered so keenly. I am often, I see, unfortunate in the choice of my expressions. I seem frequently to mean that which is farthest from my intention, and to convey subject for offence, in terms that are only designed to express esteem and attachment. Let us not, therefore, in a world where we can hardly afford to throw away any rational enjoyment, suffer the sentiment which we may entertain for one another, to be disturbed by any misconceptions to which a letter may give occasion. If a sentence should occur to furnish a subject for doubt, let us meet and speak clearly; and then, if either should be found unworthy of the other's confidence, let him be punished by losing it.

"I have seen, during the last few weeks, an announcement of a new work, from the author of the O'Hara Tales,—'The Croppy,' the action of which is fixed at a period of strong interest—a period worthy of being celebrated by a writer, who is not afraid to encounter a stern and tumultuous subject. I am not familiar with the history of those times, but I remember hearing (indeed it must be known to you) of the burning of a barn—in Wexford, I think—which would have supplied the subject of a forcible episode. But you felt no want of materials for such a work, neither did this circumstance, now I remember, reflect much honour on the insurgents.

"I have to return you my sincere thanks for the kind manner in which you speak of my hasty volumes. I have been long since made aware of their numerous faults, and am endeavouring, as all well-disposed people ought, to proft by experience. But though I am sensible that I should have acted more wisely by delaying their publication and devoting nore time to their improvement, yet I do not regret having put them forward, even if they should procure me no other advantage than that of recovering an old and valued friend. I remember your speaking to me on one occasion, of a work which is greatly wanted at the present moment—a History of Ireland. I should be sorry to think that you had wholly relinquished the idea. It is a subject, however, which affords a fairer field for the pursuit of fame than that of fortune, and on that account is little likely to be popular with writers who are able to accomplish both. I have seen one lately announced—from the pen of some Colonel, I believe.

"Were we now to meet, you would I dare say, find a considerable alteration in many of my opinions. One I do not think it right to withhold from you. You may remember some conversations we had at a time when you lent me a little edition of 'Paley's Evidences.' The sentiments which you then expressed surprised me a little, when I remembered some former remarks of yours with which they contrasted very strongly.

This circumstance, joined with others, led me to a course of study and reflection, which, with (I hope) the Divine assistance, ended in the complete re-establishment of my early convictions. The works which I read were (after Paley's) Milner's 'End of Controversy,' and Massillon's sermons, both very able works. I mention my change of opinion on this great subject, because it is a slight part of the great reparation that is due from me, and I mention the occasion of that change, to show how much good or how much evil a person may do by the expression of his opinions in the presence of others, and how very careful he ought to be in assuring himself that his opinions are correct, before he ventures to communicate them to those with whom his talents and his reputation may give him an influence. An author, my dear friend, has a fearful card to play in domestic society as well as before the public. But why should I take the liberty of pursuing such a theme as this so far? Forgive me for it this single time, as I was tempted only by a deep anxiety for your happiness. I thought, too, that the circumstance above mentioned would give you a pleasure.

"If your brother should not be at present in England with you, will you do me the kindness to present him my best remembrances when next you write. One of those 'fair occasions gone for ever by,'—yet no, not for ever, I hope—which I regret to have lost during my residence in London, is the opportunity I had of becoming better acquainted with him. I had something more to say, but my paper fails me. Is our correspondence to terminate here? I anticipate a speedy and generous 'No,'—for though your time be precious, yet you would not hesitate to devote a few moments to one secluded, as I am here, if you knew the happiness that it would afford me. Present my best remembrances to Mrs. Banim, whose health, I hope most sincerely, is improved, and with the warmest esteem and affection, believe me to be, "My dear Sir,

"Yours faithfully,

"GERALD GRIFFIN."

To this letter Banim thus replied:—

"SEVEN OAKS, *May 27th*, 1828.

"MY DEAR GRIFFIN,—You see I lead the way. Be assured that your last, of April 22d, gives me heartfelt pleasure. My old harp of a heart has a string restored to it. I accept your invitation not to allow anything that may occur in letters between us to start a doubt in future of your friendship or character. Let me add my own covenant. When we meet, treat me more bluntly, off-handedly, and talkatively than you have done. I now am sure that an unlucky diffidence hitherto regulated (or rather disarranged) your social manner. However, I shall be happier with you, if amongst your other recent changes, you have acquired a knack of treating a friend differently, and I close this topic by protesting against your supposing that I here mean an iota which does not broadly meet your eyes.

"Your religious revolutions in opinion I shall not merely congratulate you upon; I do more by sympathising with them; yes, I fear, when we first met and for some time after, that my own religious creed was vague and profane, and I sincerely ask your pardon for any word of mine which may have tended to set you astray. But it is so remarkable that Paley should have been the first to call us back to the right path. And perhaps more remarkable still, that, although mixing up abuse of Popery with proofs of Christianity, he should have helped to make us Catholics, as well as believers in revelation.

"I envy you your life in poor Ireland. My health has been bad since I saw you. I nearly lost the use of my limbs, but can now limp about on a stick.

"I write you a short and hasty letter. Till this day, since I had the great pleasure of receiving your last, I have been very busy and ill enough into the bargain, and this morning I start with Mrs. Banim, to make a long-promised visit to the Rev. James Dunn (a man I wish you knew, the same whom Sheil some time ago speeched praises of) and his lady at Tunbridge Wells, but will not go till I answer your letter, and this accounts, I hope, for the kind of one it is. Pray write soon, and believe me, "Your affectionate Friend,

"JOHN BANIM." *

Not alone to Griffin did Banim thus express his satisfaction. Addressing Michael a few days after the date of the last to his friend, he writes :—

* "Life of Gerald Griffin, Esq., by his Brother," p. 238, &c.

"Another thing puts me into the best of humour—I have recovered a friend. You by this time know my doctrine—that except the loss of health, or the loss of a friend, there is nothing in the world worth fretting for. Poor Gerald Griffin! In answer to ours from the Bath Hotel before we left London, he ran down there. We were gone. Then he sent his books with a letter. I got both only lately. His note was all I could wish. I immediately answered him as I ought, recollecting all his former sufferings and inexperience. This morning I have received from him a manly, delightful letter. He tells me, among other things, that some talk of mine with him has made him, or rather re-established him, in his faith. I found him a sceptic. You may be sure this does my poor head good."

By the address of the letter last written to Gerald Griffin, it appears that Banim had changed his residence from Eastbourne to Seven Oaks, and he thus wrote to Michael, describing his condition. The reference here to his wife and child is characteristic; as the reader will hereafter perceive "sunshine, and a garden not overlooked," were necessary to his perfect enjoyment of the country. We have no more beautiful and manly letter in all these of Banim's now before us, than the following—which seems imbued by that spirit expressed by Tennyson—

> "All the land in flowery squares,
> Beneath a broad and equal-blowing wind,
> Smelt of the coming summer, as one large cloud
> Drew downward; but all else of heaven was pure
> Up to the sun, and May from verge to verge,
> And May with me from head to heel."

The letter is as follows :—

"Seven Oaks, *June* 13*th*, 1828.

"My dear Michael, — But come—my heart is lighter certainly : when I wrote last, I was very ill, shattered to pieces, and the clouds lying down on the roads and fields around me. But I am now better; my spirits capital, my self-dependence (thanks to God Almighty for his gracious protection and help) little abated, several goodly patches of corn in the land, by dint of contributions to the annuals. Ellen running about in our sunny garden, and little Mary shouting to her and to the joy-bells, this beautiful summer day. In fact, there is a delightful sense of existence—and of gratitude to the Giver of *it*, and of the humble—no, the great blessings, he vouchsafes with it, in all our hearts."

In a former part of the Biography we inserted a letter written to Michael Banim by John, and containing, in our opinion, the most admirable rules for the construction and composition of a perfect novel. The following letter is, if possible, more useful to the young novelist, and, if read in connexion with that before inserted, will prove in the highest degree interesting: indeed the outline tale here sketched is, in itself, a highly-wrought incident, and, coupled with the recollections of the fireside stories told by his mother of her relatives, reminds one of the home-pictures in Robert Southey's Recollections of his Early Life.*

This letter has also a peculiar interest, as from the hints, and directions contained in it, Michael Banim was induced to write his well-known tale, "The Ghost Hunter and his Family :"—

* "Life and Correspondence of Robert Southey," edited by his Son, the Rev. C. C. Southey. Vol. i. p. 1.

"Seven Oaks, *November 10th*, 1828.

"My dear Michael,—No matter from what class of life you take your future materials, seek as much as possible for the good and amiable in our national character and habits; as well as for the strong, the fierce, and I will say the ungovernable. How very valuable, for instance, would be a simple dramatic tale, got through by old Daniel Carroll, his wife, his sons, and his two daughters. Here no necessity exists to rake your memory for the great object, *character*. Every one of these I have mentioned, must, from your mother's description of them, live for you. Old Daniel Carroll her father, with his grotesque sun-dials, his forked pendulums—his crude system of philosophy; and his reading, during long evenings, Don Quixote and such books, although so thoroughly pious. Then his wife Betty, you recollect her defence when reprehended for some out-of-the-way expression by her husband. Questioned by him where she had heard the malediction uttered by her. She paused and taxed her memory, and then affirmed she could have heard it nowhere, except it issued from the sinful books he was in the habit of reading. Betty's character is richly primitive. Then there is the son Philip's wild irregular one. The younger Daniel's petty, selfish, cunning. Alley's retaining her anxiety to be thought very devout, not hiding her candle under a bushel meanwhile—then the eldest daughter, our own dear mother, such as she was in her maidenhood. Her industry, her thrift, her mildness—her mother-wit and natural good sense. Her lovers, her starling, her canaries. My dear Michael, if health permitted, I could use these people, and bring their real and unimagined qualities into play, with credit to the Irish character, all Papist as it is, sweetly, primitively, and amiably.

"I remember, too, an old story of our mother's, of a gaunt stone-cutter, killing a slight, delicate young man in a fight, brought on by a quarrel in a church-yard about the right of interment in a certain spot; you must recollect the occurrence, as it was described to us one cold evening as we sat close together round the fire. There was a man once in affluence, who had been a tithe proctor, if I remember rightly. After having spent a long life in acts of petty tyranny, the ban fell upon his hoard, to this day supposed to be inevitable. You and I have often heard that ban pronounced—'A proctor's money never can have luck' —so it fell out with this man; he became very poor, there was no sympathy for him, and he committed suicide—an act, in those days, of rare occurrence; he died too unrepentant and unshriven. No one can be got to inter the body; nor will any of those, whose 'people's bones' rest in consecrated ground, permit the corpse of the hardened self-murderer to rest in contact with the relics of their kindred. The coffin is laid on the public street, none will tolerate it near their dwellings, and it is cruelly dragged along the pavement from place to place, and finally brought back to the door of the house wherein the act of suicide had been committed. A compassionate young man enlists three of his associates—they take off the outcast remains and bear it to a neighbouring graveyard. It is night, and by the light of a single candle, fixed in a lump of churchyard clay, and resting on a tombstone, the three young men are hastily digging a receptacle for the begrimed coffin that lies near them. A gaunt stone-cutter surprises them at their stealthy work. His father's remains are buried close to the spot where they are delving, and he sternly interdicts further progress. The charitable young man who had induced the others to assist him, opposes the mandate; he and the stone-cutter contend fiercely over the graves; the stone-cutter is a strong and powerful man, the other is young and slight; he is struck down by his opponent, and blood gushes from his mouth; recovered a little, he assists to inter the suicide elsewhere. He has been hurt internally, and when he reaches home he is obliged to keep his bed; then the sequel of our mother's tale. Sarah, the proctor's daughter, had been, during the days of her father's prosperity, carefully brought up, and educated for a rank beyond that she could now pretend to in her poverty. While yet lamenting over the appalling termination of her parent's life, she was compelled to witness the cruel indignity practised towards his corpse; and her gratitude was overflowing to him who had charitably borne it away and placed it beneath the clay. She visited him in his illness, and nursed him to convalescence; she taught him to love her, and she married him. But consumption had fastened on the young man, and his days were numbered. His young wife imbibed the fatal malady from him, they wasted away together day by day; she was the first to die, and he followed her very quietly to the same grave."

Referring to this letter, Michael Banim writes to us thus:—

"From the first of the hints given in this letter by my brother, the tale of 'The Ghost Hunter and his

Family' had origin—the personages he indicates had been more than once graphically drawn for us by our mother. They were her own immediate parents, her brothers and sister. They, as well as herself, are faithfully depicted in the tale under the above title. 'The Ghost Hunter and his Family' was originally written by me, framed by my brother, and published in 1833, in 'The Library of Romance,' edited by Leitch Ritchie. No use was made of the second sketch. I did not like the subject. I left it in the suggester's hands, but he never wrought upon it."

In the autumn of 1828, Banim commenced writing a new series of "The Tales by the O'Hara Family"—the title adopted by him for the work was "The Denounced."

It was written amidst pain, and the dread of still greater suffering. He left his cottage at Seven Oaks, and removed for change of air to Blackheath; and from his new residence, he thus, in 1829, wrote sorrowingly to Michael:—

"BLACKHEATH, *April* 3*d*, 1829.

"MY DEAR MICHAEL,—I have been obliged to remove hither. Seven Oaks was too far from London for business, and I longed for change of air. For the last five months scarcely three weeks' work in me, and in consequence, my tale has flagged. Had it been God's will to give me health, it would have been ready before now."

The volumes passed, as usual, through Michael's hands, and appeared in July, 1829, and are not worthy the author of "The Nowlans." One does not, however, wonder that the tales are below the standard of Banim's reputation, when we recollect that they were put together hurriedly; while sickness was a frequent visitant, while the working mental power was available only at frequent and desultory intervals, and while compulsive inactivity, and the inevitable heavy outlay consequent on illness, together with the constant change of residence, in search of the health that was not to return, were causing at the same time a necessity for funds, and an incapacity to create them.

After the completion of the work, Banim's health became more feeble, and in change of air and scene lay his only hope of restoration. On the 20th of August, 1829, he wrote thus, from Blackheath, to Michael:—

"My dear Michael,—We shall be obliged to remove farther from you; I am ordered to the French coast—to a milder climate, and where constant baths can be had at a cheap rate—these I am advised to use freely. I must shift my place when there is a necessity. Anywhere in pursuit of health, for without that precious blessing—I need not conclude the sentence."

This resolution of removing to France was forthwith carried out.

CHAPTER VI.

LIFE IN FRANCE—ILLNESS—LETTERS—DISPUTES WITH PUBLISHERS—COMPOSITION OF "THE SMUGGLER," AND OF "THE DWARF BRIDE"—WRITES DRAMATIC PIECES FOR THOMAS ARNOLD—"THE DEATH FETCH; OR, THE STUDENT OF GOTTINGEN," REPRESENTED AT THE ENGLISH OPERA HOUSE: STRICTURES OF "THE TIMES" ON ITS PLOT—LETTERS—ILLNESS OF BANIM'S MOTHER: BEAUTIFUL TRAITS OF HER LOVE FOR JOHN—LETTERS—DEATH OF OLD MRS. BANIM—LETTERS—KINDNESS OF FRIENDS IN BOULOGNE—TROUBLES OF AUTHORSHIP—DISPUTES WITH, AND LOSSES BY, PUBLISHERS—WRITES FOR THE "ANNUALS"—LETTERS—ILL HEALTH AND PECUNIARY EMBARRASSMENTS—A SON BORN—SICK OF THE CHOLERA; A RELAPSE—PUBLICATION OF "THE CHAUNT OF THE CHOLERA"—PUBLICATION OF "THE MAYOR OF WINDGAP," AND OF MISS MARTIN'S "CANVASSING," IN NEW SERIES OF "TALES BY THE O'HARA FAMILY"—LETTERS—VISIT OF MRS. BANIM TO LONDON—DEBT AND EMBARRASSMENT—AFFECTING LETTER—APPEAL ON BANIM'S BEHALF IN "THE SPECTATOR," AND BY STERLING, "THE THUNDERER," IN "THE TIMES"—LETTER FROM BANIM TO "THE TIMES"—MEETINGS IN DUBLIN, CORK, KILKENNY, AND LIMERICK, IN AID OF BANIM—REPORT OF THE DUBLIN MEETING: MORRISON'S LARGE ROOM GIVEN FREE OF CHARGE FOR THE MEETING: THE LORD MAYOR PRESIDES: SHEIL'S SPEECH: THE RESOLUTIONS AND NAMES OF SUBSCRIBERS AND COMMITTEE—COMMITTEE ROOM OPENED AT MORRISON'S HOTEL: P. COSTELLOE AND SAMUEL LOVER APPOINTED HONORARY SECRETARIES—LIBERALITY OF THE LATE SIR ROBERT PEEL—LETTERS—A SECOND SON BORN—REMOVAL TO PARIS—LETTERS—LINES "TO THE COLOSSAL ELEPHANT ON THE SITE OF THE BASTILLE"—ILL HEALTH; COPY OF OPINION ON HIS CASE BY FRENCH AND ENGLISH SURGEONS—VIOLENT REMEDIES: THEIR UNHAPPY RESULT—LETTERS—ANXIETY TO RETURN TO KILKENNY—THE JOURNEY FROM PARIS TO BOULOGNE; MISHAPS BY THE WAY—LINES, "THE CALL FROM HOME."

"WHETHER Hope and I shall ever become intimate again in this world, except on the pilgrimage to the next, is very doubtful," wrote Robert Southey to Henry Taylor, when grief and sickness were upon him; so it was now with poor John Banim, praying, amidst strange scenes and ways of life in his French home, that he and Hope might once again "become intimate." Like Southey, he never ceased or paused in his labour; it was a sweet labour, which duty sanctified, and thus hoping against hope, and working despite physical pain, his first months of residence in Boulogne were passed. And what months of suffering were these! Months in which the whole past of life, with all its griefs and joys; with all its aspirations and longings— come to fruition or to failure—seemed but as the dreams of a fevered sleep, and nothing was, but the present with its woes, nothing to be, but a future at whose entrance frowned sickness, and want, and disappointment. When hope seemed brightest, when fame and fortune were about to bless him, sickness prostrated him, and, in all the bitterness of bitter grief, he felt the truth of Tennyson's thought, and knew

"That a sorrow's crown of sorrow is remembering happier things."

Ill health was not, however, the only misfortune darkening his life at this period. He had, whilst residing at Eastbourne, commenced the composition of a novel entitled "The Smuggler." In this work he entered upon new scenes of life, all the characters being English, the action being placed in the neighbourhood of Eastbourne; and the scenery being described from the landscape around his residence. The manuscript of this novel was placed in the hands of the publisher in the month of December, 1829, and the book was to have appeared early in the following year; but Banim was sick and helpless in France; disputes as to terms arose between author and publisher; wearying and violent letters passed between them; no progress as to final terms was made, and so, for a time, the matter rested.

He was not, amidst all these troubles, idle; but it seemed as if Providence had ordered that all his efforts to keep his name before the reading portion of the nation should fail. Whilst the disputes relating to "The Smuggler" continued, Banim wrote another tale, entitled "The Dwarf Bride," but the publisher in whose hands it was placed for publication, became bankrupt before the printing had been commenced, and all efforts to discover the manuscript amongst his papers were vain.

Thus, twice baffled in the pursuit of fame, and in neither instance through his own fault (and how he felt this forced absence of his name from before the public the reader knows,—he feared it as a step towards oblivion), there was yet a deeper source of regret, and one which neither money nor facile publishers could remove—his mother was dying—dying, and her own "graw bawn" far away, and never more in life was she to see him. She had been ill during all the year 1829, and at the commencement of 1830, she was only able to move, with assistance, from her bed-chamber to a little sitting-room adjoining. She loved to linger in this latter room, as in it John used to sit; here he had sketched for her a portrait of himself, which now hung upon the wall, and was so placed that it was the first object on which her eye could rest on entering the apartment. And, in this humble room, daily there might be witnessed one of the most touching scenes that the fancy could form. Moving slowly from her bed-chamber, the mother tottered to a chair placed before John's portrait; she sat, and gazed upon it, lost in thoughts—in those thoughts which have been so truly called "bitter sweet,"—then she bent her head as if in deep communion with God, and, gazing still upon the picture, she "blessed herself," and commenced her morning prayer, during which she never moved her eyes from the portrait; and as she prayed, tears rolled down her face; thus, she looked, and prayed, and wept, and exemplified that exquisite reflection of Cowper—

> "And while the wings of Fancy still are free,
> And I can view this mimic show of thee,
> Time has but half succeeded in his theft—
> Thyself removed, thy pow'r to soothe me left."

During the closing months of her life, Mrs. Banim was unable to leave her bed, and then the portrait was placed in her room, where she could look upon it constantly. John longed to see her once more, but his health was not sufficient to enable him to bear the fatigue of the journey; and he wrote to Michael as follows:—

"BOULOGNE, *May 2d*, 1830.

"MY DEAR MICHAEL,—I am now a paralysed man, walking with much difficulty. I move slowly and cautiously, assisted by a stick, and any good person's arm charitable enough to aid me. It is not to add to your trouble that I thus describe myself, I only tell you to prepare you at home for the change. I look well, and my spirit is yet uncrippled. Go to my mother's bed-side as soon as you receive this, and say what you can for me. I think she need not know that I am so lame."

In the month of June, 1830, just seven weeks after the date of this letter, old Mrs. Banim died, and the announcement of her death came with a crushing effect upon the already weakened energies of her son—a son who might most truly proclaim himself, " tender and only beloved in the sight of my mother." He declared that he had never before known sorrow, and was quite unmanned and prostrated by the crowd of calamities which had gathered around and burst upon him, in his time of sorest and most pressing need ; and in a paroxysm of grief and disappointment, he thus wrote to Michael :—

"BOULOGNE, *July 4th*, 1830.

" MY DEAR BROTHER,—You will naturally ask yourself, 'Why has not John written?' My dear Michael, I could not, and I have no explanation, only, I could not. And now I have not a single word to the purpose to say, although after a fortnight's silence, I do write. The blow has not yet left me master of myself. A blow indeed it was. Your letter was suddenly thrust into my hand, and the colour of the wax told me, at a glance, that my mother had left me. I fell to the ground, without having opened it ; I anticipated the contents. You tell me to be tranquil. It is in vain. I never felt anguish before. Yet it is true, that the certainty of the spiritualised lot of our mother, is a grand consolation ; so, also, is the certainty that she died in the arms of those she loved and who loved her.

" Not a very long time shall elapse, if I live, till we

meet in Kilkenny. My wanderings, with God's leave, must end there."

Time healed this wound; with some slight return of health his spirits revived. The quarrel with the publisher of "The Smuggler" was arranged, and it was agreed that the book should appear early in the year 1832; employment as a contributor to the Annuals and Magazines was obtained, and now, as ever, Thomas Arnold was ready to accept Banim's little pieces for the English Opera House.

These pieces were light and ephemeral, and, though generally successful, were not of a character to secure a place amongst the stock plays of the theatre. One, however, entitled "The Death Fetch; or, the Student of Gottingen," was very successful. It was an adaptation of "The Fetches," in the first series of "Tales by the O'Hara Family," and *The Times* thus commented upon it. We must, however, bear in mind that these strictures would now appear out of place, schooled as we have been, by the diablerie and double-shuffling of "The Corsican Brothers." The critique is as follows:—

"It is a dramatic resurrection of the story of 'The Fetches,' which is to be found in the 'Tales of the O'Hara Family,' and has been introduced to the stage by Mr. Banim, the author of those tales. Considering that it is exceedingly difficult, through the medium of a dramatic entertainment, to impress the minds of an audience with those supernatural imaginings, which each individual may indulge in while reading a volume of the mysterious and wonderful, we think Mr. Banim has manifested considerable adroitness in adapting his novel to the stage. We think, at the same time, that his abilities might have been much better employed. The perpetuation of the idea of such absurd phantasies as fetches and fairies—witches and wizards—is not merely ridiculous, but it is mischievous. There was scarcely a child (and we observed many present) who last night witnessed the '*fetch*,' or *double* of the Gottingen student and his mistress, and who recollects the wild glare of Miss Kelly's eye, (fatuity itself, much less childhood, would have marked it,) that will not tremble and shudder when the servant withdraws the light from the resting-place of the infant. Such scenes cannot be useful to youth; and, leaving the skill of the actor out of the question, we know not how they can give pleasure to age. This theatre was ostensibly instituted as a sort of stay and support to legitimate 'English Opera;' and we feel convinced that one well-written English opera, upon the model of the old school— that school so well described by General Burgoyne, in his preface to his own excellent work, 'The Lord of the Manor,' would do more credit to the proprietor of this theatre, and bring more money to his treasury, than 'a wilderness of Frankensteins and Fetches.'"*

The assistance derived from his pay as a play-wright and magazine contributor was not, as the reader may readily understand, sufficient to support him in his illness; and thus embarrassments became more involved. During the greater part of the year 1830, and during the whole of 1831, his letters, though few, were entirely occupied by statements of his sicknesses and of his poverty. A son was born to him in 1831, and here he found, mingled with his gladness at the event, a new sorrow for his wants; but still, as his child smiled, he hoped that Heaven would smile with it, and thus hopeful, he toiled onward until the commencement of the year 1832, when he wrote these few brave, pitiable lines to his brother:—

* "The Death Fetch" was performed in Boulogne, during Banim's residence there: it was translated into French by a friend; during the performance of the piece all children were removed from the theatre.

"BOULOGNE, *January* 20*th*, 1832.

"MY DEAR MICHAEL,—My legs are quite gone, and I suffer agony in the extreme, yet I try to work for all that."

Michael, upon receipt of these lines, wrote to him, asking information as to his position in regard of money matters, and this short note was the reply:—

"BOULOGNE, *February* 25*th*, 1832.

"MY DEAR MICHAEL,—Yes, it is but too true, I *am* embarrassed, more so than I ever expected to be. By what means? By extravagance? My receipts, and my living since I left England, would contradict that. By castle building? No,—'THE VISITATION OF GOD.'"

Whilst thus afflicted he could still serve Michael, and at this same time in which these letters were written, he was reading and correcting Michael's tale, "The Ghost Hunter and his Family," and "The Mayor of Windgap." The former was, as we have already shown, founded upon a dramatic sketch furnished by John Banim, and was published in "The Library of Romance," edited by Leitch Ritchie; the latter appeared in the third series of "Tales by the O'Hara Family," to which Miss Martin contributed her admirable story of Irish life, "Canvassing."

In this year (1832) the cholera was epidemic in Boulogne, and Banim was attacked by it. Weak and worn though we know him to have been, he struggled through the illness; then he relapsed, but, after a fearful effort, survived the second attack. Weak and shattered in body for ever, weak and shattered for a time in mind, this noble-hearted man, who had so long fought against sorrow, and pain, and disappointment, thus wrote to a Dublin friend, then a political and literary leader, and now discharging the duties of an important and onerous post:—

"*November* 28*th*, 1832.

"Sir,—Your generous letter to me on a former occasion is my sole inducement to address you now upon, literally, the question of my life or death.

"Friends, among whom were my physicians, have kindly suggested some such application as the present on their own part; but there are certain avowals which I prefer making in my own person.

"When I had last the honour of writing to you, I was engaged on two works, from which I had been promised results sufficient to re-establish my independence; one, a novel, the 'Dwarf Bride;' the other a drama, the 'Conscript's Sister.' When the first was nearly completed, my publisher, Mr. Cochrane, Waterloo Place, became a bankrupt, and legal advice induced me to lay it by, and begin three other volumes; of these I finished two, (one tale in two volumes) and was proceeding with the third volume, when I took the cholera, and had a relapse. The consequent loss of time and increased expense pressed me to dispose of these two volumes. No regular novel publisher would treat for less than three volumes, and I was glad to dispose to Mr. Leitch Ritchie, for his forthcoming 'Library of Romance,' the tale in question at a very low rate: meantime, my 'Conscript's Sister' ran at the English Opera every night till the close of the season; but owing to the necessities of the manager brought me nothing. I then set to work at other things, until struck down in such a manner that my medical advisers interdicted mental exertion for some time, at the peril of loss of life, (I refer to their certificates,) though with very good hopes, that if allowed rest, freedom from troubles, and change of climate, I should rally and be able to go on. The malady which now so sorely afflicts me has been creeping on me the last ten years, ever since I was twenty-three—(I am not yet thirty-four)— the result of too much labour. In truth, of more than twenty known volumes I have written, and of treble their quantity of matter in periodicals, within the ten years alluded to, no three pages have been penned free of bodily torture; which at last ends in depriving me (temporarily, my physicians say, should this application succeed) of the use of my limbs and brains.

" Under these circumstances, with their inevitable consequences, not only want of present and future funds, but heavy debts, incurred from sheer necessity, my literary friends, French and English, advise me to solicit temporary aid from those favoured individuals of my country who are known (as you are) for literary eminence, or as admirers and patrons of literature, and to whom, at the same time, it has pleased God to afford the means (without inconveniencing themselves) of saving for his family the life of a man who is considered by, perhaps, too partial friends, to have some claims on national sympathy and protection. The grounds assumed by those friends to justify so flattering an expectation are as follows:—

" The circulation of my books through the United Kingdom; their reprinting in America; their having been translated into French and German; and their uniform political tendency, viz. the formation of a good and affectionate feeling between England and Ireland. In my own name I add, that until the hand of Heaven visited me, I am conscious of having passed from early youth a life of industry, always with a view to independence. For instance, (and I quote facts easily ascertainable,) that at seventeen I obtained the first prize as the first draughtsman in the Dublin Academy of Arts; that at nineteen I wrote into wide circulation a Whig journal (the *Leinster Journal*) in my native city of Kilkenny; at twenty-one I received a vote of thanks from a general meeting of the artists of Ireland, for my advocacy with the Irish Government of their demands for an incorporated academy, which they now possess; that at twenty-two I produced a successful tragedy, 'Damon and Pythias,' at Covent Garden; that at twenty-five I was known, at least as a national novelist, even though of an humble order, to European literature; and that since that period, I have written twenty successful novels and five successful dramas. And I trust most respectfully that you will not consider this mere idle boast, but rather as a proof of my deep and conscientious anxiety to show that no habitual want of the pride of independence forces me now before you.

" My friends suggest to me to add, that they consider me called on to make known my position, in order to afford to the affluent protectors of literature the opportunity of saving me from death in poverty, from the misfortune of not having known in time how much might have been accomplished for my family and myself by a prompt appeal to their generosity.

"It becomes necessary to explain within what time my urgent necessities require effectual relief. During the two years and a-half of, I trust, unmerited disappointment, I am in debt 400*l.* ; this I must settle before Christmas, or, in my present state of health, go to prison. A further sum will be required for travelling hence, and living two years in a more favourable climate, every step increasing the expense of a helpless invalid ; but this latter sum would not be absolutely necessary till early next spring, before which time I am not advised to leave Boulogne. For immediate necessities Mrs. Banim would now thankfully accept a part of the first-named sum, as she leaves home without a franc in the house, and borrowing the money for her journey. And now, sir, in conclusion, if I have not minutely described my melancholy feelings on this occasion, or sufficiently expressed my sense of the very great trouble to which I expose you by this application, believe me it is not from a want of understanding my own position, or of duly estimating yours.

"I have the honour to be, &c.

"JOHN BANIM."

The effects of the attacks of cholera on Banim's health were very and lamentably evident. He found himself incapable of continued exertion ; and at a time too when the price of exertion was most needed ; for, at the close of 1832, a second son was born to him ; but life, they told him, could only be preserved by a total cessation from all occupation. This was a hard sentence, and, much perplexed, he thus, announcing it, wrote to Michael :—

"BOULOGNE, *December* 30*th*, 1832.

"It is impossible for me to go on. For the last six months I am under the ban of the physicians, not to work, at the risk of my life. The ban continues for a year. In fact, the cholera so shook me, that the partial paralysis of my limbs extended, and made free with my head. Idleness has made me better, and they give me hopes of health, and continuation of life, if I go on idling, and going about in hired vehicles, and so forth. How is all this to end?"

About three weeks after the date of this letter, Mrs. Banim visited London, for the purpose of arranging the payment of the bills which had been given in part payment of the copyright of "The Smuggler" by the publisher: and she took this opportunity of calling upon some of Banim's literary friends, chiefly his fellow-countrymen, and represented to them her husband's state in health and fortune. All aided her, by placing the matter before the public, but her best and most hearty advocate was the editor of *The Times*, he whom Carlyle has nick-named "The Thunderer," the father of John Sterling.

The Sterlings, father and son, had, during Banim's residence in London, been kind to him; young Sterling had, as we have seen, taken him down on a visit to Cambridge, and had shown him its "lions," and introduced him at the Union. Old Mrs. Sterling had stood as godmother with Michael Banim, for John's first child Mary; and now, early in the month of January, 1833, Mr. Sterling crowned his kindness by writing, in *The Times*, a brilliant and truthful appeal on behalf of his sick and suffering friend. The appeal having been at once supported by *The Spectator*, Banim thus expressed his gratitude in a letter addressed to the editor of *The Times*:—

"BOULOGNE-SUR-MER, *January 20th.*

"SIR,—Accept my grateful acknowledgments for the feeling exertions made by *The Times*, and since, by the rest of the London Press. Through you, sir, I request your kind fellow-labourers to receive my cordial thanks, and perhaps you will allow me to take this opportunity of expressing my feelings on another subject.

"In a very beautiful article on my affairs, which I have seen extracted in *The Courier* of the 14th from *The Spectator*, there is one little phrase reflecting on the character of the place in which I at present reside, the only one penned by my generous though unknown advocate that did not give me the sincerest gratification; for I am bound to declare that in every—the most delicate—sense in which the noble word hospitality can apply, I have experienced it in Boulogne, from French as well as English; that here I found friends, the kindest, the truest, in adversity—in a word, sir, the day of my necessary departure from Boulogne will be to me one of deep regret and affliction, and I pray you to allow publicity to these true sentiments of my heart.

"I am, Sir,
Your obliged, obedient Servant,
"JOHN BANIM."

These appeals excited the humanity and generosity of many distinguished persons. Liberal sums were forwarded to Banim—through Dr. Bowring from the late Earl Grey, and through Mr. Ashburnham from that never-tiring friend of the struggling man of genius, the late Sir Robert Peel.

Ireland was not on this occasion inactive. Much as we neglect the memory of our great dead—of those Kings of Thought who

> "——rule us from the page in which they breathe,"

our people are generally willing to assist the needy literary man, who requires aid in misfortunes which have come upon him neither by his own faults nor by his own vices. After the appearance of Banim's letter to *The Times*, a subscription list was forthwith opened in Dublin, and in Clonmel, and the names entered, during the first day in Dublin, were these:—Matthew Boyle, 2*l.*; F. B. H., 2*l.*; Richard Barrett, 1*l.*; Michael Staunton, 1*l.*; Charles Meara, 1*l.*; Samuel Lover, 1*l.*; A Reader of "The Nowlans," 1*l.*; T. W., 5*s.*

Morrison's Great Room was offered, free of charge, for the purpose of holding a public meeting in aid of the Banim Fund, and such a meeting was accordingly held, on the 31st of January, 1833—the Lord Mayor, Alderman Archer, presiding. The following is a report of the speeches made and the resolutions adopted, with other particulars of this interesting event:—

SUBSCRIPTION FOR THE AUTHOR OF "TALES BY THE O'HARA FAMILY."

"Yesterday, there was a meeting of the friends and admirers of John Banim, the author of 'The Nowlans,' and other Irish novels, held in Morrison's Tavern, Dawson Street. The attendance upon this occasion was most respectable, and comprised men of all sects, parties, and professions. Amongst those present, we noticed the Lord Mayor; the High Sheriff, (Captain Lynar;) Richard Shiel, Esq., M.P.; Morgan John O'Connell,

Esq.; J. W. Calcraft, Esq.; Isaac Weld, Esq.; Thomas J. Mulvany, Esq.; Charles Meara, Esq.; P. Costelloe, Esq.; J. Cumming, Esq.; F. W. Wakeman, Esq.; J. D. Logan, Esq.; P. Curtis, Esq.

"The Right Hon. the LORD MAYOR in the chair.

"S. Lover and P. Costelloe, Esqrs. were requested to act as secretaries to the meeting.

"A letter was read from Mr. Howell, regretting that he was unable to attend, and enclosing 1l. as his subscription.

"Mr. Sheil, M.P. moved the first resolution. The resolution contained a statement of two facts which stood in a melancholy antithesis to each other. It asserted the great eminence of Mr. Banim, as an author who had reflected so much honour upon his country, and the deplorable need to which that distinguished gentleman had been reduced, not by any fault of his own, but by a visitation to which genius and mediocrity were equally exposed. Read a word of Mr. Banim's, and you will see him in imagination placed on the summits of literature; look to the mournful realities, and you will behold him stretched on a bed of pain, in loneliness and in sorrow, and without any other solace than that which is derived from the consciousness that his misfortunes have been the result of long-continued ailment, and not of any violation of those rules of prudence, to the infringement of which men of great abilities are erroneously supposed to be habitually prone. That Mr. Banim was a man of high and surpassing talents was beyond dispute. His works were written with that fidelity to nature which placed him at the head of the writers of fiction of our time. Pathos, derived from the purest and most natural sources—the faculty of imparting a most tender interest to scenes which in ordinary life are attended with incidents of rudeness and vulgarity, which at first view would seem to render them unfit for the excitement of that species of emotion which it is the great end of the writers of romance to produce—a rare dominion over the imagination of his readers, by which he brings the events of his narrative with such a vividness before them, that they almost appear to belong to their own existence, and to be witnessed by themselves—a great mastery of the picturesque—a vast command of diction, glowing and illuminated with brilliant thoughts — these are among the characteristics of Mr. Banim's works. They have won the suffrages of every man, whose opinion is of any value in these countries. The public, by far the best critic, has set a seal upon them which time will not break. There is not a man that hears me—there are few individuals in this great city who have not read, I might be justified in saying, who have not wept over the admirable delineations by Mr. Banim of those strange occurrences which arise in this island of ours, which is so full at once of the materials of merriment and of woe, of weeping and of laughter, and which it requires a mind with such a knowledge of mirth and sorrow, as Mr. Banim possesses, to describe. He is not inferior in his own province to Walter Scott, and if his writings have not obtained as high and lucrative a celebrity, it was perhaps to be ascribed to his having chosen Ireland (to use a professional phrase) for his venue. The English reader did not understand Ireland, and was little qualified to estimate the truth of that likeness whose original he had not witnessed; but it was incumbent on every man who loved letters, on every man who had the least sentiment of literary patriotism, to come forward and raise a man, still young, and capable of doing great things, from the calamitous posture in which the illness of years had placed him. Let Ireland, his own country, lift him up. In England, through the means of the great journal of the empire, *The Times*, a knowledge of his misfortunes had been circulated; the effect, he (Mr. Sheil) thought, would be most serviceable to Mr. Banim. But Ireland had a double office to perform—to relieve a gentleman, who had done her honour, from his difficulties, and to vindicate her own character in rescuing one of those who might be accounted among her chief ornaments, from that ruin in which he was deeply, but not irretrievably, plunged. Let him arise from the couch on which he is laid; let him feel how much he is appreciated; let him drink of that best of all restoring draughts which is to be found in the consciousness of a profound sympathy among those whose kindly opinion is of the best value. Let Banim say to himself, 'My country, from which I am far away, has not forgotten me.' The thought will be a salubrious one. It will be full of health, and confidence, and hope. His pen will fly again to those hands which despair had almost palsied, and he will live to add still more valuable contributions to those masterpieces from which we have derived so much pleasure, but many pages of which were written in anguish which none but those familiar with the calamities of literature can appreciate. (Loud cheers.)

"Mr. Curtis seconded the resolution proposed by Mr. Sheil. The resolution passed unanimously.

"Mr. Weld, in proposing the second resolution, said, that it would be in vain to attempt pronouncing a panegyric upon the great merits of Mr. Banim; these had been already touched upon by a masterly hand—the gentleman who preceded him. It would not be required to bestow any further praise upon Mr. Banim, than by referring to one of Mr. Banim's novels, or tales, for they sufficiently indicated his great invention, and his wonderfully descriptive powers. (Hear.) Mr. Weld then mentioned his first meeting with Mr. Banim, as he was travelling in the north of Ireland, and Mr. Banim reminding him that he (Mr. W.) had been the medium of bestowing upon him a prize for one of his drawings. The consequence of that acquaintance was his giving to Mr. Banim letters of introduction to literary friends in London, not one of whom did not afterwards thank him (Mr. W.) for his making them acquainted with such a man as Mr. Banim. Mr. Banim's career to prosperity was stopped short by illness, and his afflictions were increased by the failure of booksellers by whom he was engaged. When Irishmen saw how Washington Irving was treated by the people of New York—when they beheld every part of the world made tributary to the genius of Scott, he (Mr. W.) was sure that the claims of Mr. Banim upon their gratitude would not be disregarded. (Cheers.)

"Mr. Morgan John O'Connell seconded the resolution proposed by Mr. Weld. The resolution passed unanimously.

"The next resolution was proposed by Mr. Norton, and seconded by Mr. Meara.

"Mr. Burke stated that there were many gentlemen, who were, in consequence of this being the last day of term, unable to attend there, but who had promised him to give most substantial proofs of their sympathy for Mr. Banim.

"The Rev. Mr. Groves, in proposing a resolution, expressed a hope that a new era was arising, as far as literary men were concerned, and that the marks of public gratitude would be conferred upon them while living, instead of being reserved to grace their monuments when dead.

"Captain Lynar (High Sheriff of the city) felt, he said, great pleasure in giving his aid to so excellent an object as that for which they were that day assembled. (Hear, hear.) He was rejoiced to find, too, that upon such an occasion, there was a complete unanimity of feeling and sentiment amongst all parties and all classes. (Cheers.)

"Mr. J. S. Close proposed the appointment of the members of the committee.

"Mr. Kertland said, he felt honoured in being allowed in an assembly comparatively small, but one of distinguished talent, to second the motion. He was glad his friend, the Rev. Mr. Groves, had adverted to the fashion of allowing persons of genius to 'pine in want,' and after their miserable demise, the raising of splendid monuments to their memory.

> 'The poet's fate herein is shown,
> He asks for *bread*, they give a *stone*.'

It would be impertinent, in such a meeting, to do more than remind them of the fate of many a genius who perished by actual want—Otway, Butler, Chatterton, and many others, would arise before their imaginations. Let Ireland begin, and let Mr. Banim and his family feel the full effects of such beginning—

> 'For few can tell how hard it is to climb
>   The steep where Fame's proud temple shines afar,
> Ah! who can tell how many a soul sublime
>   Has felt the influence of malignant star,
> Check'd by the scoff of Pride—by Envy's frown,
>   And Poverty's unconquerable bar?'

He had only further to say, that it gave him pleasure to find in the meeting gentlemen differing on other matters, but unanimous to the call of suffering merit, and would, in conclusion, remind them that,

> 'Seven wealthy towns contend for Homer dead,
> Through which, when living, Homer begged his bread!'

"Mr. Lover pointed out the great advantages to be derived from gentlemen taking upon themselves the office of collectors amongst their friends. As an instance of the advantage to be derived from doing so, he stated that he was now able to hand in 12*l.* 10*s.* subscriptions to their treasurer.—(Hear.)

"Mr. P. Costelloe found, he said, men of all parties most anxious to contribute to the relief of Mr. Banim. (Hear.) Mr.

Banim he had known from his childhood, and no man could be better in every relation of life—it would not be possible to know a kinder friend, a better son, a warmer-hearted brother, a more affectionate husband, or a fonder father than John Banim. (Cheers.) He had known Mr. Banim to perform acts of the most disinterested benevolence, and to relieve the wants of others, when his own means were not very ample. (Hear.) The people of Kilkenny felt honoured by Mr. Banim belonging to them, and they would, ere long, give their countryman the best proof of their regard for him. He moved a vote of thanks to Mr. Morrison, who had the kindness to give them his room upon that occasion. (Cheers.)

"Mr. J. D. Logan seconded the resolution, and stated that he had corresponded with Mr. Morrison upon the subject, and could state the alacrity with which Mr. Morrison had responded to the request for his rooms. (Hear.)

"Richard Sheil, Esq. M.P. was then called to the chair, and thanks having been returned to the Lord Mayor, the meeting adjourned.

"Several subscriptions were paid by the gentlemen present. Ten pounds were given by Mr. Sheil.

"The following resolutions were unanimously agreed to:—

"Moved by Richard L. Sheil, Esq. and seconded by Patrick Curtis, Esq.:

"Resolved—That we have heard, with sentiments of the deepest sympathy, an account of the state of destitution with which our countryman, John Banim, Author of 'The Tales of the O'Hara Family,' and of many other literary productions of distinguished merit, has been reduced by the visitation of a painful and protracted malady, which, prohibiting the exertion of his intellectual powers, has deprived him of the means of support for himself and his family.

"Moved by Isaac Weld, Esq., and seconded by Morgan John O'Connell, Esq.:

"Resolved—That we feel ourselves called upon, as Irishmen and admirers of genius, to use our best exertions towards the relief of an author, whose writings have contributed largely to our intellectual enjoyments, and have elevated the character of our common country in the scale of literature.

"Moved by Thomas Norton, Esq., and seconded by Charles Meara, Esq.:

"Resolved—That a subscription be forthwith opened, towards forming a fund to relieve Mr. Banim's pecuniary privations; and that a Committee of the following gentlemen be now appointed to carry this resolution into effect, and to superintend the management and disposal of the sum contributed:—

"The Right Hon. the Lord Mayor; Mr. High Sheriff Lynar; Rev. Doctor Sadleir, F.T.C.D.; Colonel D'Aguilar, Adjutant-General; Rev. Charles Boyton, F.T.C.D.; Richard Lalor Sheil, Esq., M.P.; James Semple, Esq.; Morgan John O'Connell, Esq.; Patrick Curtis, Esq.; Joseph Burke, Esq.; Thomas Norton, Esq.; Charles Meara, Esq.; J. W. Calcraft, Esq.; George Howell, Esq.; Pierse Mahony, Esq.; Rev. Edward Groves; Frederick William Conway, Esq.; R. Sheehan, Esq.; Michael Staunton, Esq.; Patrick Lavelle, Esq.; Thomas Wright, Esq., M.D.; J. S. Close, Esq.; H. F. Wakeman, Esq.; Ross Cox, Esq.; William Cumming, Esq.; J. W. King, Esq.; J. S. Coyne, Esq.; W. Carleton, Esq.; Thomas Kennedy, Esq.

"Moved by Joseph Burke, Esq., and seconded by the Rev. Edward Groves:

"Resolved—That Isaac Weld, Esq. be requested to act as Treasurer to this Committee.

"Moved by Sheriff Lynar, and seconded by J. W. Calcraft, Esq.:

"Resolved—That our best thanks are due to the conductors of the *Times* London newspaper, for having brought into public notice the destitute situation of Mr. Banim, and for their continued exertions to direct attention to the most appropriate means of affording him relief.

"Moved by J. S. Close, Esq., and seconded by William Kertland, Esq.:

"Resolved—That the thanks of this Meeting be given to Mr. Morrison, for his kindness in affording the accommodation of his rooms on the present occasion.

"The Lord Mayor having left the Chair, and Richard Lalor Sheil, Esq., M.P., having been called to it, it was

"Moved by Thomas Norton, Esq., seconded by Joseph Burke, Esq.: and

"Resolved—That the thanks of this Meeting be given to the Lord Mayor for his dignified conduct in the Chair, and for the lively interest he has taken in promoting the objects of this meeting."

The Committee Rooms were at once opened at Morrison's Hotel, and a Kilkenny man, Patrick Costelloe, and Samuel Lover, were nominated honorary secretaries. Referring to these efforts to relieve his brother's wants, Michael Banim writes to us thus:—

"Public meetings took place, and subscriptions were entered into, in London, Dublin, Kilkenny, and many other places; and from the result, the recipient was enabled to pay heavy debts long outstanding, and I believe unavoidably contracted; and to remain in Paris for two years, while under the care of the principal members of the faculty then practising. His malady, was, however, beyond the skill even of these.

"Throughout the entire period of his embarrassments, and mental and bodily endurance, in France, no one could meet with more sympathy than did my brother. While resident in Boulogne, the English and Irish visitants were most attentive to him. In Paris, he met kindness and service from persons whom he was afterwards vain perhaps of naming as visitants of the sick couch; for a while he was unable to rise without being borne by others. Two only of his visitors I will particularise, the venerable La Fayette and the illustrious Chateaubriand. Many distinguished English residents of the French metropolis were his friends and sustainers. One wealthy Irish lady in particular, he afterwards spoke of with gratitude and affection. I refrain from giving names—those so marked out might not relish the promulgation of their philanthropy."

By slow stages Banim proceeded, towards the end of 1833, from Boulogne to Paris. He had resolved to reside in the latter city, in the hope that, amongst its distinguished physicians, some one might be found who could relieve his pain-racked and powerless limbs. He did indeed consult the most skilful and famous of the faculty, but all their efforts to restore him were unavailing, or worse, injurious.

That the reader may be enabled to comprehend Banim's condition at this period, we here subjoin a written opinion of his case, drawn up, after a careful personal examination of their patient, by two eminent physicians, one French, the other English, whose names the document bears. Banim preserved this opinion most carefully to the hour of his death; the painful remedies, and treatment recommended, and their woful results, seem to have had for him a terrible, gloomy fascination.

The opinion is as follows, but, for obvious reasons we omit the names with which it is signed:—

"The affection under which Mr. Banim labours appears to be chronic inflammation of the lower extremity of the spinal marrow. An attentive examination of its origin, progress, and actual state, has suggested to us the propriety of adopting the following treatment:—

"1st. Dry cupping, and scarifications with cupping on the lower part of the lumbar region, where the pain seems to originate. This treatment to be continued gradually along the spine to the neck: after two or three repetitions it is to be discontinued.

"2d. Small moxas, to the parts where the scarifications were made, and these moxas to be continued, at proper intervals, up to the neck; with the moxas may be used frictions of tartar emetic ointment, along the spine, until pimples appear, the extremities to be rubbed morning and evening with stimulating liniments.

"3d. An actual cautery, applied gently from the lower part of the back to the neck at the interval of two or three inches, would even be preferable to the moxas.

"4th. When this treatment has been used for some time, vapour baths, particularly sulphureous, will be of the greatest possible service.

"5th. The cure will be tedious, but the good constitution of Mr. Banim gives strong hope that he will eventually triumph over his present malady.

(Signed) ————

Paris, le 25me Avril, 1834."

Thus was he treated; "the cupping," writes Michael to us, "the moxas, the scarifications, the lubrications, et cætera, were all performed, as I suppose, very scientifically, and when the body thus experimentalised on left the hands of the operators, the limbs hung useless from the trunk from that time forward. Worse than useless, I would say they were to their owner: their appendage only felt, when they were nightly, and often daily as well as nightly, set quivering by racking pains that made the sufferer writhe and scream from excess of agony; this constant endurance of torture continued without alleviation to the period of his death."

Thus, broken in body, and with one child dead in his home, Banim was declared by his physicians incurable. He was drawn in his bath-chair through the various places of interest in Paris; his daily pleasures were few, and when the day was fortunately painless, the night came on, and with it agony. Often, as he writhed beneath his tortures, he thrust sharp pointed pins through his thighs, as if, by counter tortures, he hoped to check the pangs that came involuntarily upon him.

Still he attempted, even whilst in this state, to contribute to the newspapers and magazines, and he felt now, as he had felt eleven years before when he wrote gaily and so bravely to Michael—"By the life of Pharaoh, sir, if I did not ply and teaze the brain, as wool-combers teaze wool, the fire should go out, and the spit could not turn."

Of the various pieces, in verse and prose, contributed by him at this period to the press, the following is a fair specimen, and first appeared in *The Times:*—

TO THE COLOSSAL ELEPHANT,

ON THE SITE OF THE BASTILLE.

> I know not why they've based thee here—
>   But unto me thou art a thought,
>   With pity, doubt, and sorrow fraught—
> For now, and future, far and near,
>   Because no warning they are taught,
> Can make the careless-cruel fear.
> O'erawing thought! of a giant strength,
>   Who out of love and reason took
> From a pigmy keeper blows and spurns,
> And slight that chills, and scorn that burns,
> And bore all gently, till at length,
>   Love died, and reason could not brook
> Uncharmed by love, one other day,
> The baseness of a coward sway;
>   And then uprose the giant Strength!
>   And round his keeper did enfold
> The wreathings of his mind, and crushed
> His body till the life blood rushed
>   Thro' joint and pore, and the stronghold
>   Of his weak power the giant Strength
> Did trample down—and 'mid its stones
> Trampled upon his tyrant's bones!

Paris, November 8, 1834.   JOHN BANIM.

Friends gathered around him in Paris, and he was happy as his state of health would permit; but his continued prostration alarmed Michael, who tells us—
"In 1834, I wrote to the brother from whom I had been so long separated, urging him to return home; and I did so with the hope, that tranquillity, his native air, and the attentions of his kindred, might be more beneficial than excitement and a foreign climate."

When Banim received this letter, to which Michael here refers, he was happy in the society of some of the most distinguished literary men, French and foreign, resident in Paris; but there was no certain rest or ease from his bodily sufferings, and the "si gravis, brevis: si longus, levis" of Cicero was not a true axiom in his case. He felt his health becoming each day more weak, and thus he wrote to his brother, in reply to the letter advising him to come home once more to his native place :—

"PARIS, *January* 19, 1835.

"I got your letter, my dearest Michael, long enough ago, to have replied to it before now. Nothing but the want of power has kept me so many weeks silent. How could I be willingly silent to it?

"I will go home to you, and to the grave of—another: still, I cannot do so, so directly as you propose.

"Besides, spring will be better than the present season, better than the biting January, for poor cold I."

Poor fellow! he was not, however, to leave France until he had passed through another and most bitter sorrow. The death of one of his children, a boy, has been already mentioned; he had now two, a girl and a boy, surviving at the date of the last letter. He loved them dearly, and none knew better than he the tender, holy truth expressed in those lines of Martin Tupper, which teach that,—

"A babe in a house is a well-spring of pleasure, a messenger of peace and love;

A talent of trust—a loan to be rendered back with interest;"

and the faces, the voices, the laughter of his boy and girl had cheered him in many a weary hour, and now his boy was about to be snatched from his arms for ever. "Tell us," we said to Michael, "of this death, and how your brother withstood the shock:" and Michael wrote to us thus:—

"His daughter was now (1835) in her eighth year, his son beyond four. That dreadful and dangerous malady, the croup, attacked his boy, and he fell a sacrifice to it. I have listened to him for hours of an evening, after his return home, describing the noble qualities, and the affection of this child to him. I have heard him tell how the little fellow would come in from his play, steal gently to the back of the father's sick sofa, and press his soft lips on the hand that lay listlessly hanging over. The first intimation of the child's presence would be this affectionate salutation. And when the father turned his eyes to greet the saluter, then there was a spring into the parent's arms, and a fond, lengthened embrace between them. Other and various excellences he would repeat, when he lay helplessly and discoursed of his affections. Immediately after the date of the last letter, this attached, fond boy was taken from him. He did not write himself, his wife announced to me the fatality.

"' *January* 27*th,* 1835.

"'DEAREST BROTHER,—The first real sorrow I ever experienced came on me this morning. I have lost my noble little son; noble, generous, and good-natured as if he were grown up; and, no doubt, if the Lord had spared him, he would have done honour to his father's name. He is, I hope, this moment communing with your sainted mother.

"'I know not what I write, but I had rather you should learn this through me than through any other channel.

"'When I am more composed I will tell you more about him. The event has almost killed his father; their affection for each other was unbounded.'"

Residence in Paris, after the death of his boy, became painful to him. His life there had been gloomy, and he would now be at home, amidst old scenes and faces, "with memories not all sad." And yet what were these memories not all sad? The dream-land of those days when he wandered with Anne D——; the lost love; the dead mistress; his own long sickness; the debts of the wild days; a dead mother; a broken, ruined body; fame dimmed as it shone most brightly; and now a forced return to all these scenes. Truly might he exclaim of memory:—

> "To me she tells of bliss for ever lost;
> Of fair occasions, gone for ever by;
> Of hopes too fondly nursed, too rudely cross'd;
> Of many a cause to wish—yet fear to die."

But to be at home, to be at Kilkenny, was henceforth his constant longing. There was a beauty in the scenery, a balm in the air, a charm in the Nore, which no other place on earth could now supply to him; and he thus wrote to Michael, explaining his wishes as to the house he desired to secure:—

"PARIS, *April* 30*th*, 1835.

"MY DEAR MICHAEL,—What I require is this. I must have a little garden, not overlooked, for with eyes on me I could not enjoy it. Herein paths to be, or afterwards so formed as to enable three persons to walk abreast. If not paths, grass-plats formed out of its beds, for with the help of your neck or arm, dear Michael, I want to try and put my limbs under me: this is the reason for my last, and to you, perhaps, strange request; but indeed there is a reason, connected with my bodily and mental state, for all the previous matters to be sought for in my contemptible abode, and which I have so minutely particularised.

"If possible, I would wish my little house to have a sunny aspect; sun into all possible windows every day that the glorious material god shines. I am a shivering being, and require, and rejoice in, his invigorating rays as does the drooping sickly plant.

"If this little house could be within view of our Nore stream, along the banks of which you and I have so often bounded, but along which I shall never bound again, it would enhance my pleasure.

"I will begin to go home the 10th of the next month (May): travelling is to me a most expensive and tedious process. Every league of the road will take a shackle off me. My mind is fixed on a little sunny nook in Kilkenny, where I may set myself down and die easily, or live a little longer as happily as I can." *

He was impatient, as we have stated, to leave Paris, and commence his homeward journey ; and so, to use the words of Mrs. Banim, he "bundled everything," and started for Boulogne. Even here, on his journey, his invariable attendant, sickness, pursued him—Mrs. Banim was attacked by typhus fever. He thus announces his position to Michael :—

"BOULOGNE-SUR-MER, *May* 20*th*, 1835.

"MY DEAR MICHAEL,—I left Paris the 10th, as I told you I should do, although much weakened from a regimen to arrest throwing up blood, which happened to me some weeks before. I arrived here the 13th, and was about to cross to England the 16th, when my poor Ellen was struck down by typhus fever, which, fastening on a previous cold, has so inflamed her chest

* This description of the house in which he would pass his future life is very beautiful, and it may interest some readers to mark the similarity between it and that poet's home which Tennyson has so exquisitely described in "The Gardener's Daughter :"—

"Not wholly in the busy world, nor quite
Beyond it, blooms the garden that I love.
News from the humming city comes to it
In sound of funeral or of marriage bells;
And, sitting muffled in dark leaves, you hear
The windy clanging of the minster-clock ;
Although between it and the garden lies
A league of grass, wash'd by a slow broad stream,
That, stirr'd with languid pulses of the oar,
Waves all its lazy lilies, and creeps on,
Barge-laden, to three arches of a bridge
Crown'd with the minster-towers."

and side, that I don't yet know if she is to be spared to me. At any rate, do as well as she can, I must not stir for a month at least—God's will be done. There is always something to be grateful for. Had Ellen taken ill on the road from Paris, amongst strangers, instead of here, surrounded by real affection, how much more must I have suffered.

"Indeed, from men and women, French and English, and Irish, in Boulogne, we find nothing but great kindness."

"*May 24th.*

"I am glad I did not send this yesterday; Ellen is better to-day, and the chances are all in her favour."

As "Ellen is better to-day, and the chances are all in her favour," and as he is on the road towards home, towards Kilkenny, with the garden not overlooked, and the flowers, and the sunshine, and the sparkling, winding, shady Nore, and with the soft warm wind of summer playing around him, and with kind English and French friends smiling by him, and helping him to restore Ellen, he must take up his pen, and he writes, and encloses, in the last quoted letter to Michael—

THE CALL FROM HOME.

"From home, and hearth, and garden it resounds,
From chamber, stair, and all the old house bounds,
And from our boyhood's old play-grounds.

"And from my native skies and airs, which you
Tell me must nerve my wretched form anew,
Breathing forth hopes of life, alas! how few.

"And from the humble chapel path we've trod
So often morn and eve, to worship God,
Or kneel, boy penitents, beneath His rod.

"And from its humble grave-yard, where repose
Our grandsire's ashes and our mother's woes,
That saint, who suffered with a smile to life's last close.

"Brother, I come, you summon and I come;
From love like yours I never more will roam,
Yours is the call from brother and from home.

"From the world's glare and struggle, loving some
And hating none; to share my mother's tomb,
Hoping to share her bliss, brother, I come."

CHAPTER VII.

THE RETURN HOME—LONDON: OLD FRIENDS—LINES TO BANIM BY THE LATE THOMAS HAYNES BAYLY—DUBLIN: MICHAEL BANIM'S DESCRIPTION OF JOHN'S APPEARANCE AND SUFFERINGS—WONDERFUL CHEERFULNESS OF MIND: HEROIC COURAGE—KINDNESS OF IRISH FRIENDS—"DAMON AND PYTHIAS" PLAYED FOR BANIM'S BENEFIT AT HAWKINS' STREET THEATRE—ARRIVAL IN KILKENNY—TAKES POSSESSION OF WINDGAP COTTAGE: LIFE IN THE COTTAGE: THE "SHANDERADAN"—"THE MAYOR OF WINDGAP" DRAMATIZED, AND PLAYED FOR BANIM'S BENEFIT, IN KILKENNY, BY GARDINER'S COMPANY—LITERARY LABOUR—QUARREL WITH MESSRS. GUNN AND CAMERON, PROPRIETORS OF "THE DUBLIN PENNY JOURNAL:" BANIM'S INDIGNANT LETTER TO THEM—DISTINGUISHED VISITORS AT WINDGAP COTTAGE—BANIM'S ENTHUSIASM WHEN THE EARL OF MULGRAVE, THE LORD LIEUTENANT, VISITED KILKENNY: THE "SHANDERADAN" DECORATED, AND BEARING THE INSCRIPTION, "MULGRAVE FOR EVER!"—A PENSION GRANTED—DESCRIPTION OF A DAY WITH BANIM—"FATHER CONNELL" COMMENCED—VISIT FROM GERALD GRIFFIN—HIS LETTER TO MICHAEL BANIM—THE STAGE DARKENING ERE THE CURTAIN FALLS: THE TREE DYING FROM THE TOP.

WHEN Mrs. Banim was pronounced by her physician sufficiently recovered to bear the fatigue of travelling, the poor, broken pilgrim of health commenced his homeward journey.

He rested some days in London, and the old familiar faces, the friends of earlier, and, amidst all their sorrows, brighter days, gathered around his sofa. Amongst these friends, the late Thomas Haynes Bayly was one of Banim's most attentive and constant visitors.

All through life, Bayly was on terms of intimacy, or friendship, with most of the literary men of his time; and we find letters addressed to him from Moore, Rogers, Theodore Hook, Crofton Croker, Galt, and others; but John Banim was his dearest friend.

It was after he had called to see his sick friend, thus returning from France, that Bayly wrote the following lines:—

I.

"I saw him on his couch of pain,
    And when I heard him speak,
It was of Hope long nursed in vain,
    And tears stole down his cheek.
He spoke of honours early won,
    Which youth could rarely boast;
Of high endeavours well begun,
    But prematurely lost.

II.

"I saw him on a brighter day,
    Among the first spring flowers;
Despairing thoughts had pass'd away,
    He spoke of future hours;
He spoke of health, of spirits freed
    To take a noble aim:
Of efforts that were sure to lead
    To fortune and to fame!

III.

"They bear him to a genial land,
    The cradle of the weak;
Oh! may it nerve the feeble hand,
    And animate the cheek!
Oh! may he, when we meet again,
    Those flattering hopes recall,
And smiling say—'They were not vain,
    I've realized them all!'"

London, even with friends like Bayly, could now offer nothing to the poor, broken, world-weary man, comparable to the quiet beauty of the humble resting-place which his fancy had created, and which he hoped to discover amidst the green and leafy scenes of his native place. He quitted London for ever, and arrived in Dublin, at the close of the month of July, 1835.

"When," writes Michael Banim to us, "I hastened up to Dublin in August, 1835, to meet my brother, I could not at once recognise the companion of my boyhood,—the young man, who, thirteen years before, had been in rude health, robust of body, and in full vigour, could scarcely be identified with the remnant I beheld.

"I entered his room unannounced. I found him laid listlessly on a sofa, his useless limbs at full length—his open hand was on the arm of the couch, and his sunken cheek resting on his pillow. I looked down on a meagre, attenuated, almost white-headed old man. I spoke; my voice told him I was near. He started, and leaning on his elbow, he looked eagerly into my face. His eyes were unlike what they had been,—there was an appearance of effort in his fixed gaze, I had not seen before—I had been prepared to meet a change, but not prepared for such a change as was now apparent,— we were not long, however, recognising each other, and renewing our old love.

"When we thus met, John was the wreck of his former self. He was unable to change his position; dependent altogether on extraneous help. To remove from one place to another, he should clasp with both his hands the neck of the person aiding him, and sitting on the arms of his assistant, be carried wherever it was necessary to bear him. He should be conveyed in this manner from the bed to the sofa, and from the sofa elsewhere. It required expertness more than strength to convey him safely,—and when one unaccustomed to be his carrier, undertook the task, his apprehension of falling affected him strongly. His extremities hung uselessly from the trunk, and were always cold,—it appeared as if the vital warmth had no circulation through them; and when out of bed, his legs and thighs should be wrapped closely in rugs and furs, or the heat of the upper portion of the body would pass away through them.

"No day passed without its term of suffering,—for two, or at most three hours after retiring to bed, he might, with the assistance of opiates, forget himself in sleep,—he was sure to awake, however, after a short repose, screaming loud from the torture he suffered in his limbs, and along his spine : the attack continuing until exhaustion followed, succeeded by, not sleep, but a lethargy of some hours' continuance. This was not an occasional visitation, but was renewed night after night. It was not during the hours of darkness only, that he suffered — frequently the pains came on in the daytime—after he endured them all night long, if the weather lowered, or the atmosphere pressed heavily, they were present in the day : to say nothing of his decrepitude, few of his hours were free from agony.

"The account of one day and night will answer for every succeeding day and night; the only difference, a greater or lesser degree of torture. On one occasion, after his establishment at Kilkenny, I visited him about noon, and found him, as at the same hour was often the case, languid and drooping after the night and morning. With a melancholy smile he said, as he took my hand, 'My dear Michael, I can be food for the worms any time I please. If I wish for death, I need only stay abed, and resign myself to what must inevitably follow. If I make no effort against my malady, all will be over in three or four days,—I will not act thus, however,—I will live as long as God pleases. But, come, come, my honest fellow, let us talk of something cheerful,—cheerful conversation is a balm to me. The sun is banishing the clouds; we will have a ride together in the Shanderadan—and look about us, and talk of something else besides my crippled body.'

"In the intervals between one attack of pain and another, and when recovered from the consequent exhaustion, the spirit of the enduring man seemed to rebound, as it were, from its prostration.

"He cheered up,—his brow relaxed from its compression; his eye brightened; and as a smile displaced the contortion of his lip,—and he enjoyed with a high relish everything from which he could extract a temporary gleam of pleasure, anything that could induce a forgetfulness, the mere negative good—the absence of actual suffering—was an enjoyment, and he became even mirthful.

"In the intermissions of extreme illness, his conversation, if I do not judge partially, was very attractive. His youthful sense of nature's beauties would return; and he would become enthusiastic as he pointed out favourite bits of landscape. He would indulge in pleasant badinage. He would discourse of books and theories, or he would sketch vividly the varieties of human character he had encountered through life. It was a blessing to him he had the power to forget, and to make his companions forget also, that he was enjoying no more than a short vacation."

In Dublin, as in London, old and new friends gathered around Banim: literary friends, friends of the early days of artist life, came to him; and the Viceroy, the Earl of Mulgrave, was most attentive and thoughtful in his endeavours to aid the poor, broken sufferer.

As a graceful means of increasing his resources, it was resolved that Banim's fellow-countrymen should be invited to show their appreciation of his genius by attending a performance for his benefit, which it was proposed should take place at the Theatre Royal, Hawkins' Street; and accordingly the following announcement appeared in all the Dublin newspapers of Thursday, July 16th, 1835:—

"Theatre Royal.—Under the immediate patronage of His Excellency the Lord Lieutenant. Mr. John Banim, the author of 'Damon and Pythias,' 'Tales by the O'Hara Family,' and several other National Tales and Dramas, being now in Dublin, his friends deem this a fitting opportunity to call upon his fellow-countrymen to testify the respect and admiration in which they hold his talents. The Theatre will open for this purpose on Tuesday Evening, 21st July, when will be performed, for his benefit, 'The Sergeant's Wife,' dramatised by Mr. Banim from one of his own Tales, and 'The Sister of Charity,' also written by him. There will be a Comic Interlude, with a variety of other Entertainments; the particulars in the bills of the day. Tickets to be had at all the Newspaper Offices; of Mr. G. R. Mulvany, Secretary to the Committee,

24, Upper Sackville Street; and of Mr. Eyre, at the Box Office, where places may be secured."

The entire press supported this attempt to assist our sufferer, and the tone of all their appeals was as in the following, from 'The Morning Register,' of Friday, July 17th, 1835, the day following that in which the benefit was first advertised.

"MR. BANIM.

"It does not surprise, but it affords us, nevertheless, infinite gratification to find, that even already there is a stir, and a great one, for our suffering, but, thank God! not forlorn countryman. High and worthy names, in some number, were put upon the box sheet yesterday. The press, of all colours, lends its willing and creditable aid. We shall, then, have a bumper; but let it *be* a bumper. Posterity will weave garlands for the grave of John Banim, and while they pay the merited tribute to his exalted genius, let there be in their memory nothing giving them ground to cast the reproach of a base and unfeeling niggardness on those who dwelt in one town with him, and were aware of his misfortunes, in July, 1835."

And the following day the same journal thus declares for him :—

" MR. BANIM—DEBENTURE TICKETS.

"There are over one hundred debenture tickets on our Theatre. These, we understand, are for the most part sold— and their action, night after night, on the profits of the concern, help to explain why it is running fast to total ruin. It would be lamentable, we had almost said scandalous, if they were suffered to interfere with the receipts on Tuesday night. We are told that some of the ordinary vendors of these tickets have come to the laudable resolution of suspending their sale, at least on this sacred occasion. We hope an observance, so deserving from its generosity of the highest commendation, will become general, or if it do not, that there will, at least, be few willing to go in a cheap, and sort of back-stairs way, to poor Banim's benefit. The prospects of a bumper are increasing; but let there be no relaxation in the efforts of the friends of genius. Much must be done before that which is intended as an advantage is secured from the risk of becoming a source of new embarrassment. In plain words, to cover the very EXPENSES will require an exertion in the present state of the town."

The performance took place on Tuesday, July 21st, —the Lord Lieutenant attended; the house was filled by a rapturous, overflowing audience; Banim reclined on a sofa in a private box, surrounded by a few of his oldest, and firmest friends; and the following address, written by George F. Mulvany, Esq. was spoken by one of the performers :—

> " This night to welcome to his native land
> A long-lost brother—and to grasp his hand,
> In friendly brotherhood, as warm, as true,
> As erst a 'Damon or a Pythias' knew;
> To-night to cry *caed mile failthe* home,
> I see bright eyes, and beating bosoms come !
> I see the fair, still ever first to breathe
> Soft word of welcome, and still first to wreathe
> For brows victorious in the field of fame—
> Or warrior, or poet—still the same—
> The laurel crown—the dearly—toil-won prize ;
> Ever most treasured when their sunny eyes
> Smile on its freshness.—I behold around
> The noble ! and the brave ! who too have found
> The while from state's, or war's high trammels freed,
> A pleasing pride to win the author's meed,
> And still a crowd—perchance to fame unknown,
> But yet with hearts which Irish bosoms own—
> All here assembled, with soul-beaming smile,
> To welcome Banim to his own green isle !

> " What ! though from country and from kindred forced,
> From all the magic ties of home divorced,

> In other realms the author's lot be cast,
> Where faithful still—true *patriot* to the last,
> To add new glories to his country's name,
> Has been his beacon on the path of fame :
> What !—though his course be one of anxious toil,
> Though his lips fluid, like the fatal oil,
> That feeds the brightness of his midnight lamp,
> When his brain burns—though his brow be damp;
> Exhale too oft—too swiftly in the bright,
> And rapt conceptions of its spirit's light;
> Sapping the system, till the treacherous stealth
> Drives him a *pilgrim* to the shrine of health;
> Bidding him wander back renerved to be
> At life's true spring—the scenes of infancy ?
> Though dark clouds lour—must not the gladd'ning sight
> Of friends assembled as around to-night,
> Repay in part the grateful tribute due,
> And bid Hope's flow'rets blossom forth anew !
> So may it prove to him, whose ev'ry hope
> Hath been concentred in the patriot scope
> Of country's cause—whose labour to unfold
> Th' historic records of her days of old,
> To draw oblivion's dusky veil aside,
> And paint his country's claims with filial pride—
> To him whom HOMEWARD now a soft voice calls,
> Th' awakened echo of O'Hara's halls;
> There, in the magic of his native hearth,
> To feel, fresh springing in *Antean* birth,
> New strength to cope in *Herculean* strife
> With toils and care that track the poet's life,
> To work afresh the unexhausted store
> Of Irish character and Irish lore,
> Rich mine of hidden wealth, of unwrought ore—
> To dare new labours in his country's cause,
> And win reward—and impetus in your applause ! "

Back he went, in the month of September, to his longed-for home. He was so worn and weak, that he could only travel by post-chaise, and the journey from Dublin to Kilkenny required three days in its completion. He went first to the old house, where so many years of hope, of dreaming, of love, of pain, and of memories, "bitter sweet," were passed.

The "little octagon table" in the "sanctum sanctorum" of his father, with the dear mother, and Michael, and the schoolmaster, and the sister around it, reading his praises, and weaving the laurel crown, were the dreams of the dead, cold, forgotten past,—and now he came to the grave of all those things, and even hope itself was dead, and nothing was in memory but pain and woe, nothing in the future but rest which was poverty, and life which was worse than death, in its pains and in its inutility.

Early in the month of September, 1835, John Banim, accompanied by his wife and daughter, and by his brother Michael, arrived in Kilkenny, and his fellow-townsmen received him warmly and kindly. They assembled to consider the best method of showing their regard for him, and their appreciation of his genius; and after some debate, they resolved, unanimously, to present to him the following address :—

"*Address, from the Citizens of Kilkenny,*

TO JOHN BANIM, ESQ.,

AUTHOR OF 'THE O'HARA TALES,' &c.

"SIR,—Influenced by personal regard, and by that esteem which your talents have won, even in far distant lands, your fellow-citizens hail with sincere pleasure your arrival amongst them, though that pleasure is accompanied by the regret that your health is not such as the desires of your countrymen would have it; but they trust that native scenes and air shall tend to your restoration, and that, ere long, a fostering legislature shall extend to you that liberal aid which a good and wise government is ever ready to bestow upon distinguished literary worth.

"Your fellow-citizens have resolved to offer to you some testimony of that respect which native and well-directed talents ever merit—respect due from every Irishman who recollects that your writings have pourtrayed his country in the colours of truth—delineated, without concealment or exaggeration, its national character—sketched its peasantry as they really are, placing their virtues in relief, and tracing their misfortunes and their crimes to the true sources whence both spring —showing this country to the sister-kingdom as it really is, and begetting there commiseration for its sufferings, and esteem for those social virtues and ennobling qualities, which centuries of wrong and bondage have shrouded, but not entombed.

"As citizens of Kilkenny, your claims come still more forcibly upon their esteem. Your pen has preserved many of the beautiful localities in and around this city—given new charms to most of its popular legends, and delineated, with truth and accuracy, many of its original characters, blending the charms of truth with the creations of a powerful fancy, and directing all to the noble purpose of elevating the national character, and vindicating a too long-neglected and oppressed land.

"The citizens of Kilkenny, therefore, hope that you will accept of the token of your countrymen's regard which accompanies this address, and they venture to express their ardent wish that you may live to use it in an advanced and honourable old age, with bodily powers then as vigorous as is that intellect which has won you the proud distinction of fame, conferred an honour on Kilkenny, and an important benefit upon Ireland.

> "Signed, for their Fellow Citizens, by
> "C. JAMES, *Chairman*,
> "R. CANE, *M.R.C.S., Secretary.*"

This address was written by Dr. Cane, and was engrossed on satin, and was presented to Banim with a silver snuff-box, containing in it a subscription of 85*l.*; the snuff-box bore the following inscription :—

> "THIS BOX, CONTAINING A TOKEN OF REGARD
> AND ESTEEM FOR HIS TALENTS,
> WAS PRESENTED TO
> THE AUTHOR OF 'THE O'HARA TALES,'
> BY HIS FELLOW-CITIZENS,
> AT KILKENNY.—SEPTEMBER, 1835."

Banim thus replied to the address of his fellow-citizens :—

"MY DEAR SIRS—With a son's deep affection I returned to my mother land—with a child's delight I re-entered my native city ; and from the moment that I touched Irish ground, after attentively regarding, during many years, other countries, my mind has been gradually and irresistibly impressed with the proud and happy conviction, that among strangers Ireland is at present ignorantly, and, I may add, presumptuously underrated, and that to no country that I have seen is she, in my humble opinion, inferior—except, alas ! in the disunion, and in the consequent poverty, misery, and crime, caused by the born-blindness of those who, unfortunately, cannot perceive that their own proper interests are naturally, derivatively, and inevitably identified with hers. *Superior* to any other country I am not enthusiastic enough to wish to make her; but, in some instances, she has made herself so; yes, in the social and domestic relations—in that glorious quality which we all agree to call *heart;* and, taking one class with another, in true urbanity of manners—and of good manners, too—we may, although her sons, safely venture such an assertion.

"All this you may call the exaggerated glee of a boy sent away to his school, and now asked home to spend his holidays. I will, however, hazard another remark, which perhaps may sound even more like flattery to you, and more like home-prejudice on my part:—no matter, this it is—that of any city or town of Kilkenny's population and resources—considering it also as an inland city—it has not yet been my chance to have observed one equal in beauty of scenic appearance, in the pervading intelligence of its citizens, in unostentatious morality, and above all in public and private charity, to my own dear native place. As to the flattering mention made by you of my Tales, I beg to say that they were inspired simply by a devoted love of our country, and by an indignant wish to convince her slanderers, and in some slight degree at least to soften the hearts of her oppressors; although that in writing in her cause to other nations, I saw the necessity of endeavouring, cautiously and laboriously, to make fiction the vehicle of fact; and while thus, for the first time, called upon to reply to compliments paid to me as the writer of these volumes, I cannot hesitate to mention that a considerable portion of the success of some of the stories they contain, is attributable to the assistance of a dear and respected brother.

"MY DEAR SIRS, I return through you, to my fellow-citizens, my proudly-grateful acknowledgments of their tasteful as well as munificent present; and for your and their kind wishes for my continued possession of it, I also beg leave to offer my heart-felt thanks, assured that no spot on earth can so much contribute to the re-establishment of my health as that of our unique Kilkenny. Allow me to subjoin, that upon this, the earliest occasion when I have had a fitting opportunity to express my sense of national kindness, I hope I may avail myself of it to remind you, that in the beautiful though half depopulated metropolis of our Ireland, I have, on my way here to you, experienced friendships and services, such as even you could not have excelled, and that I now anxiously request my numerous Dublin creditors, to whom, one and all, I own myself a bankrupt in gratitude, to accept this passing allusion as part payment of my deep debt to them. And again I pray you to allow me a parting word. In Dublin, as well as here, flowers of every tint of the political parterre have been condescendingly wrought into a little holiday garland for a very humble brow; and may I not, therefore, take the liberty of asking you, is not this a slight proof at least that Irishmen of all opinions *can* unite in recognising, through the medium of no matter how unmeriting an occasion, that principle, of the perfect and universal establishment of which we all stand so much in need—namely, the great and glorious principle of nationality!

I remain, my dear Sirs, and my dear fellow-citizens, with profound respect and esteem, your faithful humble servant,

JOHN BANIM.

To Christopher James, Esq., and Robert Cane, Esq., M.R.C.S."

Thus was Banim received by the people amongst whom he had passed his boyhood; and as the words of the address told him of their appreciation of his genius, of their pride in his fame, of their sympathy in his sorrows, the brave, strong heart must have grown bright once more, as in the old times when the battle of life was as nothing, but a thing to rouse every faculty, with no doubt or pause; when hope was too weak a term to express the knowledge of certain success,—when to secure success required but work and thought; and then, with John Banim, work and thought made up the whole sum of life, with all joys and griefs centred in them.

We asked Michael Banim to tell us the story of his brother's return; and, of John's first months of the new life in Kilkenny, he writes thus:—

"John was received, in the old house where he was born, by the remaining members of his family: not now, as on his last visit, to boast of his hopes and aspirations: but to tell the tale of his wreck and failure. When I saw him in the old room, where we had been all assembled together thirteen years before, giving credit to the bright visions of prosperity and distinction he then described as in store for him, I could scarcely regret that his mother was no longer with us to witness the present contrast.

"After some preliminary arrangements, the object of our solicitude was established in a suburban cottage close by the road leading to and from Dublin. This cottage was on a height above our river, at the outlet called Windgap, and the scene of one of the tales by 'The O'Hara Family.' After a short residence here, the neighbours knew him *sotto voce* as 'the Mayor of Windgap,'—the title of the tale I have referred to. There were at this cottage dry air, as much sun as any other spot was favoured with, the view of green fields— and from one of the windows a glimpse of our crystal Nore, wending through a beautiful valley—these recommendations, joined to seclusion from observation, were desirable, and guided the choice of 'Windgap Cottage' as the future abode of the ailing resident.

"There was a slight inconvenience, however, which to another would have been trivial in the extreme, but which annoyed my brother to some extent.

"In the spring of 1836, the occupant of Windgap Cottage set to work at the formation of a flower garden, outside his parlour window; and, when the weather permitted, he sat without doors propped in his Bath chair, superintending the operations of his man of all work, as he planted shrubs and flowers, laid down sods, and formed broad sanded walks, in contact with which the invalid still hoped to place his feet. The Dublin road ran outside the high boundary wall of the enclosure, and as the public coaches passed to and from the metropolis, those seated on the outside could look down into the little garden. My brother soon discovered that he had become an object of curiosity and comment; regarded as one of the shows of the road, exhibited by the driver for the entertainment of his fare—he could notice the coachman's whip pointing him out, the exhibitor at the same time turning his head from one passenger to another, as he answered their queries, and then there was the stretching of necks for a view, and comments going the round of the coach.

"On one occasion he overheard a portion of the dialogue passing from the rear to the front of the vehicle.

"'He'll never see the bushes an inch higher,' said a rear passenger: 'He's booked for the whole way, and no mistake,' responded the coachman, chirping to his horses, and smacking his whip artistically, in satisfactory appreciation of his own wit—a laugh went round as the coach drove on. It showed a weakness of mind in the subject of the jocularity, to be so sensible to ridicule; but for the future, he never sat out in the sun, directing the plantation of his shrubs or flowers, when the passage of the coach was expected."

Shortly after Banim had become the occupant of Windgap Cottage, some strolling players, under the management of Gardiner, who, about twenty-three years ago was a performer of Irish characters, in Power's line, at the Abbey Street Theatre, Dublin, happened to be on circuit at Kilkenny; and amongst the company was an actor named De Vere, of very considerable ability, and who was also an excellent scholar, and a man of cultivated taste. This De Vere had been attracted by the admirable "situations" of the tale by "The O'Hara Family," entitled "The Mayor of Windgap," and had, at his leisure hours, dramatized it. This circumstance became known to Banim's Kilkenny friends, and after some consultation it was arranged "The Mayor of Windgap," and "Damon and Pythias," should be performed by Gardiner's company for Banim's benefit. The plan was speedily carried out, and a crowded house and full treasury were the welcome results.

But, it may be asked, how did Banim pass his time? how did he visit his friends? how was he able to leave his garden in search of changed scene, and other air? We asked these questions, and Michael Banim thus replied:—

"Motion and air, for a portion of each day, were prescribed as indispensable for the sufferer's endurance of life: a postchaise and pair was the only vehicle he could use, as he should be supported at his back to the height of his shoulders, and have something to hold by with his right hand. This mode of conveyance, having been indulged in for some months, was found too expensive, and it became necessary to provide some kind of carriage for his own particular use. A gentleman having an old four-wheeled chair lying by, presented it to him, and it was gratefully accepted. On examination this was found unsuitable; but as it had been a gratuitous offering, it was deemed worth remodelling, and much consultation there was as to the mode of adaptation. It was a low chair, in which two persons could sit facing the horse, while the driver took his place immediately in front; there was no support for the back, no grasp for the hand, and no defence against the weather. All these defects were to be remedied. On a stout iron frame, a roof of oilcloth was raised; projecting to the front over the person, a lap of leather, or apron, was contrived, folding over the occupant, nearly breast high; and a stout loop of leather was attached to the iron stauncheon of the roof, through which the arm could be passed.

"Thus added to; the nuts, and bolts, and so forth put into gear, and the whole newly painted, it was tolerably convenient for use; and being unique in structure and appearance, it received from its owner, in one of his lapses from pain, the title of the 'Shanderadan'—a translation, he said, of its rattle and rumble as it went along. After a little use the Shanderadan gave way bit by bit; the axle, the springs, the shafts, the wheels, all of it in fact, became disjointed and broken, and a year had scarcely gone by, when my brother would entertain his visitors with a humorous description of its several dislocations, and his 'hair-breadth 'scapes' in consequence; and he would enlarge on the joint skill of himself and Geoffry Grady, the neighbouring carpenter, who had, the one by plan the other by operation, displaced scrap by scrap, the entire vehicle, so as to leave scarcely any of the primary Shanderadan existing.

"The conveyance held together, however, by constant patching, longer than its occupier. For six years he daily took his seat therein, in his little garden, whenever the weather, and his ailment, allowed him to be abroad—seated in this, or in his Bath-chair, should the Shanderadan be under Geoffry Grady's hands, he received his visitors; and almost daily, while his life continued, he was to be met driving about on one or other of the roads in the neighbourhood of Kilkenny. In the Shanderadan he frequently penetrated into the demesnes of the gentry of our locality, and even into their gardens, and he visited any of the contiguous villages not too distant, to continue his acquaintanceship with the native resorts of his youth. He was seldom without a companion as he went along; at times his wife, at times his brother, but most frequently his daughter, a lovely and loveable child, bore him company. Very frequently he invited any of his visitors, whose conversational powers gave him pleasure, to sit with him during his little excursions. Gerald Griffin was his guest for a fortnight, shortly preceding the death of that eminent writer. And during the term of the visit the brother authors drove out every day together. Griffin was tall, and he was forced to bend his knees uncomfortably to adapt himself to the inconvenient mode of conveyance, that he might enjoy his friend's society."

Poor Griffin! the old times were around him in memory; many a pleasant hour they had at this period; and yet these were hours snatched from physical pain by Banim, and from pangs of a tender conscience by Griffin, for he had begun to think of the past as a void in life, and to look forward to the future years as a period of expiation. He fancied that his novels might be injurious, and as he expressed it, he felt the horrors of "the terrible idea, that it might be possible he was mis-spending his time," or as he wrote to a friend,—

> "Because the veil for me is rent,
> And youth's illusive fervour spent,
> And thoughts of deep eternity
> Have paled the glow of earth for me,
> Weaken'd the ties of time and place,
> And stolen from life its worldly grace;
> Because my heart is lightly shaken
> By haunts of early joy forsaken:
> Because the sigh that Nature heaves,

> For all that Nature loves and leaves,
> Now to my ripening soul appears
> All sweetly weak, like childhood's tears.
> Is friendship, too, like fancy, vain?
> Can I not feel my sister's pain?
> Aye, it is past! where first we met,
> Where Hope reviving thirsted yet,
> Long draughts of blameless joy to drain,
> We never now may meet again.
> At Sabbath noon or evening late
> I ne'er shall ope that latchèd gate,
> And forward glancing catch the while
> The ready door and L——'s smile;
> I ne'er shall mark that sunset now,
> Gilding dark Cratloe's heathy brow,
> Blushing in Shannon's distant bow'rs,
> And lighting Carrig's broken tow'rs;
> No more along that hedgy walk
> Our hours shall pass in lingering talk;—
> For vanished is the poet-queen,
> Who deck'd and graced that fairy scene,
> And stranger hands shall tend her flow'rs,
> And city faces own her bowers."

However, with his "long shanks doubled up," and sitting in the Shanderadan beside John Banim, Gerald Griffin was, as in the old days when he wrote to his brother William, of Banim,—"What would I have done if I had not found Banim? I should never be tired of talking about, and thinking of Banim. Mark me! he is a man—the only one I have met since I have left Ireland, almost."

As they sat by Banim's humble table, he gathered there, to do honour to his guest, all in Kilkenny who were likely to appreciate the mind-gleanings of himself and his friend.

Amongst those thus invited to meet Griffin was an artist, now distinguished in his profession in Dublin, who tells us—" I met them often during Griffin's visit, alone and with others; and 'twas charming to mark their love of each other; Griffin's buoyant spirit seemed to make Banim forget his pains; and he appeared, when speaking of their London life, to fancy himself once more in London. It was all—don't you remember, Gerald?—or, Griffin, my boy, do you recollect? and then, when Griffin sang for him his, Banim's, own songs, he seemed happier than I ever knew him, even in his best days."

In fact, his love for Griffin was so tender and anxious, and yet so proud of its being returned by Griffin, that it took the hue of a kind man's loving regard for a woman: he loved him as Southey might have loved poor Hartley Coleridge, had Hartley shunned the enemy that stole away his life and brains.

Griffin return to Pallas Kenry, and a few weeks afterwards he thus wrote to Banim. The letter is now first published, but one more creditable to the writer's heart we have never read:—

"PALLAS KENRY, *October*, 1836.

"MY DEAR BANIM,—It is with no little gratification I find myself writing to you once more as of old, to ask you how you are, and all who are about you. I have often thought since I left Windgap, that it must have been an ease to you to get rid of me, you kept such continual driving about while I was with you; besides the exhaustion of the evenings, which I fear must have been too much for you in your present state of health. To enable me to pass my time pleasantly I am afraid you made it more unpleasant to yourself, than I ought to have permitted; but I am a great hand at seeing what I ought to have done when the occasion is passed. And now, in the first place, I will ask you—How have you been since? and have you yet had any relief from those terrible pains and sinkings, from which you used to suffer so much and so continually while I was with you? I believe you would think well of the Munster folks, if you knew how kind and general have been their inquiries respecting you since my return. How fervently do I wish that time, and home, and patience, may bring about in you the same happy change which they have often done in other invalids, and enable you again to take, and long to hold, your rightful place at the head of our national literature. This sounds mighty like a fine speech, but let it pass. Would it be unreasonable to ask you to send me that song—*your* song—when you can conveniently do so. I would also wish to have that beautiful little poem you read for me one evening—the lines in a churchyard: some of them have been haunting me ever since I heard you read them. It is time for me to say something of the other members of your family, and to make inquiries for Mrs. Banim and for your sweet little daughter. It is a great blessing that Mrs. Banim's health has held out so well under the severe trials and fatigues to which it has been so long subjected, and most sincerely do I hope that her devotedness and patience may ere long meet some reward, in seeing you restored to at least a portion of the health you once enjoyed. I would be most ungrateful indeed, very ungrateful, if I could ever forget the attention I received both from her and you in London, when friends were less than few. In your present state, it must be a great source of satisfaction to have your sweet little Mary near friends who feel for her the interest which only, or almost only, relatives can feel. Farewell, my dear friend : God bless you, and all you feel an interest in. This is my sincere and fervent prayer. Remember me to your father and brother (who I find was perfectly right about action and re-action), also to your sister. Hoping that you will find my 'shalls' and 'wills,' 'shoulds' and 'woulds,' 'weres' and 'have beens' in the foregoing, orthodox, and hoping far more ardently that they may find you better in health and hope than when I left you—I remain,

" My dear Banim,
" Your sincere friend,
"GERALD GRIFFIN."

About this period the Earl of Mulgrave, now Marquis of Normanby, was Lord Lieutenant, and was hailed by the populace as the greatest and truest friend of Ireland that had ever held the Viceroyalty. Banim joined naturally in the popular opinion, and when the Lord Lieutenant, in the course of his "Progress" through Ireland, was reported to approach Kilkenny, Banim called, in the Shanderadan, upon his artist friend, to whom we have already referred, and, having been carried to the studio, said,

"I want you to paint something for me."

"Do you?" said the artist; "only tell me what and I'll go at it at once."

"Well," replied Banim, "you see there will be a procession to meet the Lord Lieutenant, and I want you to give a touch to the Shanderadan."

"I was," says our friend, "rather taken aback by being requested to make myself something between a coach decorator and a sign-painter; but, upon reflection, I could not refuse the poor fellow, so I enquired what kind of 'touch' he wished me to give the Shanderadan. He said, 'I want you to paint the top and front of it *green*, and to put on the front, in *orange* letters,

MULGRAVE FOR EVER!'"

This wish was gratified; and as John Banim, in the Shanderadan, drove through the city, on the day of Lord Mulgrave's entrance, not a truer or more honest admirer of the Viceregal politics greeted the Viceroy on his way.

Of Banim's every-day life at Windgap Cottage, Michael Banim thus writes to us:—

"His habits or occupations could be but little varied. Reviving from the exhaustion of the night, he arose generally at a late hour; from his bed he was removed to his sofa, and thence to the Shanderadan, or to his chair in the open air. There was then his drive before dinner, again to his sofa, and then to seek such rest as he could find. He could accept of no invitations, owing to his decrepitude; he was sometimes his father's guest, up to the old man's death which took place before John's; he dined now and then with his brother-in-law, and his relatives partook in turn of his family meal—chance guests might call on him of an evening, and then, if not in pain, he was merry, and his spirits cheerful.

"It will be easily credited, that leading the life I have particularised, it was impossible he could employ himself with any continuity at his pen. He said to me once,—

"'Michael, I shall never be able to do anything worth

notice again; I am now only fit for stringing a few loose and pawky verses together; giving out the same odour as the archbishop's sermons in Gil Blas—the energy of my mind is gone with the health of my body—neither of them ever to return.'

"Yet he was not altogether idle—he sent a few contributions to Tait's Edinburgh Magazine—the manuscripts prepared at his dictation by his devoted little daughter, and he put together some songs; many of them sweet and plaintive, but little of power about them. I cannot point to the particular song or verses referred to by Gerald Griffin.

"Before he had been a year residing at home, the welcome news came that the Queen had bestowed a pension on him of £150 per annum—never was the royal bounty more needed, or bestowed on a more helpless claimant. I had hopes at the time that this certainty of the future might tend, by easing his mind, to the abatement of the disease—his own hopes were similar to mine—but there was no amendment.

"I have heard him say, that for this boon, which by removing pecuniary anxiety lightened his sense of endurance, and helped to smooth his passage to the grave, he was principally indebted to the present Earl of Carlisle,* aided by his early friend, Mr. Sheil.

"Amongst other persons of distinction who came to visit him, the Earl of Carlisle, then Lord Morpeth, favoured him more than once by calling at Windgap. My little niece, then twelve years of age, attracted his lordship's observation. The father spoke about his anxiety on her account, and a further pension of £40 was granted for the child's behoof. This was another

* Now, 1857, Lord Lieutenant.

great cause of uneasiness removed—my brother never spoke of this nobleman's kindness and commiseration without evincing the most lively gratitude."

Michael Banim here refers to the tales and poems contributed by John Banim to the periodical literature of the time. Indeed, these short pieces were his sole means of subsistence previous to the grant of his pension ; and to the last hour of his life, literary composition was his best, and surest, and chiefest security against the depressing effect of pain.

Amongst his poetic pieces written at this period are two little poems suggested by his love for the memory of his dead child, his son. How he loved this boy, Michael has thus already told us :—

"I have listened to him for hours of an evening, after his return home, describing the noble qualities, and the affection of this child to him. I have heard him tell how the little fellow would come in from his play, steal gently to the back of the father's sick sofa, and press his soft lips on the hand that lay listlessly hanging over. The first intimation of the child's presence would be this affectionate salutation. And when the father turned his eyes to greet the saluter, then there was a spring into the parent's arms, and a fond, lengthened embrace between them. Other and various excellences he would repeat, when he lay helpless and discoursed of his affections."

It was a beautiful trait in the sick man's character, that frequently, during his bitterest pangs, his memory bore him back to the child's grave at Montmartre ; the following are the lines to which we have referred :—

"TO MY CHILD.

By the quiverings of thine eye, my babe, so quick and sharp, they seem
Revealings of meridian mind before thy time to gleam,
By thy knowledge of our words to thee, although the knowledge come,
We know not by what promptings, for as yet, my babe, thou'rt dumb—

By thine answers in thine actions, babe, so rapid and so true,
Is all that by a word or look we want thee, babe, to do—
By signs like these 'tis whispered, babe, in moments as of fear,
That a spirit winged so early forth, not long can settle here.

In pride, alone, and humble thanks for promised gifts so rare,
That foolish whisper comes to me, of my little boy so fair,
Because by sickness only, I am sure God lets us know,
When he doth wish a living soul back to Himself to go.

And yet, my babe, while you and I this day communed alone,
A creeping of that vain surmise I inwardly did own,
There was such meaning in thee, babe, so startling and intense—
A power in thine up-cast eyes, a pure intelligence—

In accents strange and primitive, in a language bold and strong,
Once spoken in the infant world, though now forgotten long,
I almost thought to hear thee shape the question of that look,
To which, as to a spirit's glance, I for a moment shook.

My dreams! my dreams, I also fear! they do so picture thee,
A little corpse laid at my feet, in sage tranquillity,
And in the middle of the night, my own weak moans do start,
The desolating sorrow from my cramped and quailing heart!"

"AN INFANT'S BURIAL.

Little child, for you
  No passing bell was rung:
Little child, for you
  No burial chaunt was sung:

Little child, for you
   Before your coffin head,
No priest led on the way
   Unto your church-yard bed:

Little child, for you
   No mourning weeds were on,
To show a double grief
   That you to God had gone.

But people paced around,
   With grave and sober tread,
In awe, not tears, to heaven,
   For a gracious infant, dead.

Behind, your father walked,
   Linked with his brothers, two,
And alone, because infirm,
   Another followed you.

And why tolled not the knell,
   Why was the death-chaunt mute—
Why were the mourners there,
   Without a mourning suit?

Why did no follower shed
   A tear, sweet child, for you;
Nay, father and his kin,
   Why were they tearless, too?

Although it taxed them sore,
   And him, the mourner-chief,
Although *he* could have wept
   Aloud, aloud in grief.

Because each well did know,
   Priest, people, father, kin,
That for your loss to us,
   Sorrow were almost sin

That life is misery,
   The more when life is long—
That life is weakness all,
   When life should most be strong.

> And more than this they knew,
>   That God had willed away
> From earth a child of His,
>   Unsullied by earth's clay—
>
> As yet unstained by crime,
>   Before his Maker's face—
> And therefore sure to find
>   In heaven a resting place."

The lines are not, we are well aware, either very poetical or very striking; but they show the phases of a longing, loving mind; of a soul all love and hope, of a heart young amidst care and grief—a heart that would not be crushed.

A friend who visited Banim, at this period, thus describes his conversation and mode of life:—

"I had left the town behind, and my route led along the Dublin road, when a small dwelling overlooking the path announced the author's villa. A wooden door opened to my summons, and admitted me into a small court-yard bordered by a trimly-kept plot of garden ground. A lad was wheeling an invalid in a Bath chair round the gravelled walk. I needed not to ask; I knew it must be Banim.

"Quickly I approached, and put my card into his hand. 'Mr. Banim,' I said, 'pardon this intrusion; but I could not be a day in Kilkenny without paying my homage to a genius to whom Ireland owes so much. I have written a little myself, and therefore felt bound to come and see you.'

"He took my hand, and pressed it warmly. 'I have read your work with pleasure,' he said, 'and am thankful for your visit. Come in and rest after your walk.'

"'Pardon me,' I replied, 'if I decline just now. The walk here is nothing, and you are enjoying this lovely day. Continue your jaunt, and I will walk and talk with you.'

"The boy resumed his propelling motion, and I chatted with the gifted Banim. I had full leisure to observe his features, which were long and delicately formed; his high forehead, denoting intellect, and soft eyes ever lit with flashing thoughts. When he removed his hat, his hair seemed grey, 'but not with years,' for I do not think he was much more than forty; but with mental excitement, and much privation and acute bodily suffering, (he then laboured under rheumatic paralysis, which deprived him of the entire use of his lower limbs,) had told upon his brown tresses, and silvered his head.

"We spoke chiefly on literary topics. He declaimed powerfully against the low state of literature in this unhappy country, which he attributed to the prohibition of learning in the time of the Penal Laws, from the effects of which the great mass of the people were but slowly recovering—how it was impossible to derive any considerable pecuniary emolument from writings in Ireland. 'Moore told me,' he said, 'if he had confined his labours to Ireland, he would be a beggar.' He spoke rather feelingly of the neglect of men who had the means, but not the will, to make his sojourn in his native place more agreeable, and hinted at the Marquis of Ormond. Tears of gratitude sparkled in his eyes as he related a visit not long before paid him by the Lord Lieutenant, the Marquis of Normanby. If men of that class only knew how prized a few kind words—some pithy notices of judicious praise—are to the sensitive minds of authors, methinks they would be less chary in giving what, at all events, costs nothing.

"I mentioned my regret at his invalid state, and asked whether change of air might not be serviceable? 'Ah!' he said, 'I have tried that, and it was of no use. I was in France—at Boulogne and in Paris—and the contrast between my reception at Paris and here is painfully great. There I was made too much of. My soirées, which, unlike the extravagant parties in this country, I would give for about a dozen francs, lights, cakes, café, and eau sucré forming the chief items in our bill of fare, were attended by the élite of the French capital. The nobles, by birth as by talents, took pleasure in attending. I found my health rapidly declining, and indeed I came home to die. My God! I shall never forget the humiliation of feeling I experienced on landing at Kingstown. Judging from the misery that everywhere met my sight, I felt as if the Irish had nothing to be proud of except their beggars.'

"I described my ramble over the city that forenoon, and the interest which his tale of the Roman Merchant gave to the churchyard of St. Canice.

"'That is a singular incident,' he replied, 'and well worthy of being wrought into three volumes: I wrote that tale one evening between dinner time and tea. It is quite true. The stranger's tomb is in the wall, near the entrance.'

"Banim now directed his servant to turn his steps towards the door, and, by the help of crutches, entered his dining-room. Here we were shortly joined by a gentle little girl, with pale, thoughtful face, and auburn hair, Banim's only child; she spoke but seldom during my stay, but her remarks betokened an intellect far beyond her years. She seemed a great pet of her father's, and no doubt the fervour of his genius communicated a warmth which caused hers to expand.

"Of those we love, unconsciously we learn. Mrs. Banim also entered, and I was introduced to her; she showed great solicitude about her husband, enquiring how his drive agreed with him, and appeared obliged for my visit. She was evidently proud of the renown he had acquired, and felt every call the homage he had a right to receive. She spoke rather reproachfully of the conduct of his countrymen in general, who seemed to take little interest in the declining health of one who had done such honour to the soil.

"Banim soon resumed his literary conversation, and we talked much of poets and poetry. He took down a volume, and read part of Shelley's 'Faust,' and I sat by entranced—never was poetry more eloquently written, and never was poetry more eloquently read. It was a glorious thing to hear such strains so sung.

"But Ireland was the theme most upon his lips, and the love of country glowed in his bosom ever and always. 'We have been sadly neglected,' he said, 'and the works which are written on this country seldom give a correct notion of the people. Mrs. Hall writes too like Miss Mitford, and therefore too English to be correct. We want a cheap periodical.'

"I mentioned the 'Dublin University.'

"'It is a good magazine for the hands into which it falls,' he replied; 'but too much devoted to party to be national.'

"He repeated some of his own poetry—very touching and intensely Irish. I remembered an incident which occurred, as he thought, at the Clare Election, when two adverse factions were reconciled by the amicable meeting of the leaders long at variance. Banim wrote the following stanzas on the event, which he called 'The Old Man at the Altar:'—

> "An old man, he knelt at the Altar,
>   His enemy's hand to take,
> And at first his weak voice did falter,
>   And his feeble limbs did shake;
> For his only brave boy, his glory,
>   Had been stretch'd at the old man's feet,
> A corpse, all so haggard and gory,
>   By the hand which he now must greet.
>
> "And soon the old man stopp'd speaking,
>   And rage which had not gone by,
> From under his brows came breaking
>   Up into his enemy's eye—
> And now his limbs were not shaking,
>   But his clench'd hands his bosom cross'd;
> And he looked a fierce wish to be taking
>   Revenge for the boy he lost.
>
> "But the old man he glanced around him,
>   And thought of the place he was in,
> And thought of the promise that bound him,
>   And thought that revenge was sin—
> And then, crying tears, like a woman,
>   'Your hand!' he cried, 'aye, that hand,
> And I do forgive you, foeman,
>   For the sake of our bleeding land!'"

When Messrs. Gunn and Cameron resolved to publish "The Irish Penny Journal," they were anxious to engage the services of Banim, as a contributor; the monetary differences, too usual between author and publisher, arose, and bitter complaints were made by Banim, answered by declarations of the publishers, that he was irregular in his promised assistance.

Sick, weary, and irritable, Banim became impatient, and enclosed the following letters to his ever faithful friend, Michael Staunton, then the editor and proprietor of " The Dublin Morning Register :"—

"KILKENNY, *September 17th*, 1840.

" MY DEAR STAUNTON,—Should you consider the accompanying letters fair matter for the notice of the Irish Press, I beg to leave them at your disposal.

" Ever truly yours,

" JOHN BANIM.

"M. STAUNTON, Esq."

" Office of the General Advertiser,
"DUBLIN, *August 21st*, 1840.

" SIR,—For anything new, and which will be suitable, we shall, if it be first-rate, pay as high a price as any one; and more can hardly be expected from the publishers of such a work as ours.

" When we commenced the PENNY JOURNAL, we certainly were foolish enough to suppose that 'patriotism' (that is the word) might possibly induce *some* ONE Irishman to aid us with his pen in our arduous undertaking—not certainly gratuitously, but at a moderate rate. We have, however, already lived long enough to be undeceived. We have always, it is true, found Irishmen exceedingly kind in their professions of patriotism, and verbally, very fervent in their hopes, that every Irishman capable of contributing to the PENNY JOURNAL, ought to aid us with his talents, and so forth. But we are constrained to say, that we have always found these loud professions coupled with an immediate demand for not only the highest price for their contributions, but a greedy desire to clutch as much as possible from those who, if not more patriotic in reality than themselves, have not had the disgusting hypocrisy to avow a feeling they did not possess. It is not the demand for remuneration, for this is but fair; but it is the invariable profession of patriotism which is so offensive—that patriotism, we find, being bounded by their lips and pockets. At the time we first wrote to you, we were very desirous of obtaining your contributions, because we then thought that your name as an author and contributor would assist us in launching our little work successfully.

"We have now, however, found that its unparalleled progress has depended more upon our own efforts than upon the aid of others; and are, therefore, much more indifferent. If you had assisted us then, you would have obliged *us;* if you contribute now, it will be to oblige yourself.

"We are, Sir,
"Your obedient Servants,
"GUNN & CAMERON.
"To JOHN BANIM, Esq."

"KILKENNY, *September 17th*, 1840.

"Messrs. GUNN AND CAMERON,—When you first applied to me to contribute to your penny periodical, a member of my family informed you that from illness I regretted I could not do so; lately I repeated the assertion to account for my not sending at a later date anything new; but the respect due to at least severe suffering—I put forward to *you* no other grounds for your forbearance—has not been at hand to protect me, and, through me, the whole literature of my country, nay, the character of that country itself, from the gross, though absurd and contemptible insolence of your letter of the 21st of August.

"But I have no further answer to that impudent shop-boy letter; trusting, however, to make such use of it as may help to deter future adventurers in Ireland from repaying with offered insult, the hearty support of, perhaps, a too generous people.

"Continued indisposition must again account for my delay in answering your communication.

"JOHN BANIM."

This was an unhappy quarrel; and one must regret that the publishers had so little consideration for the author's condition. As Johnson said of Collins, "When sickness or want are at the door, a man of genius is little calculated for abstruse thought or glowing flights of airy fancy."

There are,—there have been,—hundreds of men who, with not one-half John Banim's genius, and afflicted with not one-hundredth part of his sufferings and his sorrows, would have become misanthropic, and cold, and harsh, even to those nearest and dearest to them by every bond of relationship, of sympathy, and of friendship. Not so with Banim; broken in health, powerless for work, weak in all that a brave, strong soul would wish to possess in full, complete, and vigorous strength, still he was the MAN as in other days, and sickness, or pain, or grief could not depress his spirit.

Thus writing, talking, suffering, and—amidst all his sources of despair—ever hoping, John Banim lived on. He was happy in one blessing,—his mind was as strong as ever; and he, like Johnson, had prayed that his intellect might continue vigorous to the last; like Swift, that he might not die from the top, while the leaves and branches were undecayed.

But strength to do was passing away, even while the will to do was eager; and in the following sketch, Michael Banim gives us an account of the last joint literary work of the authors of "Tales by the O'Hara Family:"—

"I had laid by my pen to devote myself entirely to business from the period of my coadjutor's break down in 1833. It will be recollected, that in one of the letters from which I have extracted, my brother threw out the suggestion, that we should write a novel, of which an old parish priest might be the hero. In 1840, five years after his return home, relinquishing on his own part all hope of being able to take up anything requiring continuous application, he urged me to resume my occupation, under his immediate supervision.

"I had, some time before, filled a note-book with materials referrible to the latest agrarian confederacy, that had disturbed our neighbourhood, the actors in which had bestowed on themselves the fantastical name of 'Whitefeet.' With some of the principal leaders of this lawless and wide-spread combination I had held intercourse; I had gained a knowledge of their signs and passwords, and obtained an insight into their views and proceedings. I proposed a tale wherein my materials could be used; my adviser differed with me.

"'We have given,' he said, 'perhaps too much of the dark side of the Irish character; let us, for the present, treat of the amiable; enough of it is around us. I once mentioned our old parish priest to you; the good, the childishly innocent, and yet the wise Father O'Donnell; we have only to take him as he really was, and if we succeed in drawing him life-like, he must be reverenced and loved, as we used to love and reverence him.'

" I sat down as proposed, when time, not indispensably engaged otherwise, enabled me to do so; I read for my brother each chapter as the tale progressed; when I had put it out of hand, he took it up for revision and amendment. I have, ever since, regretted having allowed him to do this. According to his conception, the tale required extensive alterations as to style and management : I may have differed with him; but, adhering to our original mode of proceeding, I did not object either to substitution or condensation. The task was too continuous for his disorganized brain, and I fear that, although his daughter, then fifteen, and a young man who resided near the cottage, acted as occasional amanuenses, his death was hastened by his more than usual occupation on the tale of ' Father Connell.' In some instances the original was condensed; and one entire chapter substituted.

" 'Father Connell' was the last joint work of the O'Hara Family. John's attending physician, although not pronouncing positively, led me to think he might have held out longer, if he had not wrought, for him, too ardently at this book.

" Not presuming for one moment, that the tale of ' Father Connell' possesses merit as a novel, I may be permitted to remark, that it is so far of value, inasmuch as the character of the old priest who governed the parish of St. John, in Kilkenny, when my brother and I attended in our muslin surplices at his vesper choir, and partook of his twelfth-night feast of cakes and ale, is attempted to be faithfully pourtrayed. No matter how meagre may be the colouring, or how ill-disposed the lights and shadows, and relief, the likeness is a true one, without flattery or exaggeration; no virtue feigned, or habit imagined: such as he is given under the name of 'Father Connell' was our parish priest, the Rev. Richard O'Donnell, Roman Catholic Dean of Ossory, when the writers of the tale were young."

From the period of the publication of 'Father Connell,' Banim's health began to decline, and, more perceptibly than ever, he was wearing away. How his life faded into death; how his last literary labours were performed; and how his last hours passed, we shall now relate.

CHAPTER VIII.

CLOSING DAYS OF LIFE—DEATH—PENSION GRANTED TO HIS DAUGHTER—DEATH OF HIS DAUGHTER—PENSION GRANTED TO MRS. BANIM—MEETING CALLED IN KILKENNY TO ERECT A PUBLIC TESTIMONIAL TO BANIM—RESOLUTIONS AND NAMES OF COMMITTEE—TESTIMONIAL ERECTED—CONCLUSION.

WE left John Banim with the shadow of death around him; the mind was waning—the tree was dying from the top—the stage was darkening as the curtain fell. Yet life was about him, and he longed for life. Those who watched by his bed in these days tell us of the time, in memories bright and gloomy—recollections which have in them as many smiles as tears.

One friend, not his brother, who lived in daily intimacy with Banim during these times—who knew his phases of thought, his modes of composition; who watched the clouds and sunshine of his mind—has written, at our earnest request, the following narrative of Banim's last months of life :—

"*February,* 1857.

" MY DEAR SIR,—In consenting to your request that I would supply you with some written recollections of the late John Banim, I have had to overcome a great deal of reluctance, which I very naturally felt when reflecting on the extreme delicacy of such a task, and the readiness with which many people take offence in matters of biography, where none is even remotely intended. Your urgent importunity and my own desire to oblige you, however, have prevailed in the present instance, but I must observe *in limine*, that I greatly fear you will be disappointed, if you calculate on finding much, or any at all, of what I have to say worthy of being transferred to your pages.

"I had some notion of putting what I had to say into the shape of a consecutive narrative; but considering there was so very little incident in the life of Mr. Banim, after his return to his native city, and during the period of my intimacy with him, that the history of one day might well be regarded as embracing this whole term, I feared I should produce a rather dull chapter, and, therefore, concluded it would be better to throw the substance of my recollections and observations under the headings suggested by a reference to your first note to me respecting the points on which you were desirous of obtaining information.

"First, then, as to his

MODE OF LIFE AND HABITS.

"My acquaintance with the author of the 'O'Hara Tales' began in the latter months of 1836, about a year after his return to Ireland. He was then residing in Wind-gap Cottage, which does not require to be described by me, as, if I rightly remember, it has been fully noticed in a former chapter. Here, sheltered from the public gaze, and safe from intrusion, he received only such visitors as he chose, and at such times as he thought proper to admit them. Though his limbs had now, for some time, refused to obey his desire to move, his mind was still vigorous and active, and enabled him, under an incredible amount of bodily suffering, to continue his literary pursuits, indulge his natural tastes, and labour to form those of his daughter.

"He seldom rose in the morning earlier than eleven o'clock, and, if the weather at all permitted, had himself conveyed from his bed-chamber to a Bath-chair in the little enclosure that fronted the drawing-room window. The chair was provided with pillows and cushions, which it was Mrs. Banim's or Mary's special duty to see properly arranged, as the organization of his poor frame had become so sensitive that even a crumple was sufficient to cause a momentary agony. After a few turns round the circular bed of flowers which occupied the centre of the garden, he would order breakfast—a morsel of thin, dry toast, a rare egg, and a cup of tea. This despatched, the chair would be again put in motion, and the exercise continued for an hour or so, when he would have himself placed under the shade of either of the two trees which stood at opposite points of the enclosure, and devote the intermediate hours between that and three o'clock to writing or the care of his flowers, of which he was so passionately fond, that he frequently insisted on being carried out at night to ascertain, by the light of a lanthorn what progress his favourites were making. He bestowed particular pains on the culture of a rose unique, which was afterwards affectionately transferred, by his daughter's hand, to the turf under which he rested, and, when last I visited his grave, was the only mark by which it could be distinguished from the narrow dwellings of the humbler dead around.

"When three o'clock approached, the business occupying him, whatever it might be, was immediately laid aside, orders given to have the horse put to a little 'machine' in which the pillows and cushions had been previously arranged with the same care as the adjusting of the chair required in the morning, and, accompanied by his wife or daughter, or some other esteemed friend, for he feared going out alone, he would proceed on the drive which, at this period of the day, he never under possible circumstances failed to take. This exercise seemed to be essential to his existence, for, if anything occurred to debar him from its enjoyment, he could not resume his occupation for the remainder of that day, but became dull, peevish, and uncomfortable, making every one about him share more or less in his unhappiness. On returning from his drive another process was to be gone through before undertaking the *labour* of dining—the table had but little *pleasures* for him for years before. An extraordinary chilliness invariably seized his whole body, particularly his lower extremities, on the cessation of the rapid motion of the carriage. To get rid of this disagreeable sensation he used to submit himself to a particular operation which he humorously termed 'shampooing.' A field-labourer who lived close by was generally called in, by whose rough, horny hand, he had himself briskly pinched from head to foot for a full half-hour, when his natural warmth would begin to return, and the business of the dinner become practicable. The shampooing was regularly repeated before retiring to bed at night, and before leaving it in the morning.

"Whenever the little carriage was disabled, which was a circumstance of frequent occurrence, or that a horse could not be procured—he had not always one of his own—recourse was had to the Bath-chair as a substitute for the drive, and, accompanied by Mrs. Banim and Mary, who occasionally lent it an impulse from behind, some friend of the other sex having generally volunteered to place himself at the front, the scheme sometimes succeeded exceedingly well, while it almost as often involved its peculiar difficulties and even perils. When once equipped, if there was any spot sufficiently near commanding a prospect which he once admired, or presenting a natural beauty with which in youth he had been familiar, an endeavour was made to reach it, every practicable route being sought, and none considered too circuitous to avoid the public road, and escape the public gaze. Many were the obstructions which the unfortunate chair had, in such excursions, to encounter; many an intricate way was entered without ever reflecting on the possibility of effecting a return; and often and often the limbs of the poor invalid had to repose on the grass till the chair had been carried over obstacles there were no other means of surmounting. His eagerness on one of these occasions to reach a spot on the banks of the Nore, endeared to him by some early recollection, was near having a fatal termination. The spot alluded to was to be gained by descending a gentle slope, as it appeared to him, at the base of which the stream flowed smooth and deep; none of the party present apprehended the slightest danger in gratifying his desire, and the chair was at once, and without reflection, turned in the direction indicated. But a very little progress, however, had been made when the motion of the little hand-carriage became too rapid for the control of the ladies who were to act as a drag in the rear; and had not the gentleman in front, by a sudden twist of the guiding wheel, and by dexterously placing his own person right in its way, succeeded in arresting its onward movement before it had acquired its full impetus, no human power could have prevented his being precipitated into the river, whereby the 'stubborn Nore' would have obtained with posterity the melancholy interest of having afforded Banim a grave. It would be impossible to describe the terror that, for the moment, took possession of him, heightened, as it was, by the consciousness of his inability to help himself; but the arrangements for effecting a return were no sooner completed than he commenced jesting at the probable catastrophe from which he had escaped, and ridiculing Mrs. Banim and Mary for their weakness in having yielded to womanly fears on the occasion.

"There was another circumstance, too, connected with his excursions productive of no small inconvenience to Mrs. Banim in the way of domestic arrangements, but which her 'hereditary generosity' enabled her patiently to support. The roads and green lanes in the neighbourhood of Kilkenny, in the latter of which the little carriage of our poet was frequently seen to pause on summer evenings, abounded at that time, at all events, in specimens of human misery which a sensitive heart, however well acquainted with the devices of mendicant hypocrisy—a species of knowledge in which he considered himself deeply skilled—could scarcely help commiserating. Whenever anything in the appearance or the story of one of these unfortunates seemed to speak of better days, or deserve a better fortune, he or she, or they—sometimes the case would comprise a whole family—had orders to follow the carriage or the chair home to Wind-gap, where, when their comforts had been attended to, lodgings would be procured, and, if the subject was a fitting one, an effort made to procure a service, or some kind of permanent employment. Some act of theft or ingratitude was generally the return for his excessive kindness; still, the very next day, a tale of woe would find as ready entrance to his heart as if he had never erred in his judgment of the narrator of one. Amongst the guests here alluded to was a deaf and dumb boy, of about fifteen years of age, who had been discharged, or else had made his escape, from the Glasnevin Institution. Picked up one summer evening in the usual way, as Banim was enjoying his customary exercise, he was, of course, directed to come to Wind-gap, where his quick intelligence, docility, and eagerness to make himself useful, soon rendered him a general favourite. For nearly a month he presented himself regularly at the cottage, at the hour its master was wont to make his appearance in the garden. His face would beam with pleasure whenever Banim began to interrogate him, or invited him by means of slate and pencil or the telegraphic movement of his fingers, to draw the chair or water the flowers. He disappeared, however, like a young wolf, when he was thought to be quite domesticated, and without any apparent reason. He is mentioned here merely as an instance of the changes men's opinions often undergo with respect to the theories of their earlier days. The 'Revelations of the Dead Alive' shows what a sceptic Banim was in the doctrines of phrenology, and his sincerity in the ridicule of that science at the time the above-mentioned work was published; at this period, however, so firm was his creed in the soundness of its principles, that he never left this boy at the cottage when going out to drive, without placing him in charge of the man who was employed to do the 'shampooing,' as he apprehended some dreadful consequences might result from an opportunity being presented for gratifying the animal propensities which he fancied were indicated by his cerebral conformation. Here are facts to illustrate his

LOVE OF KIND,

which, far from being confined to his own immediate friends, was for ever displaying itself in some one or other species of action, having for its object the moral or social improvement of so much of the humbler classes, collectively or individually, as came within the scope of his influence.

"In close proximity to Wind-gap Cottage stood a newly-erected school-house, a fine spacious building, and at the time, perhaps, superior to any provincial structure of the kind in the kingdom; it was the work of Michael Banim's untiring zeal in the cause of education. He spared neither time nor labour in collecting subscriptions, soliciting donations, or superintending the tradesmen engaged in the work. Indeed, in his eagerness to complete the undertaking, he made considerable advances from his private means, which were never repaid him. The national system was then in its infancy, and by no means popular; Michael Banim was, however, amongst the first to perceive its advantages, and he entertained sanguine expectations of achieving the happiest results for the children of the poor of his native city from a combination of those advantages with the free character of 'Father Connell's' charitable institution. With this view the idea of a National Free School, to supersede the theatre of 'Mick Dempsey's' labours, to be still governed by a committee of the Society which had been founded for the support of the honoured seminary, which, it is hoped, Banim's pages have now immortalized, the members whereof (comprising every respectable individual in the community) still met occasionally and paid their small quarterly subscriptions; and to differ only from its predecessor in the enjoyment of a Government grant, was conceived and executed.

"The result of Michael Banim's labours was not what he expected. The building being pronounced fit for occupation, the committee met, and, through improper interference, from private motives, an incompetent person was elected to take charge of the new school, in opposition to the wishes and advice of the gentleman who had originated the plan, and done so much to carry it out and secure its success. Michael Banim, of course, ceased to take further part in the proceedings of the committee; the members of the Society began to refuse subscriptions, on the ground of the support to be derived from the Board of Education, and to declare off altogether; few or no pupils made their appearance, on account of the prejudice that existed regarding the National system, and finally the Board of Education withdrew the gratuity, not recognising the claims of a school, in which no effort was made to promote the objects for which the Board was instituted. Such was the condition to which 'Mick Dempsey's' once flourishing realm was reduced on Banim's return to Kilkenny. He regretted the disappearance of the old thatched roof under which the shivering limbs of so many poor children were made to experience annually the blessings of Father Connell's charity, and that of many another benevolent spirit long after the pulse of that commiserating heart had ceased to beat. The handsome edifice which replaced it was but a poor compensation, in Banim's opinion, for the good that had departed with it, and in the general apathy that prevailed with regard to the matter, he resolved to take upon himself the task of reviving the society, and of turning the fine new schoolhouse to some practical account at least, if the ancient utility of the old one could not be restored. For this purpose he put himself at once in communication with the Education Board, to request a renewal of the connexion, and with the local clergy, to secure an attendance of pupils. Both these objects attained, he succeeded in interesting Mr. Keoghan,—one of the Catholic curates of the parish, and a gentleman for whose zeal as a minister, and acquirements as a scholar, he had the greatest esteem,—so much in the furtherance of his views, that the latter readily consented to accompany him on a questing excursion amongst the quondam subscribers. On a fixed day, accordingly, the carriage was ready at an hour much earlier than usual; and, Mr. Keoghan being punctual to his appointment, both gentlemen proceeded on their mission; the following day was devoted to the same object, and a sum was collected far exceeding all expectation. Banim's glee was great on the evenings of both these days, he and the clergyman congratulating themselves over a glass of sherry (which being plentifully diluted with water, formed his favourite beverage) on their eminent success, and laughingly relating how, by judiciously flattering the wives, they succeeded in obtaining both arrears and current subscriptions, when the surly husbands would persist in obstinately refusing payment of either. Alas for the mutability of human things! the good Father Keoghan was carried away in a few months after by a malignant fever, caught in his attendance on a patient at the County Fever Hospital; Banim is scarcely remembered in his native city; while few, if any, know if there ever existed such a body as the once famous 'St. John's Parochial Society.' But to return. One week after Banim had formed his resolution, the school was in efficient working order, and had an impetus communicated to it which bore it beyond the chance of again sinking into the condition from which his efforts had raised it. Nor did his solicitude in regard to it stop here; many an hour was snatched from other important business in order to pay a visit to the school. On these occasions it was necessary that the chair and cushions which he used at home should be sent before him, by which there was given timely intimation of his approach—a circumstance which frequently caused him to allude to his infirmity in terms of mingled pleasantry and sadness, and to observe how lucky it was for both teachers and pupils that they need be in no apprehension of ever being taken by surprise. And yet he would sometimes express himself on these and other occasions so as to lead one to think that he did not, at least at that time, quite despair that such might one day be the case.

"Having taken possession of his chair in the schoolroom he would summon before him the various classes in turn, explain the subjects of the different lessons, lecture on the elements of grammar and geography, in the latter of which he would use his clenched hand with great effect as a substitute for a globe, when it was necessary to explain why the figure of the earth was usually represented by two circular pictures, &c., and communicate all sorts of knowledge in such popular language, and in a manner so fascinating, that the little students were always sorry when his visit terminated. He bestowed many marks of favour and encouragement, too, on such of the boys as exhibited marks of talent. There was one in particular for whose future way in the world he was resolved to interest himself; but chancing, during an evening drive, to surprise him in the act of lighting a collection of straw which he had heaped on an unfortunate hedgehog, for the purpose of forcing the poor animal into a state of activity, and thereby furnishing pastime to a crowd of associates, he abandoned all his kind intentions towards him, and, save reading him a severe lecture on his cruelty, never again noticed him in any of his subsequent visits to the school, which were only given up when increasing feebleness rendered it impossible to continue them longer.

Besides the improved system of education which he was the means of introducing into the school, he had in contemplation another project for still further elevating the taste of the generation then springing up around Wind-gap Cottage. It was the establishment, if possible, of light theatrical performances, in connection with the school, somewhat after the fashion of educational institutions of loftier pretensions. The practicability of the scheme was often gravely discussed, and its success considered certain. The musical and dramatic talents of the artisans of the 'faire citie' had been celebrated even before the time of Moore's theatricals there, and I may safely add were sufficiently noticeable at this time, at least, to be considered characteristic. From those, in conjunction with the pupils attending the school, he reckoned on being able to form a tolerably efficient company; the school-room he pronounced admirably adapted for the purpose of a theatre; and one of his own short pieces, which required but simple scenery and moderate artistic skill, would afford suitable material for a first attempt. The rehearsals and other details were to be an affair of personal superintendence, and the recovery of a little even of his former strength was all that was required to put the design in immediate execution. This he kept fondly promising himself was some time or other to return; the hope of renewed health, as long as he was capable of hoping, never completely deserted him; it was a vain expectation, however, and so the experiment was destined to remain untested. The same cause prevented him from giving the world a work, the plan of which had been conceived some years before, and for which considerable materials had been collected; it was to have been entitled the 'Lies of History,' and dedicated to his daughter.

"When discussing his theatrical project, he would lay it down as a maxim, that a high moral style of drama was a test of a country's greatness; that it fostered the seeds of nationality, and matured its fruits; that it should be regarded as amongst the most powerful instruments of refinement and order; and that to cultivate and spread a taste for it was a task becoming every man truly desirous of regenerating his country or protecting her independence. His impressions in this respect seemed founded on grounds furnished by his own special case; for questioning his daughter, one day, on the subject of her school exercises, and looking through the little pile of books from which she had been preparing her various lessons, he expressed some surprise at not being able to discover amongst them the one which of all others he most wished to see in her hands; and to her request to be informed to what particular book he alluded, he replied that it was the old 'Scott's Lessons,' or 'Speaker,' as that once popular treatise on Elocution was more generally called, adding, that—taking into view the whole circle of his youthful discipline—the study of the dramatic selections comprised in it had had by far the largest share in the process which formed his mind. Indeed, the 'rival near the throne' of the realm of theatrical recitation, whom James Charles Bucmahon, (Buchanan, for he was a real character, as I need scarcely say almost all Banim's were,) the master of the English Academy, suspected he was one day to encounter in the person of the young hero of 'Father Connell,' was no other than little John Banim himself. It was little John Banim's forefinger of the right hand that used to define with such exactitude the orb of Norval's shield; his little head that was wont to drop as naturally asleep on the form in the old schoolroom, as if it were the genuine royal couch on Bosworth field, and then express by such unmistakeable signs the mortal terror that had disturbed his slumber; and it was from his little fist, when personating Will Boniface that 'the imaginary ale' was quaffed with the smack and relish that were accustomed to draw tears of laughter from the good old priest, and throw the rough but warm-hearted housekeeper, who had never in the course of her life seen anything approaching a veritable actor, into a fever of delight, forcing her to vent her approval in terms so near the line in Shakspeare, 'He doth it as like one of those harlory players as ever I see!' that a listener unacquainted with her unromantic nature might easily be betrayed into the belief that she actually meant a quotation from the bard.

"He was not, however, by any means so much of a visionary as to allow a theory, no matter what it might have for its object, or how large a share of his attention it might claim, to interfere materially with his serious occupations; indeed, it was only under the most favourable circumstances as to health and leisure, that he purposed his present plan should be worked out. Whilst the chance of such a happy state of things was becoming every day more unlikely, though not so as to assume the appearance of an utter impossibility, a portion of a company, just then disengaged by the periodical closing of one of the Dublin theatres, arrived in Kilkenny, and the local newspapers were requested to acquaint the public that a series of performances would be forthwith given in the 'Assembly Rooms' of the 'Tholsel,' under the management of Mr. Gardiner, a comedian of established reputation, assisted by some of the most distinguished names in the profession. Amongst other great feasts to which the citizens were to be treated, there appeared announced in very prominent characters, 'Banim's "Mayor of Windgap," dramatised for the occasion by a member of the company.' Mr. Banim regarded the announcement with pleasure; believing that the story could be effectively used in that way by a skilful hand, and that the thing would not be attempted in his immediate presence, unless executed in commendable fashion. He awaited the performance, therefore, with some interest, hoping that the result would prove creditable both to himself and the dramatiser. It was evident, however, from the first scene, that the gentleman who undertook the task was possessed of more temerity than talent. Mr. Gardiner's humour, indeed, secured him some applause in his personation of the Mayor's Bailiff, a character which had been sketched with such fidelity in the original, that, much of its individuality as it had lost in its transmutation, it was still easily recognised, and 'Bryan Sweeny' resounded from all directions of the house each time he made his appearance. Bryan Sweeny was the real name of the worthy who sat for this portrait to Banim, and though some years had elapsed since the decease of himself, and the corrupt old corporation of which he had been an officer, the identity was at once admitted by all who had been familiar with that model official. In the remainder of the details the piece bore so little resemblance to the original, that it would seem the title of 'Mayor of Wind-Gap' was bestowed on it only as the best means that could be resorted to for the purpose of 'filling the house.' This report of the affair annoyed Mr. Banim, and for a time he felt almost as mortified as if the failure could be attributed to his own production. He bitterly observed that he believed there never yet was a scribbling fool who did not fancy he could write a play, and who, failing to give the world some ridiculous production of his own, did not disfigure somebody else's. Anxious to impress his fellow-citizens with a more favourable opinion as to his powers as a dramatic writer than what they could be expected to entertain from witnessing the performance just alluded to, and ambitious of having one of his own pieces represented in his native city, he proposed to Mr. Gardiner to bring out 'The Conscript Sisters,' which had been written for Arnold's Theatre, and acted there with eminent success. Gardiner perused it, but finding it did not come quite within the range of his own or his company's talents, he returned it to the author, who was thus debarred the only remedy that presented itself for the outrage committed on one of the most exquisite of his O'Hara Tales."

Taking up the narrative from this point, Michael Banim writes to us :—

"Late in July, 1842, I left home to spend a fortnight with some friends forty miles from Kilkenny: when parting from my brother, I could perceive no change for the worse in his symptoms or appearance. I was suddenly summoned home in consequence of his dangerous illness. I returned at once. I found him barely able to recognise me—only able to take my hand and look in my face, but incapable of speaking. I saw at a glance that his time of suffering was nearly over. I attended on him until I closed his eyes. His struggle against death was an enduring one. His chest and lungs were sound and healthy, and he continued to breathe strongly, but not painfully, for a day and night after all consciousness had left him. Death was rather the extreme of exhaustion than a violent separation of the spirit from its prison. Life passed from him almost unperceived.

"Frequently, during the last six years of his life my brother and I had been together, he engaged my promise that I would stand by while his grave was digging, that I would see the side of his mother's coffin laid bare, and that when his body was lowered to its last resting-place, I should be certain the side of his coffin was in close contact with that of his beloved parent. His instructions were religiously observed.

"There are two portraits extant of the subject of your memoir; one, in my possession, painted by himself* when in his nineteenth, or approaching to his twentieth year; the other remaining with the talented artist of whose pencil it is the production, Mr. George Mulvany, of Dublin; the last mentioned taken after the total failure of health. Both these pictures are excellent likenesses of the original at the different periods of life when they were painted. Placing them side by side, it would require almost a stretch of the imagination to trace a resemblance between them, or to acknowledge them as representations of the same person.

"I have not attempted, in any of my notes furnished you, to measure my brother's claims to literary distinction. His merit as a poet or novelist I have not sought to weigh or to decide on. I have contented myself with giving a faithful account of his early and more mature endeavours to establish the reputation he thirsted to attain. The range and quality of his genius as a writer I leave to more disinterested parties than myself to ascertain and define. I think I may claim for him, however, numerous amiable qualities, springing directly from the heart, the seat of the affections; and many valuable qualities emanating from the head, the formator of character.

"His affections were ardent, impulsive, and uncalcu-

* This is the portrait of "her own graw-bawn," before which old Mrs. Banim, John's mother, used to pray.

lating. He was industrious, persevering, and self-reliant, so long as his physical capabilities enabled him to be so.

"It will be borne in mind that he died while yet young, and that, for fully thirteen years preceding his demise, the physique of his mental power was not in health, nor the full force of his mind at his command. At forty-four, his age when he died, men of genius begin to train the flights of imagination and fancy within the scope of reason, to prune exuberances, and to contrast with judgment.

"I think I may affirm that, had it pleased Providence to have given him health during the thirteen years he was an ailing and incapable aspirant for fame and independence, and to have prolonged his life until he had descended even but little from the summit of existence which he had not reached, he would have made good way towards the goal he had marked out ultimately to reach. I am confident that, had health and life been his, he would have advanced much closer than he did to 'Fame's Magnetic Altar,' the bourne to be attained, as expressed in one of his early rhymes.

"About to close my subject, I will here reiterate the opinion I mentioned to you when relating the termination of his boyish passion. I still think that the peculiar ailment causing death, and which for some time baffled the skill of the most eminent medical men, had its origin at the period of this early calamity. I judge that his brain was then injured, and that the subsequent overworking of the seat of thought brought on the spinal disease, which first paralysed his limbs, and finally extinguished life.

"My brother left behind him a widow and an only child, his daughter Mary. I have stated that this beloved daughter had been, through the kind interference of the present Earl of Carlisle, placed on the pension list at 40*l.* a-year. Shortly after her father's death she was placed at the convent school of Waterford, under the special care of the sister of Mr. Sheil, Mr. Sheil himself being one of her guardians. In the October of 1843 I visited her there, and spent the day in private discourse with her. She was then a very lovely girl, full of talent, full of endearing affection, giving promise of doing credit to her parent's name. The February following I received notice that she was very ill. She had shown symptoms of chest disease at Christmas, at first thought lightly of. When I visited her in February, consumption had painted two vivid spots of dazzling red upon her cheeks, and given a flaring lustre to her dark eyes. The June following she died, in her eighteenth year, and her coffin was placed on the yet sound timber encasing her father's remains."

When John Banim's daughter, his only surviving child, thus died, his fellow-countrymen feared that his widow might not be considered a fit object for the bounty of the State. Such fear, however, owing to the active interposition of the late Sir Robert Peel, was not well founded. The following paragraph, from "The Nation" of Saturday, May 10th, 1845, describes all the matters of interest connected with the case, and the names appended show how warmly and how generally, despite opposite feelings of politics and religion, the memory of John Banim, the Scott of Ireland, was cherished :—

"Mrs. Banim.

"Sir Robert Peel has acted most kindly and creditably with reference to this lady. A Committee of twenty-one, including the most active of the Conservative and Repeal writers and speakers, undertook to procure subscriptions for the purchase of a small annuity for her; but at an early meeting it was agreed to make one more application to Government for the re-grant to the widow of that pension so freely and so worthily given to the orphan of John Banim. The application was made through Mr. E. B. Roche,* the Member for Cork County, and Sir Robert Peel has answered by saying that the pension list applicable to such a purpose is full; but that he will give 50*l.* from the Royal bounty now to Mrs. Banim, and will guarantee her 40*l.* a-year on the first vacancy.

"Such acts, so done, introduce an amenity and generosity into public life; and whether Peel did this from feeling or policy, he deserves equal credit, and we thank him for it. Nor are we less pleased at another instance of the successful co-operation of Irishmen, differing in creeds and minor politics, when a matter of national duty or sentiment is involved.

"This was the Committee that took up Mrs. Banim's case, and carried it to this fortunate issue:—

Daniel O'Connell, Esq., M.P.	Torrens M'Cullagh, LL.B.
John Anster, Esq., LL.D.	Thomas Davis, Esq., M.R.I.A.
Smith O'Brien, Esq., M.P.	Samuel Ferguson, Esq., M.R.I.A.
Isaac Butt, Esq., LL.D.	
Dr. Kane, M.R.I.A.	Thomas O'Hagan, Esq.
John O'Connell, Esq., M.P.	William Carleton, Esq.
Charles Lever, Esq.	E. B. Roche, Esq., M.P.

---

* Now Lord Fermoy.

Joseph Lefanu, Esq.	Dr. Maunsell.
Charles Gavan Duffy, Esq.	J. Grey Porter, Esq.
J. Huband Smith, Esq., M.R.I.A.	James M'Glashan, Esq.
Thomas Mac Nevin, Esq.	M. J. Barry, Esq."

The county being, after its fashion, grateful, the fellow townsmen of John Banim resolved to manifest their belief in the fact that Kilkenny, the College, Wind-gap, and some other places existed, and that John Banim had done a little to make them stand before the world as something more than names in an atlas. Accordingly, in the Kilkenny and other Irish papers of December, 1852, the following announcement appeared:—

"BANIM TESTIMONIAL.

"At a Public Meeting of the friends and admirers of the genius of the late JOHN BANIM, held in the Tholsel, Kilkenny, on Wednesday, 15th December, 1852, the Mayor of Kilkenny in the Chair, the following resolutions were unanimously adopted:—

"Proposed by the Rev. Dr. Browne, Kilkenny College, and seconded by J. M. Tidmarsh, Esq., T.C.—

"1. 'That it is the opinion of this Meeting, that a suitable Testimonial to the memory of the late JOHN BANIM, be erected in this his native City.'

"Proposed by Robert Cane, Esq., M.D., and seconded by the Rev. James Graves—

"2. 'That the best mode of evincing our respect for the name of JOHN BANIM, would be to erect (if the funds admit thereof) a Public Testimonial, which would be, at the same time, ornamental to the City, and prove of use and convenience to the Public at large.'

COMMITTEE.

- The Most Noble the Marquis of Ormonde, Kilkenny Castle.
- Right Hon. W. F. Tighe, D.L., Woodstock, Co. Kilkenny.
- John Potter, Mayor of Kilkenny.
- Daniel Cullen, Ex-Mayor of Kilkenny.
- Rev. Dr. Browne, Kilkenny College.
- Rev. James Graves, Kilkenny.
- M. Sullivan, M.P., Kilkenny City, Inch House, Kilkenny.
- John Greene, M.P., Kilkenny County.
- William Shee, Sergeant-at-Law, M.P., Kilkenny County.
- J. St. John, LL.D., Nore-View House, Kilkenny.
- H. Potter, J.P., High Sheriff of the City of Kilkenny.
- Thomas Hart, J.P., Windgap Cottage.
- Richard Smithwick, J.P., Birchfield, County Kilkenny.
- Abraham Whyte Baker, Ballytobin, County Kilkenny.
- Robert Cane, M.D., Kilkenny.
- Captain Helsham, Kilkenny.
- John James, M.R.C.S.I., Kilkenny.
- Z. Johnson, M.D., &c., Kilkenny.
- John Kearns, M.R.C.S., Kilkenny.
- James Tidmarsh, T.C., Kilkenny.
- C. O'Callaghan, Kilkenny.
- John Lawson, Solicitor, Kilkenny.
- Michael Shortall, Solicitor, Kilkenny.
- Thomas Power, Kilkenny.
- M. Davis, Kilkenny.
- A. Colles, Kilkenny.
- R. Molyneux, V.S., Kilkenny.
- P. Watters, Town Clerk, Kilkenny.
- J. Poe, Solicitor, Kilkenny.
- T. Dumphy, Kilkenny.
- F. Devereux, Ringville, County Kilkenny.
- J. M'Creery, St. John's Place, Kilkenny.
- James O'Neill, John Street, Kilkenny.
- John Campion, Patrick Street, Kilkenny.
- Thomas Hewetson, T.C., Rose Inn Street, Kilkenny.
- Thomas Cody, T.C., Rose Inn Street, Kilkenny.

"*Treasurer*—Daniel Cullen, Ex-Mayor of Kilkenny.

"*Secretaries*—John Thomas Campion, John's Bridge; John G. A. Prim, Editor of "Kilkenny Moderator;" John Reville, Editor of "Kilkenny Journal."

"Subscriptions will be received by the Treasurer, Secretaries, or by any of the gentlemen of the Committee."

The Testimonial selected was a bust in marble, executed by Hogan, the resemblance being caught, for the most part, from Mulvany's picture, and in the year 1854 it was placed in the Tholsel of Kilkenny.

We lately visited the burial-place of this noble-hearted Irishman, and we with difficulty discovered it. He is buried in the grave-yard of the Roman Catholic Chapel of St. John, Kilkenny, where also are interred Dr. Burgo, the ecclesiastical historian, and the Rev. Mr. O'Donnell, the "Father Connell" who gave the title to Banim's last novel.

When Banim was dying he said to Michael, " I have only one request now, lay me so that I may be nearest to my mother, with my left side next her." And so they buried him, more than fifteen years ago, and so for fifteen years and some months he has lain without stone or monument to mark his grave. Thomas Hood died in 1845; he has a public monument: Moir, Blackwood's "Delta," died in 1851; he has a public monument. Have these examples of public gratitude no teaching for Irishmen? is the only memorial of John Banim to be a bust, quite unlike him, in the Tholsel of Kilkenny? must Michael Banim drag, from his own small funds, the money to purchase a tombstone for JOHN BANIM'S GRAVE?

Michael Banim is now, after many struggles with care, the Post-master of Kilkenny, and the gay roamer by mountain and stream for whom, as Barnes O'Hara, Cauth Flannigan and Peggy Nowlan selected that shirt which " was not a shirt entirely," is the grave official, looking back upon the bright scenes of golden youth, as the pleasant dream-land which can be traversed never more. Patiently has he borne his lot in life; his mind was ever impressed with that truth contained in the motto, *Le vin est versé ; il faut le boire ;* and so he passes on to the quiet of a happy old age, looking backward with a smile, and expecting the future with the hope and faith of a Christian.

APPENDIX I.

KILKENNY COLLEGE.

Of its most famous pupils, the present master of Kilkenny College, the Reverend John Browne, LL.D., names the following:—

"The famous men who have received their education in this foundation have been most numerous. On this subject I may quote a passage from Stanihurst, who, in his historical work, *De Rebus in Hibernia Gestis Libri Quatuor*, p. 25, again gratefully blazons the achievements of his old master:—

"'Hic ludum aperuit, nostrâ ætate, Petrus Whitus, cujus in totam Rempublicam summa constant merita. Ex illius enim scholâ, tamquam ex equo Troico, homines litteratissimi in reipublicæ lucem prodierunt. Quos ego hic Whiteos, quos Quemefordos, quos Walsheos, quos Waddingos, quos Dormeros, quos Shethos, quos Garueos, quos Butleros, quos Archeros, quos Strongos, quos Lumbardos, excellentes ingenio et doctrinâ viros, commemorare potuissem, qui primis temporibus ætatis in ejus disciplinam se tradiderunt.' Amongst this array of names, comprising those of most of the old gentry of the Pale, many hold a distinguished place in the annals of literature and of the state,—Lombard, the historian and Roman Catholic Archbishop of Armagh; Wadding, the annalist; Dormer, the poet (author of 'the Decay of Ross,' in ballad-royal); Walsh, the translator of Cambrensis, and White, whose refutation of that author's statements regarding Ireland has lately been brought to light by the labours of the Rev. M. Kelly; Gerald Comerford, an eminent lawyer, Queen Elizabeth's Attorney for Connaught, and second Baron of the Irish Exchequer; Elias Shee, 'a gentleman of passing good wit, a pleasing conceited companion, full of mirth without gall, who wrote in English divers Sonnets;' Butler, who translated Corderius' 'Book of Phrases' in 1562; Archer the Jesuit, for whose actions the 'Pacata Hibernia' may be referred to; and, not the least notable amongst these distinguished individuals, Stanihurst himself, who, besides his celebrity as a man of letters, may also be mentioned as the uncle of Archbishop Ussher. Amongst the names entered on the Register of the School, as re-founded by the first Duke of Ormonde, I find those of Baldwin, afterwards Provost, and a benefactor of Trinity College, Dublin; Bishop Berkeley, with regard to whom it is difficult to decide whether his fame as a man of letters, or as a Christian philanthropist, stands highest; his friend and correspondent, the patriot Pryor; Armaker, Archdeacon of Armagh in 1690, and author of several works; Congreve the dramatist; and Harris the historian. As we draw nearer our own day, many a famous name also stands out proudly from the throng of less distinguished *alumni* of Kilkenny College—Harry Flood *the* orator of his day; Yelverton Lord Avonmore, and Sir Hercules Langrishe, also luminaries of the Irish House of Commons; Michael Cox, Archbishop of Cashel; Hugh Carlton, Solicitor General; and though last not least, John Banim. Scions of the noble Houses of Desart, Inchiquin, Colooney, De Vesci, Waterford, Llandaff, Mornington, Lismore, Charlemont, Hawarden, Ashbrook, Rosse, Howth, Thomond, Clifden, Boyle, (ancestor to the Duke of Devonshire), Bandon, Shannon, &c., appear amongst the names entered on the Register; in which also will be found frequent mention of the families of note and mark in this and the surrounding counties, viz., Cavanagh, Staples, Cuffe, Cooley, Penefather, Vandeleur, Wemys, Flood, Langrishe, Bryan, le Hunte, Butler, Cramer-Coghill, Wheeler, Izod, Barker, Greene, Warburton, St. George, &c. &c. Whilst amongst the names by some chance omitted therefrom, may be enumerated the far-famed Dean Swift, and Farquhar the dramatist, who are known to have received their education at Kilkenny College. Sir Richard Steele, the friend and com-

peer of Addison, whose father was private secretary to the
Duke of Ormonde, it is likely also spent his early years at
this school. The names now enumerated fully justify the
remark of Banim, that it was after the restoration of its
original charter 'this seminary rose to the height of its fame,
and that young Irish noblemen and gentlemen crowded its
classes for the most approved preparation for University
honours. It might be called the then Eton of the sister
country.' Dr. Ledwich, in his History of Kilkenny, says of
the institution—'This school has had a succession of eminent
masters, has produced men of great learning, and is justly
esteemed the first school for the education of youth in this
kingdom.' The names of the masters since the Duke of Ormonde's foundation are as follow:—

1670. Edward Jones, D.D.	1776. Richard Pack, A.M.
1680. Henry Ryder, D.D.	1781. John Ellison, D.D.
1684. Edward Hinton, D.D.	1793. Antony Pack, D.D.
1702. William Andrews, D.D.	1810. A. O'Callaghan, A.M.
1714. Edward Lewis, A.M.	1820. William Baillie, LL.D.
1743. Thos. Hewetson, LL.D.	1842. John Browne, LL.D.

"Amongst these, Dr. Edward Jones was afterwards made
Bishop of Cloyne, and Dr. Ryder Bishop of Killaloe; but
alas! 'tempora mutantur'—the masters are no longer made
Bishops; our great men and our little men are not satisfied
with education in Ireland, and the lamentable consequence,
obvious to all, is an unlearned and mentally dwindled race,
instead of the giants of those days when Ireland educated her
own sons. The earlier portion of the Register, which I have
caused to be transcribed for the library of the Society, commences with October, 1684, and ends with July, 27th, 1688;
after this occurs a *lacuna* of nearly three years, an omission
which is explained by the heading prefixed to the next entries,
viz.—'The names of such as were admitted into His Grace
the Duke of Ormond's Schoole at Kilkenny *since the Warre
ended in Ireland* in the year 1691.' The first entry of this
portion is dated January 20th, 1691-2, and the series is com-

plete up to August 6th, 1716, from which date no entry occurs until the year 1743, from whence the Register is continued in regular series up to the present day. There are also some notices of the pupils who left the school for College, or to enter into various professions, &c., which are very curious; these entries commence with the date 1684, and end with the year 1704; since which period, with the exception of a few entries commencing 1743, this portion of the Register has been discontinued. We learn, on the authority of Ledwich, that there formerly existed, in Primate Marsh's Library, Dublin, a book of poems, intitled 'Sacri Lusus,' by the young gentlemen of the College of Kilkenny, which, I am sorry to say, is not now to be found there. I may also mention in conclusion, that I have heard from Mr. B. Scott, sen., of this city, an interesting anecdote connecting Dean Swift's name with Kilkenny College, which is as follows:—When the old College was pulled down, Dr. Ellison was master of the school. The oak timber-work was purchased by his (Mr. Scott's) uncle, the father of the late Mr. Martin Scott, of Kilkenny, who therewith erected his tenement in High-street. After the work was finished it came to Dr. Ellison's knowledge that the name of 'Jonathan Swift' existed, carved in school-boy fashion, on some part of the woodwork. Anxious to obtain this treasure, Dr. Ellison obtained permission from Mr. Scott to pull down that part of the work in which the particular board had been used; but after considerable progress in the work of demolition, *Mrs.* Scott declared that she could no longer suffer the business of the establishment to be interrupted, and put a stop to the search. I understand that the timber-work of the house erected at that period remains, the frontage only having been re-built within a few years back. If such prove to be the case, I will use every exertion towards the recovery of this interesting relic." *

* See a most interesting paper entitled "Kilkenny College." By the Rev. John Browne, LL.D., in the "Transactions of the Kilkenny Archæological Society," for the year 1851. Vol. I. Part ii. p. 221.

APPENDIX II.

DAMON AND PYTHIAS.

To many of our readers this tragedy and its plot must be quite as little known as *The Celt's Paradise;* it is as follows :—

The Senate of Syracuse chooses as its President, *Philistias,* a tool of *Dionysius,* an ambitious soldier. *Dionysius* directs another of his creatures, *Procles,* to induce the populace, by divination, to name him ruler, and he succeeds. *Damocles,* another tool, urges *Dionysius* to revenge himself upon *Damon,* who is a friend to the old laws of Syracuse, and a foe of the Dictator, and as the soldiers return from storming and plundering the citadel, they encounter *Damon,* who, incited by a love of country, calls them " obstreperous traitors," and reproaches *Procles,* as—

> "Thou most contemptible and meanest tool,
> That ever tyrant used."

The soldiers are about to kill *Damon* for this bold speaking, when his friend, the warrior *Pythias,* rushes in and saves him, crying—

> *Pyth.* Back, on your lives!
> Cowards, damn'd, treacherous cowards, back, I say!
> Do you know me? Look upon me: Do you know
> This honest sword I brandish? You have seen it
> Among the ranks of Carthage: would you now
> Taste its shrewd coldness in your quaking selves!
> Back! back! I say. He hath his armour on—
> I am his sword, shield, helm; I but enclose
> Myself, and my own heart, and heart's blood, when
> I thus encompass him—
>
> *Damon.* False-hearted cravens!
> We are but two—my Pythias, my halved heart!—
> My Pythias, and myself; but dare come on,
> Ye hirelings of a tyrant! dare advance
> A foot, or raise an arm, or bend a brow,

And ye shall learn what two such arms can do
Amongst a thousand of ye.—My good friend,
The gods have sent thee to me—Who had deem'd
To find thee here from Agrigentum? [Soldiers *advance.*
   Pyth. Off!
Off, villains, off!—Each for the other thus,
And in that other, for his dearer self.
Why, Procles, art thou not ashamed,—for I
Have seen thee do good work in battle time—
Art not ashamed, here on a single man
To rush in coward numbers? Fie upon thee!
I took thee for a soldier.
   Pro. For thy sake,
Who art a warrior like ourselves, we spare him—
'Twas a good star of his that led thee hither
From Agrigentum, to lift up thine arm
In the defence of that long robe of peace
Wherein he wraps his stern philosophy.
Come, teach him better manners. Soldiers, on.

Pythias has come to Syracuse for the purpose of wedding *Calanthe;* he informs *Damon* of this circumstance, and it is agreed that he shall attend the nuptials of his friend.

The Senate debate as to the guilt of *Dionysius,* and the punishment to be inflicted for his attack on the citadel. The faction in the assembly devoted to the traitor's interests, declare that for his great services to the state on former occasions, he shall be pardoned; and proceeding yet more boldly it is proposed to the Senate, and agreed by them that he shall be King. *Dionysius* had surrounded the building with his most trusted soldiers; he knew that *Damon* would oppose his election, and this was to be the great day of his triumph. He had wrought out the triumph—

> " In all that biting bitterness of heart
> Which clings, and gnaws, by inches, to its object,
> More keen, because a first essay hath fail'd,
> In shame and suffering, failed, thus have I sped
> My work, in silence, on. It did become
> A thought inwoven with my inmost being."

Damon had been his chiefest opponent in all his schemes,

and against him were the most strict precautions taken. When the Senate are upon the point of decreeing that *Dionysius* shall be King, a noise is heard without the Senate-house, and *Damon*, having broken through the guards, rushes in and cries, referring to the proposed decree—

>*Damon.* And all ! are all content ?
>A nation's rights betray'd,
>And all content ! O slaves ! O parricides !
>O, by the brightest hope a just man has,
>I blush to look around and call you men ;
>What ! with your own free willing hands yield up
>The ancient fabric of your constitution,
>To be a garrison, a common barrack,
>A common guard-house, and for common cut-throats !
>What ! will ye all combine to tie a stone
>Each to each other's necks, and drown like dogs
>Within the tide of time, and never float
>To after ages, or at best, but float
>A buoyant pestilence ? Can ye but dig
>Your own dark graves, creep into them, and die ?
>>*Third S.* I have not sanction'd it.
>>*Fourth S.* Nor I.
>>*Fifth S.* Nor I.
>
>*Damon.* O ! thanks for these few voices ! But alas !
>How lonely do they sound ! Do you not all
>Start up at once, and cry out liberty ?
>Are you so bound in fetters of the mind,
>That there you sit as if you were yourselves
>Incorporate with the marble ? Syracusans !——
>But, no ! I will not rail, nor chide, nor curse ye !
>I will implore you, fellow-countrymen,
>With blinded eyes, and weak and broken speech,
>I will implore you— O ! I am weak in words,—
>But I could bring such advocates before you ;—
>Your fathers' sacred images ; old men
>That have been grandsires ; women with their children,
>Caught up in fear and hurry, in their arms—
>And those old men should lift their shivering voices,
>And palsied hands—and those affrighted mothers
>Should hold their innocent infants forth, and ask,
>Could you make slaves of them !

All these appeals are vain, the Senate kneel to the usurper, and salute him King. Enraged by this act, *Damon* runs upon him, attempts to stab him, is baffled in the deed, and is condemned to die. *Lucullus* flies to the Temple of Hymen, where the marriage of *Pythias* and *Calanthe* is being celebrated. He whispers in the bridegroom's ear the fate of his friend, and, pale with terror, *Pythias* abandons *Calanthe* even at the altar, and hastens to the rescue or assistance of *Damon*.

Damon had entreated that *Dionysius* would liberate him but for six hours, that he might bid his wife and child farewell; the entreaty was refused, but at the request of *Pythias*, and upon his offering to take the place of his friend, as a hostage for his return within the six hours, *Damon* is permitted to go forth; and it is agreed that if he return not before the expiration of the sixth hour, *Pythias* shall die. *Pythias* is chained and placed in the dungeon, and *Damon* hastens to his villa, accompanied by *Lucullus*. Whilst he is bidding adieu to his wife and child, *Lucullus*, hoping to delay his return beyond the six hours prescribed, kills his horse. *Damon*, committing his wife and child to the care of the gods, rushes forth from the house, eager to mount his steed, and hasten to release his friend from chains and prison. He cries :—

> 'Tis o'er, Lucullus—Bring thou forth my horse.
> I have stayed too long, Lucullus, and my speed
> Must leave the winds behind me : By the gods,
> The sun is rushing down the west !
>   *Luc.* My Lord—
>   *Damon.* Why dost thou tremble? Fetch the colour back
> Into thy cheek, man, nor let thy weak knees
> Knock on each other in their cowardice !
> Time flies—be brief—go bring my horse to me !
> Be thou as swift as speech, or as my heart is !
>   *Luc.* My Lord—
>   *Damon.* Why, slave, dost hear me? bring him here !
> My horse, I say ! The hour is past already
> Whereon I bade old Neucles summon me.
>   *Luc.* My generous master, do not slay me !
>   *Damon.* Slave !

APPENDIX II.

Art mad? or dost thou mock me in the last
And fearfullest extremity?—Yet you speak not!

Luc. You were ever kind and merciful, nor yet
Commended me unto the cruel whip,
And I did love you for it!

Damon. Where's my horse?

Luc. When I beheld the means of saving you,
I could not hold my hand—my heart was in it,
And in my heart, the hope of giving life
And liberty to Damon; and——

Damon. Go on! I am listening to thee!

Luc. And in the hope to save you, I slew your steed!

Damon. Almighty heavens!

Luc. Forgive me!

Damon. I am standing here to see if the great gods
Will with their lightning execute my prayer
Upon thee! But thy punishment be thine!
I'll tear thee into pieces! [*Seizes him.*

Luc. Spare me! spare me!
I saved thy life—O do not thou take mine!

Damon. My friend! my friend! O that the word would
kill thee!
Pythias is slain!—his blood is on my soul!
He cries, Where art thou, Damon? Damon, where art thou?
And Damon's here!—The axe is o'er his neck,—
And in his blood I'm deluged!

Luc. Spare me! spare me!

Damon. A spirit cries, "Revenge and Sacrifice!"
I'll do it—I'll do it—Come!

Luc. Where should I go?

Damon. To the eternal river of the dead!
The way is shorter than to Syracuse.—
'Tis only far as yonder yawning gulf—
I'll throw thee with one swing to Tartarus,
And follow after thee!—Nay, slave, no struggling!
Pythias is grown impatient! His red ghost
Starts from the ground, and with a bloody hand
Waves to the precipice!

Luc. Have mercy!

Damon. Call for mercy on the furies—not on me!
[*Exit* DAMON *dragging* LUCULLUS *with him.*

During the six hours, *Dionysius*, disguised, visits *Pythias* in his dungeon, and tells him that soldiers have been sent forward to stay the return of *Damon*, and endeavours to induce him to escape from the prison; *Nicias*, the father of *Pythias*, and his own *Calanthe* are introduced, each imploring him to go forth, but he is firm to his trust in *Damon's* honour. The following is the closing scene of the fifth, and concluding act, and is extremely effective; the characters are *Calanthe, Dionysius, Pythias*:—

The gates of the prison are flung open, and PYTHIAS *is discovered. He advances.*

   Cal. Pythias!
   Pyth. Calanthe here!—My poor fond girl!
Thou art the first to meet me here at the block,
Thou wilt be the last to leave me at the grave!
How strangely things go on in this bad world—
This was my wedding-day: but for the bride,
I did not think of such a one as death!
I deemed I should have gone to sleep to-night,
This very night—not on the earth's cold lap,
But, with as soft a bosom for my pillow,
And with as true and fond a heart throb in it
To lull me to my slumber, as e'er yet
Couch'd the repose of love.—It was, indeed,
A blissful sleep to wish for!
   Cal. O, my Pythias, he yet may come!
   Pyth. Calanthe, no!—Remember
That Dionysius hath prevented it.
   Cal. That was an idle tale of this old man,
And he may yet return.
   Pyth. May yet return!
Speak!—how is this? return!—O life, how strong
Thy love is in the hearts of dying men!
Thou art true he did'st say, the tyrant would prevent
His coming back to Syracuse.
   Dion. I wrong'd him.
   Pyth. Ha! were it possible!—may he yet come?
   Cal. Into the sinews of the horse that bears him
Put swiftness, gods!—let him outrace and shame

The galloping of clouds upon the storm !
Blow breezes with him ; lend every feeble aid
Unto his motion !—and thou, thrice-solid earth,
Forget thy immutable fixedness—become
Under his feet like flowing water, and
Hither flow with him !

Pyth. I have taken in
All the horizon's vast circumference
That in the glory of the setting sun
Opens its wide expanse, yet do I see
No signal of his coming !—Nay, 'tis likely—
O, no—he could not ! It is impossible !

Cal. I say, he is false ! he is a murderer !
He will not come ! the traitor doth prefer
Life, ignominious, dastard life !—Thou minister
Of light, and measurer of eternity
In this great purpose, stay thy going down,
Great sun, behind the confines of the world !
On yonder purple mountains make thy stand
For while thine eye is opened on mankind,
Hope will abide within thy blessed beams—
They dare not do the murder in thy presence !
Alas ! all heedless of thy frantic cry,
He plunges down the precipice of Heaven !
Pythias—O, Pythias !

Pyth. I could have borne to die,
Unmoved by Dionysius—but to be torn
Green from existence by the friend I loved—
Thus from the blossoming and beauteous tree
Rent by the treachery of him I trusted !
No ! no ! I wrong thee, Damon, by that half thought—
Shame on the foul suspicion ! he hath a wife,
And child, who cannot live on earth without him,
And Heaven has flung some obstacle in his way
To keep him back, and lets me die who am
Less worthy, and the fitter.

Pro. Pythias, advance !

Cal. No, no ! why should he yet ? It is not yet—
By all the gods, there are two minutes only !

Pro. Take a last farewell of your mistress, sir,
And look your last upon the setting sun—
And do both quickly, for your hour comes on !

Pyth. Come here, Calanthe! closer to me, yet!—
Ah! what a cold transition it will be
From this warm touch all full of life and beauty,
Unto the clammy mould of the deep grave!
I pr'ythee, my Calanthe, when I am gone,
If thou should'st e'er behold my hapless friend,
Do not upbraid him! This, my lovely one,
Is my last wish—Remember it!

Cal. Hush! hush! Stand back there!

Pyth. Take her, you eternal gods,
Out of my arms into your own!—Befriend her!
And let life glide on in gentleness,
For she is gentle and doth merit it.

Cal. I think I see it——

Pro. Lead her from the scaffold!

Pyth. Arria, receive her!—yet one kiss—farewell!
Thrice—thrice—farewell! I am ready, sir.

Cal. Forbear!
There is a minute left—look there! look there!
But 'tis so far off, and the evening shades
Thicken so fast, there are no other eyes
But mine can catch it—Yet, 'tis there! I see it—
A shape as yet so vague and questionable
'Tis nothing, just about to change and take
The faintest form of something!

Pyth. Sweetest love!

Damo. Your duty, officer.

Cal. I will not quit him
Until ye prove I see it not!—no force
Till then shall separate us.

Damo. Tear them asunder!
Arria, conduct your daughter to her home.

Cal. O, send me not away—Pythias, thine arms—
Stretch out thine arms, and keep me!—see, it comes!
Barbarians!—Murderers!—O,'yet a moment—
Yet but one pulse—one heave of breath! O, Heavens!

[*She swoons, and is carried away by* ARRIA *and* Guards.

Pyth. [*To the* Executioner.]
There is no pang in thy deep wedge of steel
After that parting. Nay, sir, you may spare
Yourself the pains to fit me for the block.
Damon, I do forgive thee!—I but ask

APPENDIX II.   319

Some tears unto my ashes!

[*A distant shout heard*—PYTHIAS *leaps upon the Scaffold.*
By the gods,
A horse, and horseman! Far upon the hill
They wave their hats, and he returns it—yet
I know him not—his horse is at the stretch.
Why should they shout as he comes on? It is——
No!—that was too unlike—but there, now—there!
O, life, I scarcely dare to wish for thee,
And yet—that jutting rock has hid him from me—
No!—let it not be Damon!—he has a wife
And child! gods! keep him back!

  Damon. Where is he?

    [*He rushes in, and stands for a moment looking round.*
Ha! He is alive! untouched!   [*Laughing hysterically.*
  Ha! ha! ha!

                          [*Falls upon the Scaffold.*
  Pyth. The gods do know I could have died for him!
And yet I dared to doubt!—I dared to breathe
The half-utter'd blasphemy!
He faints!—how thick
This wreath of burning moisture on his brow!
His face is black with toil, his swelling bulk
Heaves with swift pantings—Damon, my dear friend!

  Damon. Where am I? Have I fallen from my horse
That I am stunn'd, and on my head I feel
A weight of thickening blood! What has befallen me?
The horrible confusion of a dream
Is yet upon my sight.—For mercy's sake,
Stay me not back—he is about to die!
Pythias, my friend! Unloose me, villains, or
You will find the might of madness in mine arm!
[*Seeing* PYTHIAS.] Speak to me, let me hear thy voice!

  Pyth. My friend!

  Damon. It pierced my brain, and rush'd into my heart!
There's lightning in it! That's the scaffold—there
The block—the axe—the executioner!
And here he lives! I have him in my soul!
[*Embracing* PYTHIAS.] Ha! ha! ha!

  Pyth. Damon!

  Damon. Ha! ha!
I can but laugh!—I cannot speak to thee!

I can but play the maniac, and laugh!
Thy hand!—O, let me grasp thy manly hand!
It is an honest one, and so is mine!
They are fit to clasp each other!—Ha! ha! ha!
  Pyth. Would that my death could have preserved thee!
  Damon. Pythias,
Even in the very crisis to have come,—
To have hit the very forehead of old time!
By heavens! had I arrived an hour before,
I should not feel this agony of joy,—
This triumph over Dionysius!
Ha! ha!—But did'st thou doubt me? Come, thou did'st—
Own it, and I'll forgive.
  Pyth. For a moment.
  Damon. O that false slave!—Pythias, he slew my horse,
In the base thought to save me!—I would have kill'd him,
And to a precipice was dragging him,
When from the very brink of the abyss
I did behold a traveller afar,
Bestriding a good steed—I rush'd upon him,
Choking with desperation, and yet loud
In shrieking anguish, I commanded him
Down from his saddle: he denied me—but
Would I then be denied? As hungry tigers
Clutch their poor prey, I sprung upon his throat.
Thus, thus I had him, Pythias. Come, your horse,
Your horse, your horse, I cried. Ha! ha! ha!
  Dion. Damon!
  Damon. I am here upon the scaffold! look at me;
I am standing on my throne; as proud a one
As yon illumined mountain, where the sun
Makes his last stand; let him look on me too;
He never did behold a spectacle
More full of natural glory. Death is—Ha!
All Syracuse starts up upon her hills,
And lifts her hundred thousand hands! She shouts!
Hark, how she shouts! O! Dionysius,
When wer't thou in thy life hail'd with a peal
Of hearts and hands like that one? Shout again!
Again, until the mountains echo you,
And the great sea joins in that mighty voice,
And old Enceladus, the Son of Earth,

Stirs in his mighty caverns! Tell me, slaves,
Where is your tyrant? Let me see him now;
Why stands he hence aloof? Where is your master?
What is become of Dionysius?
I would behold, and laugh at him!
            [DIONYSIUS *advances between* DAMON *and* PYTHIAS,
                    and throws off his disguise.
  Dion. Behold me!
  Damon and Pyth. How!
  Dion. Stay your admiration for awhile,
Till I have spoken my commandment here.—
Go, Damocles, and bid a herald cry
Wide through the city, from the eastern gate
Unto the most remote extremity,
That Dionysius, tyrant as he is,
Gives back his life to Damon!

The parting scene between Damon and his wife Hermione, and his child, are exquisitely wrought up, and have ever told upon even the most fastidious audiences: the power is not alone that of situation, the language is poetical, and in no point strained or affected. The scenes between the lovers, Pythias and Calanthe, are very poetical, and marked by that intensity of passion so powerfully employed in "The Fetches," and in "The Nowlans." The following passages may be placed beside Claude Melnotte's description of the imaginary "vale," to which he would convey his mistress. Could Bulwer Lytton have had this half-forgotten tragedy in mind when writing "The Lady of Lyons?"—

               A Chamber in ARRIA'S *House.*

               Enter PYTHIAS *and* CALANTHE.

  Pyth. So, my Calanthe, you would waste the moon of
      Hymen in this lonely spot?
  Cal. In sooth
I would, for 'tis the fairest place in Sicily—
A dell, made of green beauty; with its shrubs
Of aromatic sweetness, growing up
The rugged mountain's sides, as cunningly
As the nice structure of a little nest,

Built by two loving nightingales.   The wind,
That comes there, full of rudeness from the sea,
Is lull'd into a balmy breath of peace,
The moment that it enters ; and 'tis said
By our Sicilian shepherds, that their songs
Have in this place a wilder melody.
The mountains all about it are the haunts
Of many a fine romantic memory !
High towers old Ætna, with his feet deep clad
In the green sandals of the freshful spring :
His sides array'd in winter, and his front
Shooting aloft the everlasting flame.
On the right hand is that great cave, in which
Huge Polyphemus dwelt, between whose vast
Colossal limbs the artful Grecian stole.
On the other side,
Is Galatea's dainty dressing-room
Wrought in the living marble ; and within
Is seen the fountain where she used to twine
The ringlets on her neck that did ensnare
The melancholy Cyclop.—But what care you,
A soldier, for such fantasies ?   I know
A way that better shall persuade you to
That place for our sweet marriage residence—
There Damon hath his villa—Ha ! you seem
Determined by the fast proximity
Of such a friendship, more than all my love.

Pyth. Does Damon dwell there ?

Cal. No ; his Hermione
And his young boy—O ! 'tis a beauteous child !—
Are sent there from the city's noxious air,
And he doth visit them, whene'er the state
Gives him brief respite.   Tell me, Pythias,
Shall we not see the Hymeneal moon
Glide through the blue heavens there ?

Pyth. My own adored one,
If thou should'st bid me sail away with thee,
To seek the isles of the Hesperides,
I would, with such a pilot, spread my sail
Beyond the trophies of great Hercules,
Making thine eyes my Cynosure !

APPENDIX III.

Sylla.

This tragedy, "Sylla," is neither so poetic nor so well adapted for representation, as the earlier composition, "Damon and Pythias." Indeed, its chief interest is the situation in the fifth act, in which Sylla abandons his dignity and power. He discovers that his daughter, Phryne, is secretly wedded to his enemy young Julius Marius, and with this enemy—yet the husband of his child—in chains, powerless and his prisoner, Sylla is thus, at the conclusion of the fourth act, represented soliloquising in the hall of his palace:—

>   Slaves, crawling slaves! what would they do, which they
>   Might not have left undone? Eradicate?
>   Why plant and nurture?—with their proper hands?
>   They wait a time! what time? on Sylla? no—
>   By Mars they dare not! and it shall be shown.
>   [*Sits, and writes in his tablets.*
>   Nor is the thought new-born. Thro' days of surfeit,
>   And nights of haggard slumber, it hath risen—
>   The only promise of the only conquest,
>   Change, vengeance, yet to grasp : o'er hate, o'er treason
>   A quashing, hushing vengeance—and enjoyment,
>   Because a change. A safety too—if that,
>   I did not utterly scorn.   [*He rises*
>   Gods! ye do know the very wrestling with it,
>   Were a young life to me! The thought mounts up,
>   And Sylla feels he is their master still!
>   And thou, young Marius—revenge on thee,
>   Thou didst not meditate! Phryne? she is his wife.
>   [*Sits again.*
>
>   I am very desolate. I knew, before,
>   The common mass of being cursed or hated,

Yet hoped there was one creature of my blood
Who trusted—loved. She said it was in ignorance.
Perhaps. I'll try her awfully—Catiline!

Re-enter CATILINE.

Hearken. At the first hour of morning, summon
Unto the Forum, in my sovereign name,
The people and the senators. While all rest there,
Metellus shall surround them, with a force
Of soldiers. Lepidus and Julius Marius,
Guarded, lead thither, too. And let all wait
My presence, and my will. Leave me. It shall be!
[*Exit* CATILINE.
For every cause it shall. A new, last glory!
My last audacious triumph; certainty:
Vengeance; a mystery still! a blazing wonder,
And echo to all nations and all time!

ACT V.

SCENE I.—*In* SYLLA'S *Palace. Enter hastily* PHRYNE, *followed by a female attendant.*

Phry. After my watchings all the live-long night,
A hateful, leaden sleep, uncalled, unwilled,
Unfelt came o'er me—and how long I slept
I know not—and I fear to ask or know—
Till, in the fierce ray of the summer sun,
Which, brightly angry, flashed, methought, to rouse me—
I woke and screamed. No voice replied to mine.
No creature came to me: I started up.
I have traversed all the chambers, one by one—
They are all empty, and upon the walls
And marble floors, I have looked for gouts of blood.
Speak, thou! who here at last dost wait on me—
My father and his prisoner—speak!

APPENDIX III.

Att. At dawn,
A prisoner, with Catiline, left the palace.
Your father, lady—
　Phry. At the dawn ! How old
Is the day, now ?
　Att. Yet morning tide.
　Phry. Yet morning !
Time lapsed to win, or lose, or wreck a world.
Oh, I have been accursed in my sleep.
Oh, morbid, traitor sleep ! from your death-thrall
And heavy blandishment I do divorce
Mine eyes for ever ! Or the hideous things
Which may have happened—may ?—which must ! which have !
Can well effect it ! Spake you of my father ?
　Att. 'Tis but some minutes since he parted, too.
　Phry. Whither ? You know not ?
　Att. Lady, no.
　Phry. Said he
No parting word for Phryne ? for his daughter ?
　Att. No word.
　Phry. How looked he ? sternly ? and
The prisoner ? seemed *he* sad ?—hush—thro' the streets,
Deserted by the people, bands of soldiers　　　[*At a window.*
Troop onward, heavily—returning now
Perhaps !—what *is* to happen—or *has* happened ?
Heard you ?—or any of my women ? Speak
The very truth !
　Att. Nor they, nor I, can answer.
　Phry. I will go forth ! whither I know not—but
O'er all the spreading city—and fall down
Before whatever living things I meet,
Praying a guidance to the mystery
Or explanation of it. Household gods—
House of my sires, farewell ! I go—oh, when—
And how, if ever—to return ? Fate knoweth.　　　[*Exeunt.*

Scene II.—*The Forum.* Lænas, Aufidius, Senators, Crassus, Cethegus, People.

Auf. Know ye the cause or motive of this summons?
Cras. Unless as an example to the people,
To punish in their presence, the last son
Of their old butcher, Marius, we know not.
Auf. Such circumstantial show is not his fashion.
Læn. It never was.
Auf. The people quake in terror,
And boding ignorance, as hither led
By their weak Tribunes. See, how silently
They follow hither the accused.

Enter Catiline, Julius *and* Lepidus *guarded,* First Tribune *and* People.

Cat. His air,
His brow defeat me. Could I see him wince
In look or limb, it were my dearest triumph,
And for my purpose, opportunity. [*Aside.*
Young Julius Marius. [*To him.*
Jul. Lucius Catiline?
Cat. I grieve to see you thus.
Jul. False as thou'rt foul.
Cat. No, Julius Marius, no. On public grounds
Your enemy, my heart can pity, still,
The doomed sufferings of all your race,
Now in your own to be so sadly ended.
Jul. Leave me.
Cat. And if by my poor agency
It might be otherwise—if your young life
Might from this too untimely stroke be snatched,
Here do I plainly stand, your friend, to try it.
[Julius *does not notice him.*
1st Trib. The noble senators may answer us.
Auf. We, and those good knights with us, uninformed
As Tribunes or as people, hither come
For Sylla's pleasure.

Cat. Julius, hearken to me.
You are a man—a young one—from whose eyes
The world is fading fast, with all its changes
Of wondrous, promising, and beautiful.
'Tis hard to look upon a man so young,
Standing so near the verge—encompassed,
Already, with the shadow and the silence
Of death—'tis hard to see you, Julius, thus,
And feel no wish to succour.—I cannot
Regard it passively; and altho' fate
Frown on the very dawning of the thought,
I may be bribed to zeal.   [JULIUS *is still contemptuous.*

  1st Trib. Friends! Citizens!
Behold!
  1st Citz. Metellus leading on his soldiers.
  1st Trib. They crowd upon us!
  1st Citz. Yes—and hem us in!
    [*Enter* METELLUS, *with* Soldiers, *who surround the Forum.*
  Læn. Aufidius, note you that?
  Auf. I do—and tremble.
  1st Trib. 'Tis the last day of Sylla's tyranny.
  1st Citz. Rome's lost. We are to perish!
  1st Trib. Comes *he* yet?   [*Looking off.*
  Cat. Julius, look round you. Of the shades of doom
It is the denser gathering—the deepest—
For next comes doom itself. Bethink you, and
Now answer me. There is a lady—
  Jul. Ha!
  Cat. Start not—but hear—
  Jul. Villain! excelling villain!
Why is that—here, prisoner as I stand,
I do not, from the bosom which could plot
That insult for me, tear the fetid heart out,
And—
  Cat. Traitor! unhand me!
  Jul. But—live. You are the fitter for this world,
Which now—the gods do see it—is no world
For any honest man. Go—thrive together.
In its decrepitude and worthlessness
I need bequeath to it no better curse.
Live and revenge me!—
            Romans! you look pale

And stare upon each other, asking in whispers,
Why this and this ? or, what will happen, now ?
Or what shall save us ?—Romans—no—not Romans !
That name no more—slaves then—and slaves of slaves !
But I'll speak calmer—on the day he robbed you
Of your last liberties, I met you here,
Here in this very Forum, and—

   1*st Trib.* } Hush ! back !   [*Looking off.*
   Citzs.

Jul. Pshaw ! They're not worth the breath it costs—a flock
Of sheep do not cringe closer from the growl
Of the shepherd's dog. Down with your necks, brave Romans,
That he may step on them !

Enter Second Tribune, *with* People.

2*d Trib.* Sylla !—back, back !

Enter slowly, SYLLA, *with* Lictors.

Syl. Senators, citizens, all men of Rome—
A day hath risen whose progress shall proclaim
Unto the breathing and the unborn world,
How worthy or unworthy of his place
Has Sylla proved, and in your turn, of him,
Yourselves, how worthy. A peculiar question,
Which to this great one tends, we first examine.
In me, the awful dignity of Rome
Has by assassin league been violated.
There stand the plotters. Julius Marius, and
His colleague, Lepidus. More from the Rostrum.

Jul. [*As* SYLLA *walks towards the Rostrum.*]
Now, Lepidus, your secret dagger.

Enter PHRYNE, *behind* JULIUS.

Lep. Take it.
Phry. [*Having observed* JULIUS.] Turn, Sylla ! Turn !
Jul. [*Breaking through the* Guards.] Villains, make way !
Die, monster !   [*Rushing to* SYLLA.
Phry. [*Intercepting and catching his arm.*]
Hold, parricide !—infanticide !

Cat. Guards!—Lictors!
Down with him—slay!

Syl. Lictors!—disarm that boy;
If I had wanted proof for your assurance,
Himself, the head and spirit of this treason,
Doth here supply it. Ye have seen his hand
Raised against the life of the republic—and,
By every law, civil and natural,
The days of the last Marius are now numbered.

Phry. Against all nature! against all the laws
Of natural hearts! Romans! he is *my husband!* [*Embracing him.*

Jul. Oh Phryne! I was nerved for fate—but, this—

Phry. And, Romans, plead for him, with me! ye know—
Great as his crime hath been unto your eyes,
And mine, this day—the youngest and the last
Of all the Marians, must, if he be man—
Hoard in his heart—even against his will—
Griefs, recollections, bitterness, and anger,
Which madden him, at times, to say and do
He knows not what!—oh think ye, Roman husbands,
Were he not made, by suffering, moment-mad,
He who doth love his wife, as never wife
Was loved, would raise his boyish arm upon
The sacred person of that wife's dear parent,
A parent, by that wife beloved as well—
And she will say no more—as she by him,
Her chosen husband? Romans, plead for me!
Your hands and voices here with mine! My father!
[*Kneels to* SYLLA.

Syl. I am dictator. Senators, no word.
Tribunes, beware!—Lictors, control the people.
Phryne, retire.

Phry. No! bid them strike me here!
It is the fitter place for me to fall—
Even at the feet of the unnatural father
Who spurns me here! Perish I must—I will—
If—

Syl. Lead the wife of Marius from the Forum!
[*Ascends the Rostrum.*

Phry. Off, abject slaves!—I stand by him again!
[*Rushes to* JULIUS, *who is again guarded.*
My arm around him! to be silent, now,

Since, if I am so, I have equal right
With any citizen to tarry here—
Silent until I catch a word to harm him—
My Julius, fear not !

Jul. I but fear for you.

Syl. Young Julius Marius may tell you, Romans,
He strikes but at an absolute dictator.   [*From the Rostrum.*
Wherefore, in justice ? Let the people answer.
Freely they chose me—nor unworthily—
For, ere I was dictator, I was a hero.
Deep, distant waters ye shall never see,
I bade flow round your empire, and they flowed
Rejoicingly. Kings I uncrowned and crowned ;
Avenged your wrongs ; enforced your rights ; unfurled
Your glory to earth's limits. This, abroad.
At home, I brought you peace ; by any means ;
Peace, still. Proscriptions, confiscations, blood—
These *were* the means ; on whom ? and blood of whom ?
On those who plundered ye, and first shed yours.
Who perished ? Romans—but the foes of Rome ;
What was her loss ? Citizens ?—rebels ! Sons ?
Parricides !

Jul. Friends, oh friends !

Phry. Julius—for *my* sake—
atience—forbearance !

Jul. Childless fathers, answer !
Fatherless sons ! lorn brothers, answer him !
Rome's loss ?—oh, let her women raise their voices !
And Romans, tell him, too, Rome's loss is freedom !
The freedom a perpetual dictator
Hath in his life shut up, and which his life
Alone may render !

> [*At the commencement of* JULIUS' *speech,* SYLLA *had beckoned* CETHEGUS *to his side—during it he has conferred with him ; now he resumes, without having seemed to notice it.*

Syl. Thus, the means were desperate.
Who used them ? Sylla ? No. Your Sovereign.—
In person ? No. In Rome's great Majesty.—
In personal anger ? No. In her assertion.—
For his revenge ? No—for her great salvation !
What father whose child's treason leaves him childless,

What sireless son whose father's treason shamed him,
What brother whose bad brother shamed their sire,
Will now stand up for such against his country?
If I do speak unto a Roman patriot
So circumstantial and conditional,
Let him stand forth and front—not punishment—
But the deep, broad, indelible disgrace
Of that avowal in this public forum—
Let him stand forth, I say!

   1st Trib. How should we answer?

   1st Citz. Out of our own admissions he would judge us

   1st Trib. Let no man speak!

   Syl. Your silence I do thus interpret, friends.
'Twere just to punish any, who, with cause
Of private suffering, the most peculiar,
Dares, in my sovereign person, touch the state—
Behold young Marius who hath so dared.

   Jul. Tyrant!   [*Addressing* SYLLA.

   Phry. My Julius!

   Syl. Yet—

   Phry. Hush! Hear him on!

   Syl. Yet, as the offence, to Sylla, is, at once,
Public and personal, I do waive the right
Of judging him, referring it unto
The senate and the people.

   Phry. Hear you that?

   Jul. I do—in deepest wonder—if he mean it,
I am no longer Sylla's enemy.

   Syl. But more than my permission here is urgent.

   Jul. Hark—some deep subtlety which cheats us all.

   Syl. For this you must be, once again, a people,
United to your senate, sovereign—
Without an absolute dictatorship,
Or any intervention from the presence
Of civil or of military force.
Wherefore, observe me. Lictors—yield your fasces!
Soldiers, lay down your arms!—and, all, draw off,
Or, here, as citizens, with your fellows mingle.

                           [Lictors *and* Soldiers *obey him.*

   Phry. Oh, joy, my Julius, joy!

   Jul. Let me observe him—

   Syl. This, the first step to leave your councils free,

Is the last act of my authority.
My servants powerless, myself I now
Command from power—Sylla, o'er Sylla still,
The only master. You have heard it said
That, in dictatorship perpetual,
I had shut up your freedom. Well! Attend.
My place I now do abdicate for ever;
My palm and purple I renounce for ever;
And, once again a simple citizen,
Unarmed, unsymbolled, thus advance to greet you.
        [*Takes off the golden palm and the purple cloak, and*
           descends from the Rostrum.

  Phry. Well, Julius? well!

  Jul. I am astounded—thrilled!

  1st Trib. Now, countrymen!

  2d Trib. Hush! hush! he would speak still.

  Syl. More. As Rome's magistrate, I have freely dealt
Upon the people—and the senate, too.
For *that*, yourselves have righteously admitted
I am not privately responsible.
Yet—lest my single judgment may have pushed
Authority beyond its sovereign limit—
Hear me. What I have done in Rome's great name,
I will account for in mine own. I ask
A trial from the people. I invite it.
Silent? I dare it!

  Jul. Oh, amazing courage!
Majestic boldness!

  Phry. Terrible!

  Jul. But how grand!
God-despot! His sublimity hath conquered!

  Syl. I am not answered, friends. Would the coward dagger,
A course of virtuous justice intercept?
I have heard, I know not well how many thousands,
Of those whose kindred, but contaminate, blood
Flowed at their country's doom, pronounced by me,
Waited but time and opportunity.
The time is come—if ever to come; I yield
The opportunity. That, too, I dare.
My countrymen, about the forum, here,
I now shall walk. You see I am unarmed.
My life upon a blow. To plot and poignard

I oppose my genius only ! Chæronea,
Orchomenus, and the terror of my name !
Behold, I walk among ye.
    Let that man
Who deems he has a private vengeance, take it !
Again, young Marius, strike !   [*Walks to* JULIUS.
 Jul. Her breast, as soon !
 Phry. My father !
 Syl. Well ? I cannot punish now.
 Phry. My father ! take *this* hand.
   [*Falls on* SYLLA'S *neck, holding by one of* JULIUS' *hands.*
 Syl. Tush—tush—
Freely I may depart then ? all unquestioned?
   [*Re-addressing the people while* PHRYNE *still clings to him.*
 Phry. Father !   [*Endeavouring to join his hand with that*
          of JULIUS.
 Syl.   [*Grasping* JULIUS' *hand almost*
          without regarding him.

Well, well? He is pardoned, is he not ?
Or must I plead for him unto the people
And the grave senate ? and—tush—sir, support her—
She is now more yours than mine—tho' I say not
More, in the heart—there—free me of your wife, sir—
My child—that *was*—
 Phry. [*Embracing him.*] And *is* ! *Is*, glorious father !
Say—*is* !
 Syl. Is, then—is, is—will that content you ?
Go to your husband.
 Phry. Yes ! When you call him so ! [*Embracing* JULIUS.
 Syl. Freely I may depart ? and all unquestioned ?
Take my last word, tho'. Over all my battles,
Proscriptions, decimations, hear ye, Romans ;
How I've served Rome. I found the old republic
A shadow ; scorned, insulted, braved ; I leave it
A substance ; feared, respected, trembled at—
A threat to foes—to rebels, terrible !
I found ye slaves ! I leave ye free ! By what
Inducement, ye do know, and will remember.
For myself, Romans, I give thanks for nought.
My own hand won me power. A sovereign crown
In the street-mire I found—thence caught it up,

Cleansed, placed it on my brow—and was your master!
Home, Phryne—*he*—does he walk homeward with you?

Phry. He does!

Jul. I do.

Syl. For a great ambition it was little, then—
Now, to be less or greater, I renounce it.
Whether in public or private feeling—
In patriotism, humility, or scorn—
Yourselves, your generations, ages, times
May leisurely resolve. Farewell. Come, daughter—
Julius, attend her at the other side.   *[Takes her hand.*
Farewell! The reign of Sylla hath not passed.

    [*Exeunt* SYLLA, JULIUS, *and* PHRYNE: SYLLA'S *arm round*
      PHRYNE. *Curtain falls while all the rest gaze after him.*

THE END.

R. CLAY, PRINTER, BREAD STREET HILL

The List of Titles in the Garland Series

MARIA EDGEWORTH

1. Castle Rackrent *(1800)*
2. An Essay on Irish Bulls *(1802)*
3. Ennui *(1809)*
4. The Absentee *(1812)*
5. Ormond *(1817)*

SYDNEY OWENSON, LADY MORGAN

6. The Wild Irish Girl *(1806)*
7. O'Donnel. A National Tale *(1814)*
8. Florence Macarthy: an Irish Tale *(1818)*
9. The O'Briens and the O'Flahertys *(1817)*
10. Dramatic Sketches from Real Life *(1833)*

CHARLES ROBERT MATURIN

11. The Wild Irish Boy *(1808)*
12. The Milesian Chief *(1812)*
13. Women; or, Pour et Contre: A Tale *(1818)*

Eyre Evans Crowe

14. To-day in Ireland *(1825)*
15. Yesterday in Ireland *(1829)*

John Banim and Michael Banim

16. Tales, by the O'Hara Family *(1825)*
17. The Boyne Water, A Tale, by the O'Hara Family *(1826)*
18. Tales, by the O'Hara Family. Second Series *(1826)*
19. The Croppy. A Tale of 1798 *(1828)*
20. The Anglo-Irish of the Nineteenth Century *(1828)*
21. The Denounced *(1830)*
22. The Ghost-Hunter and his Family *(1833)*
23. The Mayor of Wind-Gap *and* Canvassing *(1835)*
24. The Bit O'Writin' and Other Tales *(1838)*
25. Patrick Joseph Murray, The Life of John Banim, the Irish Novelist *(1857)*

Gerald Griffin

26. Holland-Tide; or, Munster Popular Tales *(1827)*
27. Tales of the Munster Festivals *(1827)*
28. The Collegians *(1829)*

29. The Rivals *and* Tracy's Ambition *(1829)*

30. Tales of My Neighbourhood *(1835)*

31. Talis Qualis; or Tales of the Jury Room *(1842)*

32. DANIEL GRIFFIN, The Life of Gerald Griffin by his Brother, revised edition *(n.d.)*

WILLIAM CARLETON

33. Father Butler. The Lough Dearg Pilgrim *(1829)*

34. Traits and Stories of the Irish Peasantry *(1830)*

35. Traits and Stories of the Irish Peasantry, Second Series *(1833)*

36. Tales of Ireland *(1834)*

37. Fardorougha, the Miser; or, the Convicts of Lisnamona *(1839)*

38. The Fawn of Spring-Vale, The Clarionet, and Other Tales *(1841)*

39. Tales and Sketches Illustrating the Character of the Irish Peasantry *(1845)*

40. Valentine M'Clutchy, The Irish Agent; or, Chronicles of the Castle Cumber Property *(1847)*

41. The Black Prophet: a Tale of the Irish Famine *(1847)*

42. The Emigrants of Ahadarra: A Tale of Irish Life *(1848)*

43. The Tithe Proctor: being a Tale of the Tithe Rebellion in Ireland *(1849)*

44. The Life of William Carleton: Being His Autobiography and Letters; and an Account of his Life and Writings from the Point at which the Autobiography Breaks Off by David O'Donoghue *(1896)*

HARRIET MARTINEAU

45. Ireland *(1832)*

ANNA MARIA HALL

46. Sketches of Irish Character *(1829)*

47. Lights and Shadows of Irish Life *(1838)*

48. The Whiteboy. A Story of Ireland in 1822 *(1845)*

49. Stories of the Irish Peasantry *(1851)*

WILLIAM HAMILTON MAXWELL

50. O'Hara; or 1798 *(1825)*

51. The Fortunes of Hector O'Halloran and his man, Mark Anthony O'Toole *(1843)*

52. Erin-Go-Bragh; or Irish Life Pictures *(1859)*

ANTHONY TROLLOPE

53. The Macdermots of Ballycloran *(1847)*
54. The Kellys and the O'Kellys *(1848)*
55. Castle Richmond *(1860)*
56. An Eye for an Eye *(1879)*
57. The Land-Leaguers *(1883)*

JOSEPH SHERIDAN LE FANU

58. The Purcell Papers with a Memoir by Alfred Perceval Graves *(1880)*
59. The Cock and Anchor: Being a Chronicle of Old Dublin City *(1845)*
60. The House by the Church-Yard *(1863)*

WILLIAM ALLINGHAM

61. Lawrence Bloomfield in Ireland. A Modern Poem *(1864)*

CHARLOTTE RIDDELL (MRS. J.H. RIDDELL)

62. Maxwell Drewitt *(1865)*
63. The Nun's Curse *(1888)*

T. MASON JONES

64. Old Trinity. A Story of Real Life *(1867)*

ANNIE KEARY

65. Castle Daly. The Story of an Irish Home Thirty Years Ago *(1875)*

MAY LAFFAN HARTLEY

66. Hogan, M. P. *(1876)*
67. Flitters, Tatters, and the Counsellor and Other Sketches *(1879)*

CHARLES JOSEPH KICKHAM

68. Knocknagow: or, the Cabins of Tipperary *(1879)*

MARGARET M. BREW

69. The Burtons of Dunroe *(1880)*
70. Chronicles of Castle Cloyne. Pictures of Munster Life *(1885)*

EMILY LAWLESS

71. Hurrish. A Study *(1886)*

72. With Essex in Ireland *(1890)*

73. Grania. The Story of an Island *(1892)*

74. Maelcho. A Sixteenth-Century Narrative *(1894)*

75. Traits and Confidences *(1898)*

WILLIAM O'BRIEN

76. When We Were Boys *(1890)*

ANONYMOUS

77. Priests and People: A No-Rent Romance *(1891)*